"Stuart Brioza and Nicole Krasinski exude soulfulness and authenticity in their cooking; this book is a true expression of the restaurant they created, which has changed the landscape of American dining."

KYLE CONNAUGHTON, chef/owner of SingleThread Farms and author of *Donabe: Classic and Modern Japanese Clay Pot Cooking*

"With State Bird Provisions, Stuart and Nicole have given the city of San Francisco a gift of culinary joy and delight. Not since childhood have we experienced so much fun dining out, and rarely are we lucky enough to find such an authentic and delicious expression of time and place. Now with *State Bird Provisions* they have given us yet another gift; a guide to bringing some of that magic into our homes. Thank you!"

KEVIN FARLEY and ALEX HOZVEN, owners of The Cultured Pickle Shop

"I love Stuart and Nicole's food, and State Bird Provisions has become one of my favorite restaurants in the world. So, no surprise that this is my new favorite cookbook. The bold techniques, outstanding ingredients, and fantastic flavors—they're all here. What an absolute pleasure this book is."

HUGH FEARNLEY-WHITTINGSTALL, writer, broadcaster, activist, and creator of River Cottage

state bird
PROVISIONS

STATE BIRD PROVISIONS

A COOKBOOK

STUART BRIOZA + NICOLE KRASINSKI

WITH JJ GOODE

TEN SPEED PRESS
California | New York

contents

an accidental
RESTAURANT

At State Bird Provisions, the unusual restaurant that I opened with my wife, Nicole, you eat before you even order. Before you receive a menu, you ogle an array of small plates displayed on the multitiered carts that roam a room that is about a tenth the size of the dim sum parlors that these carts probably bring to mind. You point, you chat, you wonder, and before you know it, you're slurping briny raw oysters topped with kohlrabi kraut—supreme freshness paired with fermented funkiness—or biting into delicate dumplings filled with guinea hen confit seasoned with warm spices, brown butter, and preserved lemon.

Dinner continues as the food you actually ordered hits the table—fried quail with sweet-tart stewed onions and shaved Parmesan, buckwheat pancakes topped with cured beef tongue and horseradish béchamel, and trout with hazelnuts, mandarin, and brown butter spiked with citrus and fish sauce. And all the while, the carts keep coming, adding to the array of bold flavors that shouldn't go together but do, at a restaurant that shouldn't work but does. Today, the operation runs as smoothly as we could have ever hoped, a choreographed dance on the edge of a cliff. Especially considering that almost every aspect of the restaurant was a total accident.

In 2010, Nicole and I were in search of a restaurant space. We had worked together for years, first at Tapawingo in Ellsworth, Michigan (population 400), and most recently at the wine temple Rubicon in San Francisco, which had closed after a fifteen-year run. Since then, we'd been catering from our home base in the Bay Area while we slowly sketched out a business plan for a restaurant inspired by trips to Chile and Peru, where we had eaten our favorite meals at roadside places that cooked everything over a wood fire and served it family style. Unlike so many ideas we'd had for restaurants in the past— hypothetical themes and designs and cuisines hashed out over a little too much whiskey— this one felt real. We were ready to begin the patient search for just the right space and to thoughtfully consider the menu. We felt no urgency, though. Because, for the moment, we were short on money and crazed from work, but as happy as we'd ever been.

But soon, the party would have to end. We were running our business out of our small apartment in Hayes Valley, and it was about to feel a lot smaller. Nicole was pregnant with our son, Jasper. We needed to fast-forward our plan for a restaurant, so we began scouting spaces but kept coming up empty. When Jasper was born, my paternal instinct kicked in and the pressure started building. Some might say I was freaking out. A few weeks later, we got a call from an agent about a space on Fillmore Street, in a neighborhood called the Western Addition. The next day, Nicole and baby Jasper hunkered in our apartment while I went to check it out. I rode my bike, feeling too short on sleep to drive safely.

The landlord, it turned out, had two spaces available in the same building. There was a narrow sliver that had been a pizzeria; graffiti-covered and boarded up, it smelled like an old grease trap. Then, just next door, there was the second space, built in 1911; it was 3,000 square feet on two floors with a soaring arched ceiling that hinted at the building's previous life as a movie theater. I was blown away. When Nicole saw it, she was too. Because the area was still rough-and-tumble, the rent was affordable. It was the perfect place for our first restaurant.

Except for the fact that there was no gas, no electricity, and barely any plumbing. And, oh yeah, it wasn't zoned to be a restaurant. Between the construction and zoning, the landlord guessed that opening a restaurant in the former movie theater would take years. Still, every morning for a week, I'd strap Jasper in the BabyBjörn and walk past the space, wondering how we could make it work.

● ○ ● ○ ●

Lying in bed one night, Stuart wondered out loud, "What if we rent both spaces?" It was an ambitious idea, but the purpose was purely practical. That pizzeria space next door to our dream restaurant might have been small and uninspiring, but at least it had gas and a hood over the stove. If we gave it a quick makeover, we could open it quickly, serve some simple food, and generate some income while the real place slowly came together. The landlord was into it. So we took the plunge. Now all we had to do was decide what the space would become. The key, we decided, was to keep things easy. But we should've known. Easy just isn't our style.

As we pondered, we kept catering, Jasper crawling at our feet while I piped macarons and Stuart filleted anchovies, Jasper snoozing when we got home after events and scrubbed greasy hotel pans and Cambros caked with batter. Our favorite gigs were those where we got to serve a parade of little dishes to a standing crowd—not snacks but a

dozen or so items that added up to a substantial meal. Because we cooked in people's homes in open kitchens, the work felt less like catering and more like we were part of the party. We loved interacting with the guests. We loved that they could see the food before they decided whether they wanted to eat it. That allowed us to take more risks than we otherwise would have. When you write LAMB'S TONGUE or CHOCOLATE CROQUETTES WITH CURRY on a menu, sometimes people are scared off. When you show them the dish, they say yeah!

We wanted to channel the frantic fun of those hors d'oeuvre parties. But without creating a standing-only restaurant, we didn't see how it was possible. Thank goodness for Stuart. Most people would stand inside an old pizzeria and see an old pizzeria. But

when he saw the location of the exhaust hood, near the front of the space and visible through the window, it brought to mind the setup at Chinese restaurants. He could almost see the glistening ducks hanging on hooks behind glass.

So we resurrected an idea we'd had on a plane almost a decade before, one so good that we'd scribbled it down on a napkin but so crazy we never thought we'd actually do it— a restaurant where there would be no menu and dishes came around on carts like dim sum. This had seemed absurd when we thought it up. We had cooked mainly in the high-end world, full of tasting menus and sommeliers. At the time, casual wasn't cool. Now we wondered if the idea wasn't such a crazy one after all.

At that point, all we knew was we wanted to serve fried quail with stewed onions, a dish Stuart had come up with at Rubicon but that probably didn't belong there. Back then, he occasionally brought out the dish to diners, noting as he presented it that quail is California's state bird. That's a cool name, we thought: State Bird! We added *Provisions*, because it suggests food but nothing fancy. Our free-form style of service encouraged a free-form style of cooking. We felt free to try just about anything. Pancakes with sauerkraut, pecorino, and ricotta—Stuart's sophisticated-but-fun riff on our go-to post-catering-event snack—showed up alongside duck liver mousse with duck-fat financiers and fish tartare with an aioli made from rosemary and smoky Japanese dried bonito. I was serving shards of chocolate spiked with sesame and crackly *feuilletine* to be dipped in cocoa-clementine jam and something I called "drunken cherry caramel chocolate mistake"—based on a tart I'd botched that turned out to be particularly awesome in its messed-up form. It wasn't the dead-simple food we'd first envisioned (we couldn't help ourselves), but it wasn't buttoned-up either.

●　·　·　·　●

When we opened State Bird Provisions, there was no menu. Every single dish came around on carts (fashioned for us by a woodworker friend in Seattle). Nicole and I high-fived because we had figured out how to skip writing menus, a task few chefs like. All we had to do was put food on the plate and wait for people to go nuts for it. Let's just say it didn't quite work out that way.

At the time, State Bird was even smaller than it is today. Servers barely had room to squeeze their bodies between tables, let alone navigate carts through a maze of chairs, feet, and elbows. Space was so tight near the door, where we had a small bar for people willing to stand, that both carts and diners occasionally had to pass through the open kitchen up front. Cooking during service often feels like a battle. Cooking at State Bird felt like skydiving—we were always teetering between exhilaration and disaster.

To make matters worse, not even lovers of dim sum knew what to make of the carts when dumplings and egg custard tarts were replaced by miniature Dutch ovens filled with pork belly, clam, and kimchi stew; squid stuffed with carnitas; and shot glasses of peanut milk. Customers eagerly quizzed servers about the dishes. "Are those the beets?" they'd ask, pointing to wedges that we'd crusted in rye and set on horseradish-and-ale cream. "What's in that sauce?" they'd wonder, ogling a plate of grilled bitter greens served with yogurt mixed with smoky Urfa chiles. The typical service interaction had become a conversation. It was awesome. There was just one problem: Customers would frequently let the carts roll away without partaking. They were sensibly waiting to see what their options were before they made decisions—as food got cold and desserts melted. In other words, they wanted a menu.

In fact, "Can I please have a menu?" was the number-one request. So for three days, we handed out menus. And it was the worst. That rapport between servers and diners evaporated. The carts suddenly seemed like an unnecessary, unwieldy novelty. And people tried less food. For weeks, after each service, I'd stay up way too late rethinking the restaurant's format. Every morning I woke up with some new solution. Inching closer to what State Bird was meant to be.

· · · · ·

Finally, after a month, we found a lasting compromise. Diners could order a small selection of dishes from a menu. The rest of the food remained on the carts, tempting people as it rolled by. Most important, we accepted our strange idea as something we loved and wouldn't ever abandon. So what if it took a bit (okay, a lot) of explaining? So what if it wasn't practical or efficient or sensible? We had seen the spirit those carts fostered in the dining room, the fun everyone was having—from the diners to the servers to the cooks.

Today, when we look at photos of the early days, we cringe, because we see all the restaurant's faults. The sad, empty walls. The scruffy floor. The fluorescent lights, which were supposed to create a funky diner feel but created a too-bright dining room instead. We see a space hurried into the world. But we also remember the life the place had then and still has, the vitality that comes from letting your gut guide you, then figuring things out as they come. Long ago, Stuart and I both thought about becoming photographers—we basically fell in love in the darkroom at De Anza College in Cupertino. After taking many poor photographs, I learned that my carefully calculated shots never turned out as beautifully as those I took on a whim, when something caught my eye and I just clicked the shutter.

· · · · ·

Thinking back on it, of course, we're glad we didn't have the luxury to overthink or decide to go a more conventional route. But at the time, doubts were eating at us. I'd be in the open kitchen, brushing slow-cooked pork ribs with a glaze made from their own juices or pouring sauerkraut broth over duck neck dumplings, when a diner seated across the counter would ask me to explain our unusual ways—just as the diner before him had. Every time they'd ask, I'd get about halfway through my convoluted answer before I started to wonder what the heck we'd gotten ourselves into. I'd have an existential crisis in the middle of service.

state bird

w/

PROVISIONS

There's a band Nicole and I like called Whitest Boy Alive. I've always loved the way they described their beginnings: "A band without any programmed elements." (They started playing electronic dance music but became a "band.") That's kind of how State Bird Provisions started—as a dish of fried quail without any programmed elements, with none of the expectations or the musts that can make you feel stuck.

For as long as I can remember, I'd been looking for a life without these musts. I wanted to be free to dive down whatever rabbit hole presented itself, because I loved nothing more than immersing myself in a subject until I felt I really understood it. I wasn't big on school. My fascinations tended to be physical—first soccer, then skateboarding and snowboarding, and finally cooking.

I have my parents to thank for my affection for food. I grew up in Cupertino, California, way back when *apple* only referred to something you ate. My mom was the kind of cook who talked to the supermarket produce guy and went out of her way to go to the good fish market. Twice a week, she'd steam an artichoke and serve it with a generous dollop of mayonnaise, launching my lifelong love for both. My dad was a backyard-barbecue guy, tending to coals and grilling hot dogs, burgers, and occasionally linguica sausage, appropriate for someone with a Portuguese name like Brioza. (My brother and I got along because he was a bun guy and I was a burger guy, so when Dad cooked burgers there was minimal fighting.) When the situation required, I took care of the popcorn, my specialty and the first dish I ever cooked; I tossed it in garlic butter then dusted it with Parmesan, just like my mom taught me.

My parents' spirit of culinary adventure fed mine. When they hosted Japanese exchange students, our pantry suddenly filled with seaweed, rice vinegar, and mirin. When they wanted prime rib, we all flew to L.A. just for dinner at Lawry's, the chain that gave us the famous seasoning salt. It helped that we flew for free—my mom was a flight attendant for TWA—but I still learned that food was worth a voyage. (It's possible that on planes I learned to associate a rolling cart with a sense of adventure.)

At fifteen years old, I applied for two jobs—one as a dishwasher at a place called Pacific Pasta and another at a ski and snowboard shop called Any Mountain, located right across the plaza. But only Pacific Pasta called me back. If it had been the other way around, I might have been a winter sports instructor, since I loved snowboarding.

In 1989, Pacific Pasta was ahead of its time. It sold fresh sauces and fettuccine and spaghetti by the pound, and served plates of pasta and memorable meatball heroes on garlic bread. I talked my way into doing prep—chopping carrots and making the garlic bread by splitting enormous Italian loaves, basting them with garlic butter, and piling steaming pieces in giant buckets. As part of my pay, I got a free lunch; cooked reluctantly by the young Bohemians who worked the line. Then I got lucky; instead of making the food for me, they offered to show me how to make my own.

This was a teach-a-man-to-fish moment, one of those times in your life when a door opens and you step through. Soon, on slow afternoons, I asked if I could do the cooking. Suddenly, I was tossing linguine and canned clams with cream and white wine, and simmering until the sauce clung to the noodles. I dumped them on a plate, and like that, I was a professional cook. Back then I had no clue that their renditions of spaghetti Bolognese (red sauce dolloped on noodles) and carbonara (made with prosciutto, cream, and frozen peas) didn't resemble the genuine articles.

After a year, I could make every dish on the menu and had been promoted to kitchen manager. (I was fortunate that my high school let me do independent study, sort of like online classes but without the Internet.) I rose in the ranks in part because the more experienced cooks at Pacific Pasta had greater ambitions. They had all started taking shifts at a restaurant called Blackhawk Grille. While they were tossing fettuccine with Alfredo sauce, they'd talk in hushed tones about a guy named Elliot King, who was referred to almost exclusively as "chef," and dishes like duck confit. I hadn't heard of either one. All I knew was that both sounded extremely cool.

The cooks told me that a job had opened up and if I wanted it, I should show up at 6:45 a.m., when Elliot King—the man, the legend—arrived to open the restaurant. So I did, waiting in the parking lot, a sort of punk-rock skater in black high-top Converse, cutoff shorts, and a leather vest over a white T-shirt. I even sported a floppy Mohawk. So it's no surprise that the first morning, he shooed me away. The next

morning, he didn't invite me in but didn't tell me to scram. The third day he offered me the opportunity to work in his kitchen.

This was my first real taste of kitchen life. For King and his disciples, food wasn't a job. It was a religion. The cooks had all worked at the trailblazing Bay Area restaurants of the '90s—Fleur de Lys, the Ritz-Carlton under Gary Danko, La Folie—absorbing French technique and enduring the exacting, temperamental bosses before decamping to open Blackhawk Grille. They described a new world in a foreign language. They spoke with reverence of people and places I'd never heard of—I wondered who was *Hubert Keller* and what was a *Folie*. When they referred to meat as muscle, I couldn't figure out what that meant. Regardless, I was hooked.

I began skipping school to spend all my time in a chef's jacket and toque. (Okay, *almost* all my time. I also reserved time for skateboarding and my Metallica cover band.) Instead of trying to decode Shakespeare and solve quadratic equations, I cured sturgeon and butchered hundreds of chickens. Instead of making birdhouses in woodshop, I stuffed wild rice, herbs, and liver into boned-out duck legs and pounded beef tenderloin between parchment paper for carpaccio, snipping it with scissors into a perfect circle and perfecting the lemon-caper aioli, sieved egg, and brunoise of red onion served on top.

Still a snowboarder, every winter Friday after my shift, I'd brew a big pot of coffee, climb in my '78 Volkswagen bus loaded with blankets, and drive to Lake Tahoe, arriving just in time to fall asleep in the parking lot of Kirkwood ski resort. The next day, I was the first one on the slopes. After I graduated high school, I spent the ski season in Salt Lake City. I cooked at a fancy restaurant by night and snowboarded by day, getting acquainted with my roommate's Nikon as we photographed our latest grabs and aerials. Back home, I enrolled in community college to study photography. Then, in the darkroom, I met a girl named Nicole Krasinski. She wore velvet pants, Doc Martens, and dark red lipstick; listened to the Violent Femmes and Bauhaus; and loved to crack open warm loaves of bread and inhale the smell. She was like no one I'd ever met.

An art student by day, I cooked by night at another restaurant, this time with Blackhawk Grille alum Jeff Stout, a great teacher and an adherent of French technique, though I didn't know then what that meant. Working under Elliot and then under Jeff, I cooked in a sort of trance, executing classic stocks and sauces because I was taught to. But listening to other cooks talk about *mirepoix* and *fond*, I could tell they understood something I didn't. I wanted so badly to join the conversation.

That's when I decided to attend the Culinary Institute of America in Hyde Park, New York. My education there produced a sort of *mise en place* of the mind, organizing what I'd already learned into comprehensible categories. It also rapidly expanded my universe. Until then, Jeff Stout and Elliot King had seemed like the center of the cosmos. Now, new planets suddenly came into view, celestial bodies named Auguste Escoffier, Paul Bocuse, and Michel Bras. When Bras came to school as a guest lecturer, he didn't give a cooking demo. The chef-philosopher brought photographs to show how an oil-slicked puddle had inspired a dish of monkfish. This blew my mind. Food could be more than a quest for technical perfection. There was a process to cooking that went beyond technique.

I wanted to learn more. So I started to devour cookbooks, as if their pages contained all of life's secrets. When summer came, Nicole and I traveled to Europe to eat at the restaurants of chefs I had only read about. And farther down the rabbit hole I went.

When Nicole got accepted into the Art Institute of Chicago (she'd ultimately work at a bakery instead), I arranged to have my school externship there, and was lucky enough to work under John Hogan at Park Avenue Café. An old-school practitioner with a big belly, loud voice, and glasses always perched on the tip of his nose, he had long ago mastered everything I'd just learned at school. For him, tradition and technique were just the beginning, not the end, of the conversation. His consommé was made from oxtail, enriched with bone marrow, and served with snails. He invigorated rouille, the garlicky Provençal mayonnaise that typically accompanies bouillabaisse, with an intense reduction of bouillabaisse itself. He was a force of nature, and I was eager for more. So after my externship, I joined him when he left to open his own restaurant, Savarin, first working construction on the building site, and then later on the line.

John recommended me for my first head chef job, at Tapawingo. At twenty-five, I was far from ready. But I took it, and Nicole and I moved from America's third-largest city to a town of four hundred people in Northern Michigan. Fresh from a love affair with baking at that Chicago bakery, Nicole would work for the restaurant's pastry chef, a position she'd soon take over, whether she wanted to or not.

During our first year at Tapawingo, Nicole expanded her repertoire, while I essentially cooked what I was good at—in other words, John Hogan's food—using unremarkable flown-in produce, meat, and fish that arrived in one big truck from a distribution center that was hours away. That is, until Tapawingo owner Pete Peterson reminded me where I now lived. As he put it at the time, "It's time to dance with the girl you brung."

He introduced me to the farmers and foragers who toiled at the very tip of the Michigan mitten, to the products that became my inspiration, and to the people who became my friends and teachers. I joined cherry farmers for harvest. I shared meals and discussed important matters like rabbit and pheasant breeding. Now, instead of deciding what to cook and then placing an order, I familiarized myself with what these people grew, raised, and discovered during the seven months of the year when the temperature wasn't ten below.

This was just another small decision about process. But when you added up all my small decisions and experiences, I suppose they amounted to a style of cooking. I didn't see it that way, but *Food & Wine* magazine must have. In 2003, my fourth year at Tapawingo,

I was named one of the magazine's Best New Chefs. I took comfort in the recognition that someone thought I knew what I was doing, even if I didn't.

When Nicole and I decided to return to the Bay Area, we lucked out and got hired as the chefs at Rubicon, an incredible restaurant run by restaurateur Drew Nieporent and master sommelier Larry Stone, both legends in the restaurant world. Before Larry hired us, we had to cook a five-course audition for him and several others. At least two of his invitees voted no, so we're forever grateful to Larry for believing in us. Rubicon was the big leagues—a San Francisco restaurant with a jaw-dropping catalog of former chefs and cooks, a decade-long reputation as one of the city's best, and the kind of wine cellar, twenty-five thousand bottles strong, that would make Francis Ford Coppola (one of the investors) blush.

Nicole and I cooked our butts off, creating elaborate tasting menus that would impress diners paying hundreds of dollars for dinner and pair well with their white Burgundy and fine Bordeaux. The task was challenging and exciting. The food was beautiful. I finally felt like a confident cook. Another chef might have thrived, and for a few years I did too. Then for the first time since I'd started cooking, I felt the burden of musts.

Drew and Larry gave me true creative freedom, but I still knew my food had to satisfy certain parameters of luxury and complexity. Most of my cooking at the time started from that premise, then I'd try to shoehorn my style into the mix. Yet one dish in particular helped me look toward the future: my fried quail. It didn't start by checking boxes for what's required of a tasting-menu dish; it started with soulful inspiration— the fried chicken my mom cooked for us every week when I was a kid—and blossomed from there. I used quail, because the smaller bird had great flavor and a larger proportion of the crispy skin, my favorite part. Underneath the golden-brown bird wasn't a butter-mounted reduction but a bed of sweet onions that had been slow-cooked with rosemary, then brightened with lemon. And on the top was Parmesan— not transformed into *tuiles* or infused into foam, but simple shavings. Sure, I added some fancy-food trappings of the time. I stacked the dainty little bird in the center of a comically large coupe. I garnished it with a delicate herb salad and vivid green dribbles of basil oil. Still, it felt like me.

And it was a hit. Often, diners would even ask for seconds—a request made more meaningful by the fact that they still had more rich courses on the way. Even more important, I never got tired of cooking it. I started to long for the day when I could feel this way about every dish I made.

Yet when Drew and Larry decided to close Rubicon, I mourned for them—they loved that restaurant—and for my staff, whose hard work made it great. I also struggled with a sense of failure, the thought that I had let everyone down, that this iconic restaurant had closed under my watch. It took a while, but at last, I embraced the heartbreak. Nicole and I decided the next step would be our own restaurant, driven by nothing but our passions. The next three or so years Nicole and I spent catering made for great preparation. I had time to develop some new passions, like making sauerkraut, that would come to shape my cooking. I got even more comfortable playing with tradition. Because without a professional kitchen, dedicated staff, and generous budget, certain French culinary rituals had to give. To save money and space, I kept the onion but ditched the carrots and celery in my mirepoix, the classic trio of aromatics that provided the base of flavor in classic French cooking. To save time, I skipped the step of roasting bones to make stock, and later began using less stock altogether. Often, I preferred the results, emboldening for a cook who already had a thing against must-do's.

Once the space on Fillmore Street presented itself, all Nicole and I knew for sure was that we'd serve the fried quail. We joked about opening a fried-quail shack and calling it State Bird. Quail is California's state bird, after all. But in a way, imposing any thematic concept on the food—whether it was a quail shack, northern Italian, or Southeast Asian—would mean introducing more of those musts I wanted to escape. If you're running a fried-quail shack, then you sort of have to offer fancied-up versions of sides you expect with fried chicken. But if you're just "a restaurant in San Francisco," as Nicole and I jokingly started describing the place to friends, then anything goes.

Since our restaurant fit into no category, everything was fair game. I could welcome any inspiration that came—a farro factory in Italy, a fish sauce operation in Vietnam, or a dish of Sichuan cumin lamb in San Francisco's Chinatown. My pantry could include such disparate ingredients as sambal oelek and brown butter, Japanese pickled plums and sauerkraut, kimchi and the awesome Italian oil made by pressing olives and lemons together. We never quite figured out what our food would be; we just kept cooking it.

Yet while this new freedom was incredibly exciting, the boundlessness felt over-whelming. Give me gorgeous lamb loin or a perfect fig and I'll talk your ear off for hours about what I *could* make without ever deciding what to actually cook. Of course, as I should've known, our strange little restaurant project presented its own limitations that, perhaps because they were of our own making, seemed less like musts and more like stimulating challenges.

Take, for instance, our decision, against more or less everyone's advice, to serve food on dim sum–style carts. While I didn't have any experience cooking Chinese food, I had a lot of experience watching carts heavy with tempting dishes roam vast banquet halls in Chinese enclaves around the country. Borrowing this fun, ingenious format, decided so long ago on a whim, would cause us trouble as we delved into the details, but it did end up focusing my enthusiasms, yanking my ideas from the clouds back to the earth. Dim sum evoked dumplings, so I created my own version filled with spiced guinea hen confit and perfumed with brown butter, ginger, and preserved lemon. Dim sum brought to mind ribs, but instead of aping the classic version steamed with fermented black beans, I slow-cooked them, lacquered them with a glaze made from their own juices, and dusted them with Japanese seven-spice. The thought of the golden orbs coated in sesame seeds that had always caught my eye from across the room in Chinatown guided an early, overcomplicated dish—griddled northern Chinese–style flatbread served with braised oxtail, lentil dal, and sunchoke puree, all for dipping—into a State Bird classic: an eye-catching garlicky puff of the same dough topped with burrata and sprinkled with a beguiling amalgam of six kinds of pepper.

When the cart concept created confusion, I borrowed from dim sum the idea of unspoken categories to help customers make quick sense of what was on offer. Just as the trolleys at Chinese restaurants flaunt food that can be broken roughly into dumplings, noodles, and deep-fried things, I came up with groupings of my own. There was "chip and dips," something crunchy (potato chips, fried tortillas, cacao nib crackers) meant for scooping some tasty concoction (Dungeness crab salsa, house-cured trout roe and crème fraîche, pork rillettes). There was "stab and drag," a little something enticing to poke with your fork (duck croquettes, black rice–crusted pork) and then drag through sauce (raisin verjus, apple mostarda). Some categories even made it onto the menu. A buttery pancake made with sauerkraut, pecorino, and ricotta and amped up with Nicole's sourdough starter spawned an entire selection of savory offerings. Griddled bread rubbed with garlic and fresh tomato and topped with pickled local anchovy launched a confederation of toasts. No matter how the menu changed, however, the fried quail would remain one of the few constants.

The financial realities of running this odd shoestring restaurant shaped our larder. To salvage leftover quinoa, we deep-fried it to add texture to tartares and salads. We salted and smoked extra egg yolks until they were as firm and delicious as Parmesan. We sautéed mushroom trimmings and transformed them into flavorful aioli. These joined an arsenal of vinaigrettes, fermented pickles, and other condiments that enabled us to create on the fly when the farm gave us asparagus and broccoli or one of our purveyors showed up with spot prawns or cauliflower mushrooms. They became my new tools for the old task of balancing saltiness and sweetness, acidity and richness.

I evolved as the restaurant did, my style always a work in progress. The biggest change, perhaps, came a year or so in, when the biodynamic farm we partnered with took flight. We had aligned with the farm, an hour or so south of the city, before we opened, and slowly reached the point where the vegetables and fruit were not just abundant but truly inspiring. It was exhilarating to choose some of what they grew and to learn about how great produce was cultivated. What really blew me away was my new access to vegetables that fresh. I started thinking about my radishes and lettuce leaves as "sashimi grade." As I roamed the fields, hunching over to taste snap peas or pole beans as if for the first time, I thought about a recipe I read somewhere that stuck with me. It was an oldie, written to emphasize the highly perishable pleasure of corn, which loses about half its sweetness just four hours after it's picked. It went something like "Bring a pot of water to a boil. Pick the corn and run back to the pot, shucking as you go." I wanted everything I cooked to be this perfect, an impossible standard we were suddenly that much closer to meeting.

The farm also challenged my idea of perfection as I inevitably got to know the life cycle of our vegetables. After a few seasons, I came to think of cilantro, for instance, not just as the leafy bunch you typically see at markets, but as a variety of treasures from the same source. In early spring, I'd nibble the intense little sprouts that broke through the soil. In summer, I'd taste the spirited blossoms that appeared when the plant bolted, then the spectacular citrusy green seeds that followed. I felt lucky to meet ingredients during each stage of their existence.

This, in turn, came to advise my cooking. At least, I like to say *advise*, though what I also mean is that it occasionally put me up against a wall. Every harvest gave us problems to solve—good problems, the kind that keep you thinking and wondering. Produce had to be used right away or preserved, forcing me to think on my feet. Because if that corn recipe taught me anything, it's that freshness doesn't wait. We roasted surplus eggplants to make vinaigrettes and used a food dehydrator to transform extra corn into a vividly flavored powder. To bumper crops of kohlrabi and turnips, I applied my sauerkraut obsession, using the power of salt, temperature, and time to make these members of the *Brassica* clan last. The results were so exciting, charged with acid and umami, that these makeshift solutions quickly became pantry staples.

Successful experiments led to others. A surprisingly bountiful bed of peppery nasturtium flowers inspired a flight of ingenuity. We had two gallons of flowers. We had at least that much liquid left over from fermenting turnips. So we used the latter to immerse the former, then a few days later dehydrated them to make pickled nasturtium flower salt. It sounds almost absurd, but for us it was a commonsense way to manage our bounty. Not to mention that it tasted great sprinkled on the crème fraîche accompanying anchovies.

State Bird has become a place where ideas come from other ideas, where rabbit holes are frequently dug and explored, where the food is always evolving. Where we can cook whatever we want, and a fried game bird over stewed onions can share the table with soy-glazed sea urchin pancakes and duck liver mousse with duck-fat financiers. Where anything is possible—except perhaps taking that quail off the menu.

state bird with provisions

Serves 6

marinate the quail

1 cup well-shaken
buttermilk

1 small garlic clove, finely
grated on a Microplane

¼ tsp finely grated (on a
Microplane) lemon zest

¼ tsp freshly ground
black pepper

⅛ tsp kosher salt

Six 4- to 5-ounce
semiboneless quail, halved
lengthwise and patted dry

Combine the buttermilk, garlic, lemon zest, black pepper, and
salt in a large mixing bowl and stir well. Add the quail, toss gently
but well to coat, then cover and marinate in the fridge for at least
12 hours or up to 36 hours.

bread the quail

1 cup pumpkin seeds,
toasted (see page 96)

1 cup coarse dried
bread crumbs

1 cup all-purpose flour

1 cup potato starch

3 Tbsp sweet paprika

3 Tbsp dark chili powder

1 Tbsp kosher salt

2 tsp garlic powder

1 tsp cayenne pepper

Combine the pumpkin seeds and bread crumbs in a food processor
and pulse until they are well mixed and the pumpkin seeds are
broken into approximately ¼-inch pieces. Put the mixture in
a large mixing bowl along with the flour, potato starch, paprika,
chili powder, salt, garlic powder, and cayenne and mix well.

One by one, remove a quail half from the marinade, add it to
the breading mixture, and use your hands to toss it to coat in a
generous layer of the breading, making sure the pieces, even
the wing and armpit, are well coated. Transfer the quail in one
layer to a baking sheet or large plate and refrigerate uncovered
for at least 4 hours or up to 12 hours.

make the onions

13 Tbsp unsalted butter, cut into several pieces

1 strip Meyer lemon peel (about 3 by 1 inch), white pith removed

1 rosemary sprig

4 large Vidalia onions, cut into ¼-inch half-moons

2 Tbsp kosher salt

1½ tsp granulated sugar

½ cup plus 2 Tbsp lemon juice

Melt the butter in a 4- to 6-quart Dutch oven over medium heat. Lay out a large piece of cheesecloth and put the lemon peel and rosemary on it. Gather the edges of the cheesecloth, twist the loose cloth, and tie a knot to make a sachet. Add the sachet to the melted butter.

Add the onions to the pot and cook, stirring occasionally and lowering the heat if needed to prevent them from taking on color, until wilted, 15 to 20 minutes. Stir in the salt and sugar, turn the heat to medium-low, and cook, stirring occasionally until very soft, 10 to 15 minutes. Stir in the lemon juice and continue to cook until the onions are nearly melted, about 25 minutes.

Cover the onions and keep warm over very low heat. (If you're not frying the quail immediately, let the onions cool, transfer to an airtight container, and refrigerate for up to 3 days. Warm very gently before serving.)

finish the dish

Rice bran, vegetable,
or canola oil for deep-frying

Kosher salt

2½ ounces Parmesan

2 tsp thinly sliced chives

Coarsely ground
black pepper

Pour 3 inches of rice bran oil into a large heavy pot and bring
to 335°F over high heat. Set a wire rack over a baking sheet.

Fry the quail in two batches to avoid crowding, turning them
occasionally, until they are brown and crispy, 3 to 4 minutes per
batch. As it's fried, transfer the quail to the prepared rack and
immediately season lightly with salt. If you'd like, cut each quail
half into two pieces to separate the leg from the breast.

Spoon the onions onto a large platter and top with the quail.
Use a vegetable peeler to shave thin, wide slices of the Parmesan
over the quail, sprinkle with the chives, and season with black
pepper. Serve right away.

the
SAVORY
larder

FOUNDATIONS

This section of our larder includes a collection of recipes that we consider to be fundamental to the food at State Bird, and that, with only occasional exceptions, contribute to its distinctive flavor without necessarily announcing their presence.

clarified butter, below

sweet garlic puree, opposite

state bird dashi, page 40

clarified butter

Makes about 1½ cups

At State Bird, we brown—and even intentionally burn—butter as often as we clarify it. Yet for cooking our pancakes, there's no substitute for clarified butter, a staple of the traditional French kitchen. That's why we keep vats of this pure butterfat—regular butter slowly cooked and skimmed of its milk solids—on hand. Its higher smoke point is perfect for high-heat cooking, which helps create the crispy brown patches that make the pancakes such a pleasure to eat.

2 cups unsalted butter, cut into 1-inch pieces

Line a fine-mesh sieve with cheesecloth and set it over a heatproof container.

Put the butter in a small pot, set over medium-low heat, and let it melt and bubble. When you see white foam develop on the surface of the butter, use a small ladle to skim it off and discard. Continue to cook, skimming every 5 minutes or so and lowering the heat if the butter threatens to brown at the edges, until the butter is completely transparent, about 20 minutes. Strain through the prepared sieve, discarding the solids.

Transfer to an airtight container and store in the fridge for up to 6 months.

state bird garum, page 42

salted chile paste, page 43

sweet garlic puree

Makes about 1½ cups

This is our answer to roasted garlic. Sure, the puree requires a bit of fuss—boil, drain, repeat—but it's well worth it to taste garlic stripped of any trace of its acrid flavor. What remains is strikingly clean and sweet, which is essential to our Garlic Bread with Burrata (page 153) and welcome as a more delicate alternative anywhere you typically use roasted cloves.

2 cups peeled garlic cloves
1 Tbsp olive oil, or as needed

Put the garlic in a small pot, cover with water by 2 inches or so, then bring to a boil over high heat. Drain and then rinse the garlic under cold running water. Repeat the process—boiling, draining, and rinsing—another three times. Cover with water, bring to a boil, and drain one final time.

Transfer the warm garlic to a blender and add the olive oil. Blend on high speed to a very smooth puree, gradually adding more oil if necessary to combine.

Transfer to an airtight container and store in the fridge for up to 7 days or in the freezer for up to 3 months. (Consider freezing in ice-cube trays until solid then transferring to an airtight bag.)

state bird dashi

Makes about 3¼ cups

My instinct is that if a Japanese person tasted our take on the stock called dashi, which serves as the umami-rich backbone to so much of our food, he or she would say, "This is not dashi." But my hope is that he'd like it all the same.

Ours is busier than the stunningly spare traditional version—just *kombu* (dried kelp) and *katsuobushi* (dried, cured fish) steeped in water. We engage in quite a bit of blasphemy, boosting the flavor with aromatics like lemon peel and ginger, garlic and rosemary. But I like to think these additions make sense—the ginger a familiar friend to dashi, the piney rosemary a new but amiable one to the smoky *katsuobushi*. Our dishes don't embrace the level of nuance that traditional Japanese food does. Our food is big and bold, and so is our dashi.

1 ounce kombu (Japanese dried kelp), snipped into pieces

1½-inch knob ginger, peeled and smashed

2 medium garlic cloves, smashed and peeled

2 strips Meyer lemon peel (each about 3 by 1 inch), white pith removed

1 small rosemary sprig

4 cups water

2½ cups katsuobushi (Japanese bonito flakes)

Combine the kombu, ginger, garlic, lemon peel, rosemary, and water in a small pot. Set over medium-low heat and warm until small bubbles begin to rise from the bottom but before they break the surface of the liquid, 10 to 12 minutes. Turn off the heat.

Sprinkle in the katsuobushi and, if necessary, gently stir with a wooden spoon so it's completely saturated. Let steep for 10 minutes, then strain through a fine-mesh sieve, lightly pressing on the solids. Discard the solids.

Transfer to an airtight container and store in the fridge for up to 3 days or in the freezer for up to 3 months.

Note: It's worth mentioning that you can easily double or triple this recipe by simply multiplying the ingredients. This will help you make enough dashi for Dashi-Potato Porridge with Shellfish Salsa and Pickled Seaweed (page 205), or to have plenty on hand for your own cooking adventures.

state bird chicken stock

Makes about 3 quarts

For a French-trained chef, I don't use much stock in my cooking and rarely if ever use the intense reductions that marked my food back in the day. Over the years, I've gradually replaced stock with other sources of depth and umami, like brown butter, fish sauce, and *katsuobushi* (Japanese dried, cured fish). And when I do make stock, it bears only some resemblance to the version I made half a million times as a student in culinary school and as a cook in restaurant kitchens. While I still blanch my bones, which leads to a stock that both looks and, even more important, tastes cleaner, I skip the classic trio of carrots, onions, and celery, looking to bolder aromatics like scallions, ginger, and lemon zest. Instead of letting the stock burble all day, I prefer just a few hours, and I only add the aromatics about half an hour before the stock's done, so the flavor they bring stays vibrant.

5 pounds chicken bones (such as necks and backs)

Water as needed

2 medium yellow onions, cut into ½-inch slices

5 scallions, trimmed and roughly chopped

2-inch knob ginger, peeled and smashed

4 medium garlic cloves, smashed and peeled

3 strips Meyer lemon peel (each about 3 by 1 inch), white pith removed

Put the chicken bones in a large pot and add enough water to cover. Cover the pot and bring to a boil over high heat. Immediately remove from the heat, drain the bones, and rinse them well under running water. Rinse out the pot.

Return the bones to the pot and add enough fresh water to cover by about 1 inch. Cover the pot and bring to a simmer over high heat. Remove the cover, lower the heat to maintain a very gentle simmer (with small bubbles just barely breaking the surface), and cook, stirring occasionally, until the bones begin to break apart at any joints, about 2 hours.

Add the onions, scallions, ginger, garlic, and lemon peel and cook, stirring occasionally, until the onions are fully soft, 30 to 45 minutes more. Strain through a fine-mesh sieve, pressing lightly on the solids to extract as much liquid as possible (discard the solids). Let cool.

Transfer to an airtight container and store in the fridge for up to 3 days or in the freezer for up to 2 months. Skim off the fat before using.

variation: lamb stock

Substitute meaty lamb bones for the chicken bones and add 2 star anise and 2 cloves along with the other aromatics. Simmer for 4 hours and then proceed as directed.

state bird garum

Makes about 5 cups

When you think of fish sauce, you typically think of Southeast Asia, not ancient Rome. But more than two millennia ago, Romans fermented fish to produce a powerful condiment called *garum*. What we make is *garum* in name only. Instead of fermenting fish ourselves, we buy crates of Red Boat Fish Sauce. I fell in love with the product after visiting Cuong Pham's operation in southern Vietnam, where wild anchovies caught off Phu Quoc island are salted almost right out of the water and then left to ferment in mango-wood barrels for nearly a year. Supposedly his product is pretty close to the original *garum*. Cooks in ancient Rome added vinegars and herbs to make all sorts of condiments that built on the sauce's salty, umami-filled flavor. That's what we do for ours, steeping Asian aromatics and spices into the elixir, so it tastes even more complex.

4 cups fish sauce (preferably Red Boat brand)

1 cup lime juice

1 lemongrass stalk

3-inch knob ginger, peeled and cut into a few pieces

3 medium garlic cloves, peeled

6 cloves

3 dried Indian or Indonesian long peppers

3-inch Ceylon cinnamon stick

1 whole nutmeg

Combine the fish sauce and lime juice in a blender.

Cut off and discard the bottom 1 inch and top 5 inches from the lemongrass, remove the outer layer, and cut the lemongrass into about-2-inch pieces.

One by one, coarsely crush the lemongrass, ginger, and garlic in a mortar and transfer to a blender. Focusing on one spice at a time, coarsely crack the cloves, long peppers, and cinnamon stick in the mortar and transfer to the blender. Wrap the nutmeg in a kitchen towel, whack it with a heavy pan to crack into several pieces, and then add to the blender. Pulse the mixture to break up the solids a bit more, 15 to 30 seconds.

Transfer to an airtight container and refrigerate for at least 12 hours or up to 1 month (the longer the better). Strain the mixture through a fine-mesh sieve, pressing on the solids to extract as much liquid as possible. Discard the solids.

Transfer to an airtight container and store in the fridge for up to 3 months.

salted chile paste and chile oil

Makes about 1¼ cups paste,
1¼ cups flavorful juice,
and 3½ cups flavorful oil

SPECIAL EQUIPMENT
Digital kitchen scale

2 pounds red jalapeño or
Fresno chiles (including
seeds), coarsely chopped

Kosher salt

About 3½ cups grapeseed oil

This is a fantastic way to treat a surprise haul of fresh, moderately spicy red chiles, whether that crop comes from your garden or an overeager buying spree at the market. It's one recipe that yields three ingredients for your larder. When you blend and strain the chiles, you end up with a vivid juice, full of chile flavor, that we use for vinaigrette (see page 87). The remaining solids are what you use for this recipe, curing them with salt for three days and then ever-so-slowly cooking them in oil. The result is both a pungent chile paste with a complexity far beyond that of the raw product and an oil infused with the same flavor.

Working in two batches, in a blender, puree the chiles on high speed until smooth. Strain the puree through a fine-mesh sieve into a bowl, pressing on the solids to extract as much juice as possible. Transfer the juice to an airtight container and use within a few hours or store in the freezer for up to 1 month.

Weigh the chile solids; 10 percent of this weight is the amount of salt you'll need. You'll probably have about 400 grams chile solids, which requires about 40 grams salt.

Combine the chile solids and salt in a mixing bowl and stir well. Transfer the mixture to a glass jar, cover tightly with the lid, and let cure at room temperature for 3 days.

Measure the volume of the cured chile solids; double that volume is the amount of grapeseed oil you'll need. You should have about 1¾ cups cured chile solids, which requires about 3½ cups grapeseed oil.

Combine the cured chile mixture and grapeseed oil in a medium saucepan. Cook over medium heat until the mixture bubbles gently, then turn the heat as low as it can go. Continue to cook at a bare sizzle, stirring and scraping the pan occasionally, until the paste turns several shades darker, 3 to 4 hours (the longer the better). Let cool, then strain through a fine-mesh sieve into a bowl.

Transfer the paste and oil, separately, to airtight containers and store in the fridge for up to 1 month.

smoked trout

Makes about 1¼ pounds

SPECIAL EQUIPMENT

Small electric or charcoal smoker

Fruitwood chips, such as apple or cherry, soaked in water for 30 minutes, then drained

12 cups water

1 cup kosher salt

¼ cup plus 2 Tbsp granulated sugar

2 Tbsp freshly ground black pepper

2 pounds skin-on red trout, sea trout, or arctic char fillets

This brined hot-smoked trout gives you enough fish to make trout mayo for our most popular chip and dip (see page 163), or plenty to inspire your own cooking endeavors. If you don't have a hot smoker, buy one! At State Bird, we use an inexpensive electric smoker with great results. You can get away with cold-smoking in a kettle grill (see Chicken-Egg Bottarga, page 100) to infuse the trout with smoke flavor, but then you'll have to roast it at 200°F for about 30 minutes to cook it through.

At least 2 days before you plan to serve the smoked trout, combine the water, salt, sugar, and pepper in a high-sided container big enough to fit the fillets snugly in a single layer. Stir to dissolve the salt and sugar. Add the fillets so they're fully submerged by the brine, halving them to fit in the container if necessary. Cover and refrigerate for 2 days, flipping the fillets after about 24 hours.

After 2 days, prepare the smoker with the wood chips to cook at 180° to 200°F.

Remove the fillets from the brine, pat dry, and put them on a parchment paper–lined baking sheet that will fit in your smoker, slide into the smoker, and let smoke just until the fish is fully cooked, about 30 minutes. Let the fillets cool. Remove and discard the skin (or fry it for a snack), then pick the flesh into large bite-size pieces, discarding any bones.

Transfer to an airtight container and store in the fridge for up to 4 days.

smoked mackerel

Makes about 1¾ pounds

SPECIAL EQUIPMENT
Small electric or charcoal smoker

Fruitwood chips, such as apple or cherry, soaked in water for 30 minutes, then drained

12 cups water

1 cup kosher salt

¼ cup plus 2 Tbsp granulated sugar

2 Tbsp freshly ground black pepper

2 pounds skin-on Spanish mackerel fillets, pin bones removed

While the smoked trout (facing page) is meant to be eaten flaked (and folded into mayonnaise), this mackerel is made to be sliced like the sable and sturgeon sold at Jewish appetizing stores. The overnight air-drying in the fridge is a key step; it helps form the pellicle, a sort of tacky coating on the outside of the fish that acts like flypaper for smoky flavor.

At least 3 days before you plan to serve the smoked mackerel, combine the water, salt, sugar, and pepper in a high-sided container big enough to fit the fillets snugly in a single layer. Stir to dissolve the salt and sugar. Add the fillets so they're fully submerged by the brine, halving them to fit in the container if necessary. Cover and refrigerate for 2 days, flipping the fillets after about 24 hours.

After 2 days, remove the fillets from the brine, pat dry, and put them on a wire rack set over a baking sheet. Refrigerate, uncovered, overnight.

The next day, prepare the smoker with the wood chips to cook at 160° to 180°F.

Put the fillets on a parchment paper–lined baking sheet that will fit in your smoker, slide into the smoker, and let smoke just until the fish is fully cooked, about 30 minutes. Let the fillets cool, then tightly wrap each one separately in plastic wrap.

Store in the fridge for up to 4 days. When you're ready to serve, remove the skin and use a long, thin knife (held at an angle) to cut the fish crosswise into ¼-inch-thick slices.

braised pork belly

Makes 2 pounds braised pork and 6½ cups flavorful liquid

In the beginning, the State Bird kitchen was small. Too small. Every day, our cooks took turns with counter space and bumped shoulders as they prepped. Every empty surface or unoccupied nook became sought-after real estate, including the alley behind the restaurant. Occasionally, we'd use this area to keep pork belly that we'd braised, letting it rest in its aromatic cooking liquid. When we did, it smelled good out there. Too good. One day, someone made off with nearly twenty pounds of hot belly. Nicole drove around for hours looking for the thieves, who ate really well that night.

We weren't happy, but we understood. This is seriously good stuff. It's what we make whenever pork belly passes through the State Bird kitchen, which is often. We brine the belly to infuse it with salt and tighten its texture, then braise it until the meat is lusciously tender and the fat is creamy. Finally, we press it under a weight so it cooks evenly and looks especially striking. In fact, we make so much and have it on hand so dependably that we find ourselves treating it not as a dish but as yet another larder ingredient, one that helps us showcase whatever the seasons bring. During winter's cold weather, the belly and its rich braising liquid make the base for clam-kimchi stew (see page 209). When summer brings plums or fall presents grapes, the fruits are featured beside crisp golden-brown chunks of belly that have been fried in hot oil (see page 183).

4 quarts water, or as needed

1¾ cups plus 2½ Tbsp kosher salt

¾ cup plus 1 Tbsp granulated sugar

¼ cup finely ground black pepper

3-pound piece pork belly

1 medium yellow onion, very coarsely chopped

5 medium garlic cloves, smashed and peeled

2 scallions, trimmed and cut into several pieces

3 thyme sprigs

1 large rosemary sprig

Combine the water, salt, sugar, and pepper in a large mixing bowl. Stir to dissolve the salt and sugar. Put the pork belly, fat side down, in a large Dutch oven. Pour in enough of the brine to completely submerge the belly, cover, and refrigerate for 3 days.

After 3 days, preheat the oven to 300°F. Cut a piece of parchment paper large enough to rest inside the Dutch oven with just a little room to spare. Line a baking sheet with parchment paper and have a second baking sheet ready. Clear space in the fridge.

Drain the pork belly, discarding the brine, and rinse the Dutch oven. Return the belly, fat side down, to the Dutch oven. Add the onion, garlic, scallions, thyme, rosemary, and just enough water to cover. Bring to a boil over high heat, cover the pot with the parchment paper, then cover tightly with aluminum foil.

Transfer to the oven and cook until the belly is very tender, about 2½ hours. (To test for doneness, flip the belly and carefully and gently poke the fat; it should give way like custard.) When the belly is done, remove the pot from the oven, take off the lid, and let the belly rest in the liquid for 2 hours.

Carefully transfer the belly, fat side down, to the prepared baking sheet; reserve the cooking liquid. Cover the belly with another piece of parchment paper, put the second baking sheet on top of the parchment, and top with about 8 pounds of weight (a gallon jug of water or several large cans of beans will do the trick).

Strain the cooking liquid through a fine-mesh sieve into one or more airtight containers. Refrigerate both the weighted belly and the cooking liquid overnight.

The next day, skim the fat from the cooking liquid and reserve for another purpose. Wrap the belly in plastic wrap and store it and the cooking liquid in the fridge for up to 3 days or in the freezer for up to 3 months.

FERMENTS,
PICKLES
&
PRESERVES

It all started with sauerkraut.

When Rubicon, the restaurant where Nicole and I had been working, closed, I was jobless after nearly two decades at the professional stove, and planning my next move. For the first time in a long while, I had the opportunity to lie on the couch and flip through cookbooks. One day I came across a recipe for sauerkraut. It was the opposite of the elaborate, relentlessly creative restaurant food I'd been cooking—in other words, just the kind of thing I was eager to make.

I saw that sauerkraut requires just cabbage and salt. This wasn't entirely new information, but at the time it struck me as incredible that just two ingredients—or as I came to realize, four, if you count temperature and time—could produce such complex flavor. Because as any fan knows, sauerkraut doesn't taste like salty cabbage. It has a soft crunch, a vivid sour tang, and the same mouthwatering quality that we'd all call umami if sauerkraut were not so closely associated with Germany. I had to try my hand at it. I bought a one-gallon ceramic crock, and from then until State Bird opened three years later, it was never *not* full of cabbage.

For my first batch, I followed the recipe to the letter and six weeks later had delicious sauerkraut. As soon as I finished that batch, I started another. After the first few, I started experimenting, keeping all but one component the same and assessing the effect on the final product. The chef in me converted the recipe's original volume measurements to weight, so I could have the precise ratio of salt to cabbage and apply that ratio easily to whatever amount of cabbage I had on hand. From this study, I learned how to tweak the flavor by manipulating the amount of salt, the type of cabbage, and the temperature at which I fermented. I tasted the mixture weekly to check on its progress, like a cook checking a roast or a gardener visiting his tomato plants. I peeked and poked at the kraut, looking for the gentle bubbles that told me the magic was happening.

I'm not a science guy. And to succeed at fermenting food, you don't have to be. You don't have to understand the entire process, just the contours, which are still pretty neat. In the case of sauerkraut, perhaps the most basic of fermentations, the goal is to design an environment that thoughtfully nurtures particular bacteria already hanging out on the surface of the cabbage. That's what you're doing, whether you know it or not, when you salt shredded cabbage, pack it into your crock, and cover it with an airtight lid.

In an anaerobic environment, one type of bacteria multiplies and in the process produces carbon dioxide (which helps get rid of any remaining oxygen) and lactic acid. Soon the amount of lactic acid makes the mixture too acidic for those first bacteria. They die and new bacteria take over. They continue to consume the cabbage's sugars and spit out more lactic acid. The amount of salt and the temperature regulate the feeding frenzy. Too much salt and/or too low a temperature and the bacteria won't reproduce. Too little salt and/or too high a temperature and they'll do so too quickly. As I experimented, I figured out what I liked best. I learned that I could make sauerkraut more quickly if I raised the temperature; but that at a certain point, the result wouldn't taste as complex. I learned that kraut made from sweeter cabbage retained more of its cabbage flavor, but that I preferred the opposite. I liked the way less-sweet cabbage morphed into something almost unrecognizable. I figured out my own sweet spot.

It's all so cool that you can easily get lost in the details. Yet all you have to do is follow the instructions of the many cooks who came before you. (After all, what is a recipe but wisdom passed down?) Once you do, you'll keep out the wrong bacteria, foster the right ones, and transform sweet, one-note cabbage into a vegetable alive with the thrilling funk of fermentation.

Sauerkraut, it turns out, is a gateway pickle. Soon, my love of fermenting had me making kimchi, the Korean fermented pickle that comes in infinite varieties and whose composition is as elaborate as sauerkraut's is simple. Still, despite the addition of chile, aromatics, already fermented seafood, and starch, and the idiosyncrasies they bring, making cabbage kimchi is as straightforward and relies on the same principles as sauerkraut.

Soon after we opened State Bird, and in particular once we had the farm, my affection for these two classic examples of fermentation conspired with certain challenges to shape the food we made. Fermentation became the solution to many happy problems, like how to make use of bumper crops of nasturtiums and kohlrabi. No chef wants to throw anything away, whether out of respect for the effort of farming or regard for his bottom line. Fermenting became an obsession with a purpose.

The next thing I knew, I had an ample stash of fermented foods to get through. And so they joined fish sauce and Tabasco, ginger and seaweed, as part of our quirky pantry.

As we built dishes, we'd often reach into crocks and vats of fermented turnips, cucumbers, kohlrabi, cilantro roots, and radishes for a flavor twofer—salt and acid, integral to most great food, both delivered by just one ingredient. Soon fermented turnips stood in for capers. Instead of vinegars and citrus, we started looking to flavorful brine to brighten dressings and sauces.

The recipes in this section are some of our favorite ferments. They require a little time and attention, but they're well worth the effort for the culinary firepower they bring to your pantry. If you're anything like me, however, the effort might even become part of the fun.

the basics of fermenting at home

HERE'S WHAT YOU'LL NEED

1- to 1½-gallon fermenting crock with stone weights, or a 1-gallon glass jar and a 1-gallon resealable bag

During fermenting, salt draws out liquid from the vegetables. The liquid and salt mingle to create a brine that will ultimately submerge the vegetables, creating an environment without air, which promotes the bacteria that help your fermentation and, along with the salt, prevents unwanted bacteria. As the mixture sits, these helpful bacteria eat the sugars in the vegetables and spit out carbon dioxide and lactic acid. The vegetables are preserved and their simple raw flavor evolves into a complex acidity. Some ferments are ready after 10 days, while others benefit from up to 6 weeks.

here's what to do

1. Wash your hands. Clean and dry the crock or jar. Because the stone weights are often porous, we dry them in an oven set to the lowest possible heat for 30 to 60 minutes. This helps prevent mold growth.

2. Figure out the ratio of salt and vegetables that you're going to ferment and then combine.

3. Transfer the mixture, a handful at a time, to the crock or jar, using your fist to firmly press the mixture after each addition to eliminate any air hiding in the crannies among the vegetables. More air will be forced out as the vegetables give off water.

4. Weight down the mixture. If your crock has a weight, add it and press down firmly so the vegetables are submerged in liquid. The liquid must completely cover the vegetables. It acts as a seal, keeping out air so the right bacteria can do their thing. If you're fermenting in a jar, fill the resealable bag halfway with a 6 percent brine solution, force out the air, and seal. Put the bag, seal side up, in the crock or jar and, if necessary, gently guide with your hands so it covers the mixture. The bag acts as a weight, and the 6 percent brine ensures that if the bag leaks, your ferment won't suffer.

5. Store the container in a place that's approximately 65°F (no cooler than 58°F and no warmer than 70°F) and away from direct sunlight. If it's a little hotter or a little cooler, that's fine, though it will affect the timing.

6. Let the mixture ferment, checking every couple of days. Each time I check, I taste some to see how it's progressing. I also like to remove the weight and rinse it, and wipe the empty walls of the crock or jar with a damp paper towel. Occasionally, you might spot a white film on the surface, or rarely, white clumps of mold. Carefully skim this off, weight again, re-cover the crock or jar, and continue to ferment.

7. When the vegetables have fermented to your liking, transfer them to clean, relatively tall airtight containers and add enough of the liquid to cover. Store in the fridge for up to 6 months. (Though if you're like me, you'll probably have eaten it all by then.)

sauerkraut, opposite

kohlrabi kraut, page 56

fermented turnips, page 57

dill pickles, page 58

kimchi-style pickled wax beans, page 59

kimchi, page 60

preserved lemons, page 63

meyer lemon kosho, page 64

giardiniera, page 65

sauerkraut

Makes about 2⅓ quarts sauerkraut, plus about 1¾ cups brine

SPECIAL EQUIPMENT

Digital kitchen scale

Clean 1- to 1½-gallon fermenting crock with stone weights, or a clean 1- to 1½-gallon glass jar and a 1-gallon resealable bag

5 pounds green cabbage, quartered, cored and cut into ⅛-inch slices

Kosher salt

Because the amount of salt affects the flavor of the sauerkraut and the pace of fermentation, I like to be as precise as possible, basing my measurement on the weight of the prepared cabbage. This also gives you the ability to be flexible and use whatever amount of cabbage you have. My preferred ratio is 2 percent salt by weight.

Weigh the prepared cabbage; 2 percent of this weight is the amount of salt you'll need. You'll probably have about 1.8 kilograms cabbage, which requires about 36 grams salt.

Combine the cabbage and salt in a very large mixing bowl. Mix very well with your hands, spending 8 to 10 minutes firmly scrunching, squeezing, and rubbing the mixture together until the cabbage is limp and has started to release its liquid. Loosely cover and let sit at room temperature, scrunching and squeezing again a few times, for 24 hours.

The next day, transfer the cabbage mixture, a handful at a time, to the crock or jar, using your fist to firmly press the mixture after each addition. Pour in any liquid left behind in the bowl. There should be enough liquid to submerge the cabbage. Add the weight; the cabbage should be completely submerged. (If it isn't, combine 2 cups water and 30 grams salt. Stir until the salt dissolves and then gradually add to the crock as needed.) Press down firmly, cover, and seal.

Keep the container in a place that's approximately 65°F and away from direct sunlight. Ferment for at least 3 weeks or up to 6 weeks, checking every week to assess the progress. Re-weight the sauerkraut, re-cover the crock or jar, and continue to ferment to your liking.

Transfer to clean, airtight containers, add enough of the liquid to cover, and store in the fridge for up to 3 months.

kohlrabi kraut

Makes about 5 cups kraut,
plus about 1 cup brine

SPECIAL EQUIPMENT

Digital kitchen scale

Clean 1- to 1½-gallon
fermenting crock with stone
weights, or a clean 1-gallon
glass jar and a 1-gallon
resealable bag

3 pounds kohlrabi, peeled
and grated (on the large
holes of a box grater)

Kosher salt

2 tsp finely grated
(on a Microplane)
Meyer lemon zest

After an unexpected generous harvest, I gave kohlrabi, a
knobby, alien-looking member of the cabbage family, the
sauerkraut treatment. I was thrilled when the mild-mannered,
crisp, and sweet raw vegetable morphed through the magic
of fermentation into a lightly crunchy powerhouse of flavor.
We use it as a sort of reimagined mignonette for oysters
(see page 203).

Weigh the prepared kohlrabi; 2 percent of this weight is the
amount of salt you'll need. You'll probably have about 1.2 kilograms
kohlrabi, which requires about 24 grams salt.

Combine the kohlrabi, salt, and lemon zest in a very large mixing
bowl. Mix very well with your hands, spending about 5 minutes
firmly scrunching, squeezing, and rubbing the mixture together
until the kohlrabi is limp and has released a lot of its liquid.

Transfer the kohlrabi mixture, a handful at a time, to the crock or
jar, using your fist to firmly press the mixture after each addition.
Pour in any liquid left behind in the bowl. There should be enough
liquid to submerge the kohlrabi. Add the weight; the kohlrabi should
be completely submerged. (If it isn't combine 2 cups water and
30 grams salt. Stir until the salt dissolves and then gradually
add to the crock as needed.) Press down firmly, cover, and seal.

Keep the container in a place that's approximately 65°F and away
from direct sunlight. Ferment for about 10 days, checking every
few days to assess the progress. Re-weight the kraut, re-cover the
crock or jar, and continue to ferment to your liking.

Transfer to clean, airtight containers, add enough of the liquid
to cover, and store in the fridge for up to 3 months.

fermented turnips

Makes about 6 cups turnips,
plus about 4 cups brine

SPECIAL EQUIPMENT

Clean 1- to 1½-gallon
fermenting crock with stone
weights, or a clean 1-gallon
glass jar and a 1-gallon
resealable bag

2½ pounds small trimmed
Japanese turnips

2-inch knob peeled ginger,
thinly sliced into coins,
plus 2 tsp finely grated
(on a Microplane) ginger

¼ ounce sheet kombu
(Japanese dried kelp),
snipped into several pieces

4 cups water

6 Tbsp kosher salt

2 tsp finely grated
(on a Microplane) garlic

These simple pickles, a product of my fascination with fermentation and a happy glut of sweet Japanese turnips, have become State Bird's version of capers. Since we always have them around, they end up in so much of what we make, whether a dish might typically contain capers, like salmon tartare (see page 213), or whether it just welcomes the little explosions of saltiness and acidity that these tender roots deliver.

Clean and dry the turnips well, quarter them through the stem, and then transfer to the crock or jar. Add the sliced ginger and kombu and mix well.

Combine the water, salt, and 1 tsp of the garlic in a mixing bowl and whisk until the salt dissolves. Pour just enough of this brine over the turnips to barely cover them. Add a weight and press down firmly, then cover and seal.

Keep the container in a place that's approximately 65°F and away from direct sunlight. Ferment for 10 days, checking every few days to assess the progress. Rinse the weight, wipe the visible walls of the crock or jar with a damp paper towel, and carefully skim off any white film from the surface. Re-weight the turnips, re-cover the crock or jar, and continue to ferment to your liking. Then, add the grated ginger and remaining 1 tsp garlic and stir well.

Transfer to clean, airtight containers, add enough of the liquid to cover, and store in the fridge for up to 3 months.

dill pickles

Makes about 2 quarts

SPECIAL EQUIPMENT
Clean 1- to 1½-gallon
fermenting crock with stone
weights, or a clean 1- to
1½-gallon glass jar and a
1-gallon resealable bag

2 pounds small, firm
cucumbers (such as Kirby
or Persian), ends trimmed
by about ¼ inch

6 black peppercorns

3 large garlic cloves,
smashed and peeled

3 large dill sprigs

8 cups water

¾ cup plus 2 Tbsp
kosher salt

Unlike vinegar-brined cucumbers, these lacto-fermented pickles get their more compelling acidity from the magic of fermentation. Dill sprigs work well, though we often use the bold-flavored blossoms, which appear a week or two before the plants produce seeds.

Combine the cucumbers, peppercorns, garlic, and dill in the crock or jar and mix well. Combine the water and salt in a bowl and whisk until the salt dissolves. Pour just enough of this brine over the cucumbers to barely cover them. Add a weight and press down firmly, then cover and seal.

Keep the container in a place that's approximately 65°F and away from direct sunlight. Ferment for at least 10 days or up to 20 days, checking every week to assess the progress. Re-weight the cucumbers, re-cover the crock or jar, and continue to ferment to your liking.

Transfer to clean, airtight containers, add enough of the liquid to cover, and store in the fridge for up to 3 months.

kimchi-style pickled wax beans

Makes about 2 quarts

SPECIAL EQUIPMENT

Clean 1- to 1½-gallon
fermenting crock with stone
weights, or a clean 1- to
1½-gallon glass jar and a
1-gallon resealable bag

4 cups water

¼ cup fish sauce (preferably
Red Boat brand)

6 Tbsp kosher salt

3 Tbsp Korean red chile
flakes (*gochugaru*)

2 tsp finely grated
(on a Microplane) garlic

2 tsp finely grated
(on a Microplane) ginger

2 pounds wax beans,
trimmed

Korean chile flakes, ginger, and fish sauce give these lacto-fermented pickles an unmistakable kimchi quality, even if the method for making them is far from traditional. I especially like how wax beans, carrots, radishes, and any other dense, firm vegetables we have on hand retain their crunch post-pickling.

Combine the water, fish sauce, salt, chile flakes, garlic, and ginger in a large mixing bowl and whisk until well combined. Add the wax beans and mix well.

Transfer the beans to the crock or jar. Pour in the liquid left behind in the bowl. Add a weight and press down firmly, then cover and seal.

Keep the container in a place that's approximately 65°F and away from direct sunlight. Ferment for 7 to 10 days, checking every few days to assess the progress. Re-weight the beans, re-cover the crock or jar, and continue to ferment to your liking.

Transfer to clean, airtight containers, add enough of the liquid to cover, and store in the fridge for up to 3 months.

kimchi

Makes about 2 quarts
kimchi, plus 1 cup liquid

SPECIAL EQUIPMENT

Clean 1- to 1½-gallon
fermenting crock with stone
weights, or a clean 1-gallon
glass jar and a 1-gallon
resealable bag

A couple of years into my sauerkraut mania, I had become a confident fermenter, so I decided to take the kimchi plunge. Sauerkraut has two ingredients, plus temperature and time. To tinker, you simply tweak these few variables. Kimchi, on the other hand, has many ingredients, including chiles, aromatics, already fermented seafood, and starch, just to name a few. Tinkering with these felt like trying to crack a code. My first attempt sat in the fridge for six months, not because kimchi requires the wait but because I was reluctant to try what I'd made. Yet even that first attempt, though not perfect by far, produced a "wow" moment.

The labor involved in this recipe might discourage you from making it. I get it. Kimchi takes work and time, and there are so many high-quality kimchis out there. If you substitute your favorite one in the dishes in this book, you're bound to enjoy the result. But by not making this version yourself, the dishes that call for kimchi will have a different flavor, since we developed them with our particular kimchi in mind. Without making your own, you also sacrifice a bounty of the spicy, acidic liquid in which the fermented cabbage sits, which is a fabulous ingredient in itself. And finally, you'd miss the satisfaction that comes with creating something this delicious on your own.

4 cups water

6 Tbsp kosher salt

4½ pounds napa cabbage

1 cup thin half-moon-sliced
daikon radish

2½ ounces curly mustard
greens, stem bottoms
trimmed, cut crosswise
into ½-inch pieces

1 cup julienned Asian pear

½ cup thinly sliced carrots

½ cup julienned ginger

1 Tbsp finely grated (on a
Microplane) garlic

2 Tbsp fish sauce (preferably
Red Boat brand)

Combine the water and salt in a large mixing bowl and whisk until the salt has dissolved to make a brine.

Trim and discard about ½ inch from the bottom of the cabbages. Remove the green outer leaves (reserving them for another purpose) until you reach the light green leaves. Quarter the cabbages lengthwise, cut out the cores (reserving them for another purpose), then cut the cabbages into approximately 2-inch pieces.

Add the cabbage leaves to the brine and mix very well with your hands, spending a few minutes firmly scrunching, squeezing, and rubbing the mixture. Cover loosely and let sit at room temperature until the cabbage is wilted and mostly submerged in liquid, 18 to 24 hours.

2 Tbsp Korean red chile flakes (*gochugaru*)

1 Tbsp jarred Korean salted shrimp (*saeujeot*)

2 shucked oysters (including liquor), finely chopped (optional)

¼ cup cooked short-grain white rice

The next day, transfer the cabbage to a colander and rinse well under running water. A handful at a time, squeeze the cabbage to remove as much liquid as you can and transfer to a very large mixing bowl. Add the radish, mustard greens, pear, carrot, ginger, garlic, fish sauce, chile flakes, salted shrimp, oysters (if using), and rice and mix very well with your hands. Be rough as you mix—bruising the kimchi ingredients at this point helps build flavor later.

Transfer the cabbage mixture, a handful at a time, to the crock or jar, using your fist to firmly press the mixture after each addition. Pour in any liquid left behind in the bowl. Add a weight and press down firmly, then cover and seal.

Keep the container in a place that's approximately 65°F and away from direct sunlight. Ferment for 7 to 10 days, checking every few days to assess the progress. Re-weight the kimchi, re-cover the crock or jar, and continue to ferment to your liking.

Transfer both the solids and the delicious liquid to clean, airtight containers and store in the fridge for up to 1 year.

pickled carrots

Makes about 1 cup

Thinly sliced carrots pickle relatively quickly in a simple vinegar brine. They're just one of several ways we explore the root vegetable in carrot mochi (see page 247).

5 trimmed young carrots (about ½ inch thick), thinly sliced into rounds

¾ cup champagne vinegar

1 Tbsp granulated sugar

½ tsp kosher salt

½ tsp fennel seeds

½ tsp coriander seeds

½ tsp black peppercorns

¼ tsp red chile flakes

Put the carrots in a heatproof container.

In a small saucepan, combine the vinegar, sugar, salt, fennel seeds, coriander seeds, peppercorns, and chile flakes and stir to mix. Bring to a boil over high heat and then pour over the carrots. When the liquid has cooled, press plastic wrap to the surface to help keep the carrots submerged.

Cover and store in the fridge for at least 1 day and up to 1 week.

pickled ginger

Makes about ½ cup

A relatively sweet brine balances ginger's pleasant burn and subdues the rhizome's fibrous quality. A mandoline helps you quickly and easily achieve very thin slices, which will make your ginger especially tender.

3-inch knob ginger, peeled and very thinly sliced lengthwise

1 tsp kosher salt

1⅓ cups water

3 Tbsp unseasoned rice vinegar

3 Tbsp granulated sugar

Combine the ginger and salt in a small heatproof bowl and mix with your hands to evenly season the ginger. Bring 1 cup of the water to a boil in a small saucepan over high heat and then pour it over the ginger. Let sit for 5 minutes. Drain the ginger, discarding the water, and return the ginger to the bowl.

In the same small saucepan, stir together the vinegar, sugar, and remaining ⅓ cup water. Bring to a boil over high heat and then pour it over the ginger. Let sit at room temperature for 4 hours.

Transfer to an airtight container and store in the fridge for up to 1 month.

pickled okra

Makes about 2 cups

A soak in simple brine turns okra into a crisp pickle (without the slimy quality that scares some people off the vegetable). We halve and char them for added complexity, then use them to garnish a high-summer favorite at State Bird, eggplant tonkatsu (see page 177).

8 ounces small okra, trimmed

3 cups unseasoned rice vinegar

¼ cup granulated sugar

1 Tbsp kosher salt

Put the okra in a 1-quart heatproof container.

In a small saucepan, combine the vinegar, sugar, and salt and stir to mix. Bring to a boil over high heat and then pour over the okra. When the liquid has cooled, press plastic wrap to the surface to help keep the okra submerged.

Cover and store in the fridge for at least 1 week or up to 3 weeks.

preserved lemons

Makes about 4 cups

Whether or not you make this Moroccan preserve yourself, it belongs in your larder. Salt and time turn the brightness and simple tartness of lemons into something much more complex and compelling. The whole fruit ends up edible—the tender rind is fragrant, pungent, and subtly astringent, while the pulp is still slightly sharp with acid. We turn these lemons into sauces and slip slivers of rind into the filling for guinea hen dumplings (see page 225).

6 large organic lemons, washed and dried thoroughly, plus 2⅔ cups lemon juice

1½ cups kosher salt

Wash and dry a wide-mouthed 2-quart glass jar with a lid. Slice off both ends from the lemons and stand each fruit upright on a cutting board. Working with one lemon at a time, cut the fruit in half lengthwise, stopping about ½ inch from the bottom. Rotate the lemon 90 degrees and make a similar cut perpendicular to the first.

Working with one lemon at a time, gently pull open the fruit (making sure not to break it into pieces), pack in 2 Tbsp of the salt, and add to the jar, cramming the first three lemons next to each other. Once you've added three lemons, evenly sprinkle on ¼ cup plus 2 Tbsp salt. Continue the process, sprinkling ¼ cup plus 2 Tbsp salt onto each layer of three lemons. Slowly pour in the lemon juice.

Cover tightly and let sit at room temperature and away from direct sunlight for 3 weeks. Turn the jar upside down and store for another 3 weeks.

Transfer the lemons to a clean, airtight container, add enough of the liquid to cover, and store in the fridge for up to 6 months. Rinse well before using.

meyer lemon kosho

Makes about 2 cups

SPECIAL EQUIPMENT
Digital kitchen scale

This nose-tickling Japanese condiment packs powerful fragrance and flavor into an unassuming paste. Kosho is typically made from fresh chiles and the zest of the yuzu, an especially aromatic citrus. But at State Bird, we look to Meyer lemon, which is both easier to find and has an equally complex aroma. Salt and fermentation temper the fruit's feistiness, and grassy chile adds to the aromatic quality. The result isn't as thick or intense as the Japanese original, but it's a thrill nonetheless. You'll need quite a bit of zest, so this might be an only-in-California recipe, for those lucky people who have Meyer lemon trees, or at least have a friend who does. And note that for this recipe, using a precise ratio of zest to salt is of particular importance. So weigh your zest, then be sure to use 10 percent salt by weight.

20 Meyer lemons

Kosher salt

2 green jalapeño or serrano chiles (including seeds), coarsely chopped

Cut the peel from the lemons in wide strips. One strip at a time, cut away and discard the white pith. Halve and squeeze enough of the lemons, discarding any seeds, to give you ½ cup lemon juice.

Weigh the prepared lemon peel; 10 percent of this weight is the amount of salt you'll need. You'll probably have about 400 grams lemon, which requires about 40 grams salt.

Combine the lemon peel, lemon juice, salt, and chiles in a high-speed blender and blend to a fairly smooth puree, using the wand to stir as necessary to help the mixture catch in the blades.

Transfer the mixture to a 1-quart jar. Wipe the inside walls of the jar with a damp paper towel. Press a piece of plastic wrap to the surface of the mixture. Cover the jar with a double layer of cheesecloth and wrap a rubber band around the rim of the container to secure.

Keep the container in a place that's approximately 65°F and away from direct sunlight. Ferment for about 14 days, checking every few days to assess the progress, until it is to your liking.

Transfer to a clean, airtight container, using a damp towel to wipe any stray puree from the walls of the container, and store in the fridge for up to 1 year.

giardiniera

Makes about 8 cups

Giardiniera makes a great partner for tender meat, whether it's the sloppy, wondrous slices piled on Chicago's iconic Italian beef sandwiches or the braised tongue we serve with pancakes (see page 129). The crunchy pickle—briefly cooked in vinegar and salt, then immersed in hot oil—is a great way to preserve a variety of vegetables in the same jar. The State Bird version has nearly a dozen vegetables, from peppers and turnips to carrots and cauliflower, but feel free to use whatever you have on hand. This recipe makes plenty, and you'll be happy to have leftovers.

6 cups rice bran oil

1¾ pounds assorted firm, raw vegetables (such as cauliflower, carrots, peppers, and turnips), trimmed and cut into ½-inch pieces

3 large shallots, cut into ½-inch rings

6 cups apple cider vinegar

½ cup plus 1 Tbsp kosher salt

3 medium garlic cloves, smashed and peeled

1 Tbsp coriander seeds

1 Tbsp rosemary leaves

2 tsp black peppercorns

Pour the rice bran oil into a medium pot, set over medium-high heat, and bring to 300°F. Lower the heat to maintain the temperature.

Meanwhile, in a pot large enough to contain at least four times the volume of the raw vegetables (to ensure that the hot oil won't bubble over later), combine the vegetables, shallots, vinegar, salt, garlic, coriander seeds, rosemary, and peppercorns. Bring to a gentle boil over medium-high heat, stirring once or twice to help the salt dissolve, then immediately drain the vegetables, reserving the vinegar mixture for future giardiniera making. (Strained, it can be used several times.) Return the vegetables to the large pot.

Carefully pour the hot oil over the vegetables. Let cool to room temperature, divide among several containers, and refrigerate at least overnight or up to 1 month. Let come to room temperature before eating.

state bird sourdough starter

Makes about
440 grams/2 cups

SPECIAL EQUIPMENT
Digital kitchen scale

Sourdough starter is very cool stuff, a simple project that'll remind you of the invisible magic that makes the world go 'round, like those science-fair experiments you did as a kid. Except none of those experiments ever resulted in anything delicious.

A mixture of flour and water left at room temperature becomes a breeding ground for wild yeast. Added to pancake batter (see pages 113, 117, 119, and 123) and bread dough (see pages 153 and 156), the congregation of yeast contributes flavor and improves texture. Added to sesame bread dough, it provides structure as well.

Using starter takes a little planning. First, if you're making the starter, you have to begin several days before you're ready to cook. In my experience, starter requires a good three or four days of consistent feeding—which is as easy as stirring in more flour and water—before the yeasty activity is nice and stable. Second, once you have a stable starter, you have to use it 8 to 12 hours after the last time you fed it. Why? Well, think about it. You have this beautiful sludge full of yeasty activity, then you add flour and water, effectively diluting it. The yeasts need time to do their thing—8 to 12 hours, actually—and get the mixture back to where it was.

And finally, you have to be sure you always have more starter than a recipe requires. Because if you use your entire batch in one recipe, you'll have to make more from scratch. Keeping plenty on hand isn't hard. Every time you feed your starter, it has the potential to triple in amount. If you bake a lot, this is awesome. If not, it can be overwhelming—more starter means more food, which means even more starter to feed even more food! That's why you'll notice a seemingly odd instruction in the recipe; to dump some of the starter before each feed. Yet since maintaining your starter takes a lot of your attention but not much time or money, I say don't throw out any starter— use it!

160 grams/1 cup plus
2 Tbsp bread flour,
plus about 1 kilogram/
6½ cups

30 grams/¼ cup
whole-grain (dark)
rye flour, plus
260 grams/2 cups
plus 3 Tbsp

160 grams/⅔ cup
room-temperature
(70° to 80°F) water,
plus more for feeding

Combine the bread flour, rye flour, and water in a 1-quart non-reactive (plastic or glass is fine) container and use your fingers or a chopstick to stir until there are no pockets of flour and the mixture looks like slightly wet dough. Cover with a clean kitchen towel.

Keep the mixture at room temperature (ideally around 68°F but a little warmer or cooler is fine) until it becomes bubbly and elastic, a day or so. Let the mixture continue to evolve until the bubbles get smaller and the mixture is less elastic and more fluid but before it becomes soupy, 1 to 2 days more. Take a sniff and a nibble; it will smell like sour beer and taste tangy. (If by some small chance it smells rotten or looks moldy, throw it out and start over from the beginning.)

Feed the starter by discarding (yep, discard—it's not ready to use yet) all but 100 grams of the mixture. (Since the volume varies as the starter ripens, weight is the ideal measurement). Add 80 grams bread flour, 20 grams rye flour, and 100 grams water. Stir well, re-cover with the towel, and leave at room temperature for 8 to 12 hours. For the second and all subsequent feedings, discard all but 40 grams of the starter. Add 160 grams bread flour, 40 grams rye flour, and 200 grams water. (Stir well, re-cover with the towel, and leave at room temperature for 8 to 12 hours between each feeding.)

After 3 days, you'll have about 440 grams/2 cups of healthy starter. To use in breads and pancakes, wait 8 to 12 hours from the time of the last feeding so it's good and hungry (small bubbles, slightly fluid) but not so long that it's soupy, like thin pancake batter.

Going forward, feed the starter every 8 to 12 hours, discarding (or better yet, using!) all but 40 grams. Continue to feed according to the same formula.

FEED
THE
BABY

I adopted the Polish Princess in Hawaii. When Stuart and I were still working at Rubicon, we did an event in Oahu at a fancy hotel. The guy who ran the pastry kitchen there was from Poland. He told me that when he moved to Oahu, he brought a stowaway on the plane—a quart of sourdough starter that had been made in the motherland decades earlier. In a lovely Polish person–to–Polish person moment, he offered me some of his starter. I nearly teared up.

Sourdough starter, if you're not familiar with it, is a wild yeast factory. Wild yeast, not the domesticated kind in active dry yeast or fresh cake yeast, is what you need to make great bread. Both wild and domesticated yeasts drive fermentation, turning otherwise bland, dense mixtures of flour and water into doughs that become tasty, texturally pleasing breads. How? Well, by doing a lot of scientific things that I never remember. When I need reminding, I look to Chad Robertson's *Tartine Bread* and Jeffrey Hamelman's *Bread*.

Domesticated yeasts, though, are like house cats—easy to keep, but not all that interesting. Wild yeast is like a tiger—harder to tame, but very, very interesting. Breads made with wild yeasts taste more complex and have better texture. The bad news is, you can't buy wild yeast at the store. The good news is you don't have to.

After we got home from Hawaii, Larry Stone—an incredible sommelier, winery manager, and Rubicon's founder—rushed into the restaurant holding a cluster of Pinot Noir grapes. This was a very Larry thing to do. He was excited because they were covered in so much yeast. He practically demanded that I make a starter to help the lovely yeast survive and multiply. What luck, I thought. So I did, steeping crushed grapes in the water-flour mixture and using buckwheat flour for fun. And so "Bucky" came into the world.

After Rubicon closed, I took Bucky and the Princess home. Even though I wasn't baking nearly as much, I still fed them flour and water twice a day. You have to feed your starter, because those yeasts are alive and even single-celled organisms need to eat. Then I came to my senses and mixed them together. It was kind of like Bucky and Princess had a baby. So we called it "Baby."

At State Bird, we take good care of Baby. Nothing else in the kitchen gets the kind of attention it does. When we're closed, someone takes home the starter and feeds it, like the class hamster at my son's school. We love Baby. Baby helps us make delicious breads and pancakes. It's part of the team. But the truth is, Baby isn't special.

I later learned, with the rest of the baking community, that I had glamorized starter. I loved thinking that when I was using Bucky, I was adding a special *something* from those beautiful grapes. But it turns out that wild yeast is all around us, and the source really doesn't matter. I loved thinking that when I was using the Princess, I was improving my breads by incorporating old, wise yeasts from Poland. It turns out aged starter isn't better, and that Polish starter quickly becomes San Francisco starter, since local bacteria quickly populate it.

So that's why the first instruction in my recipe for sourdough starter isn't "First, charm an old Polish man." I've accepted the fact that even if I lost Baby tomorrow, I could have new, great starter in about a week. All I'd have to do is combine flour and water and leave the mixture at room temperature. That is the perfect ambience to attract a certain kind of partygoer. The yeasts meet and mingle, imbibing the starches and sugars and burping out carbon dioxide. Keep the starches and sugars coming and they'll keep partying. Soon, there's enough yeast to make bread.

Of course, just because anyone can make great starter doesn't mean I don't have friends throughout the city with a little bit of Baby in their freezers. Just in case.

AIOLIS

In the State Bird kitchen, we take lots of liberties with the names of our larder ingredients. At least I do, and my cooks kindly play along. What I nicknamed garum (see page 42), after an ancient Roman condiment, is actually just infused fish sauce. What I casually call Arab Spice (it has such a nice ring to it; see page 99) is just a mixture of spices inspired by a cookbook on Arab cuisine. The same goes for the array of condiments in this section, which I call aiolis.

Yet when you put these dishes in a book, you butt up against certain technicalities. So I suppose I should point out that these aren't true aiolis—the labor-intensive emulsion of olive oil and garlic that is pounded in the mortar and bound in creaminess by care and patience. Mine are bound with egg yolks and by blender. They're more like mayonnaise. Now, I have nothing against mayo. Just the opposite; I love mayo! I grew up on mayo—the blob of Best Foods my mom added to a plate beside a steamed artichoke, the generous slathering I still put on hot dogs. But somehow the word *mayonnaise* doesn't do the following concoctions justice. These lush, thick sauces are excellent vehicles for flavor, and we take full advantage. We use oil infused with things like rosemary or garlic. We blend in things like miso or mushrooms cooked in butter. In some cases, we use the result to provide contrast in a dish—the way bright Meyer lemon kosho aioli perks up salmon tartare (see page 213). In others, the aioli reinforces a particular flavor—the way chanterelle mushroom aioli underscores that same awesome mushroom served on toasts (see page 151). That said, I would eagerly spread any of these aiolis on a sandwich or serve them in a bowl beside crudités.

bonito-rosemary aioli

Makes about 1⅓ cups

You know something has graduated from occasional condiment to larder ingredient when it gets a nickname, such as this aioli, now known in the State Bird kitchen as "bo ro." The *bo* is for bonito, or really *katsuobushi*, flakes of Japanese dried fish that's smoky and full of umami; the *ro* is for rosemary. The dried fish and woodsy herb go together like camping and forests. Here, the duo take a luscious, creamy form in honor of my affection (and Japan's, for that matter) for mayonnaise.

⅔ cup rosemary sprigs, leaves stripped and stems torn into small pieces

1 cup plus 2 Tbsp grapeseed oil

1 cup katsuobushi (Japanese bonito flakes)

2 Tbsp State Bird Dashi (page 40) or water

1½ Tbsp lime juice

1 Tbsp shiro shoyu (white soy sauce, such as Yamashin brand)

2 large egg yolks

Zest of 1 Meyer lemon, finely grated on a Microplane

¼-inch knob ginger, peeled and finely grated on a Microplane

½ small garlic clove, finely grated on a Microplane

Combine the rosemary and ½ cup plus 2 Tbsp of the grapeseed oil in a very small saucepan and set over medium-low heat. When the oil begins to sizzle and the rosemary becomes a shade or two lighter, about 5 minutes, remove the pan from the heat and let the mixture cool to room temperature. Strain through a fine-mesh sieve, discarding the rosemary.

Combine the katsuobushi, dashi, lime juice, shiro shoyu, egg yolks, lemon zest, ginger, and garlic in a small food processor. Process until fairly smooth. With the processor running, add the remaining ½ cup grapeseed oil followed by the rosemary oil in a thin, steady stream. Scrape the sides of the processor and process for another 5 seconds or so.

Transfer to an airtight container and store in the fridge for at least 3 hours or up to 3 days.

blue cheese aioli

Makes about 2 cups

This lively sauce is mixed with top-shelf blue cheese that stays in pungent chunks—it's essentially the blue cheese dressing you *wish* came with Buffalo wings.

2 large egg yolks

2 Tbsp lemon juice

2 Tbsp water

1 small garlic clove, finely grated on a Microplane

Kosher salt

1 cup grapeseed oil

1 Tbsp red wine vinegar

5 turns freshly ground black pepper

3 dashes Tabasco sauce

5½ ounces dense, creamy blue cheese (such as Bayley Hazen), finely crumbled

Combine the egg yolks, lemon juice, water, garlic, and ½ tsp salt in a small food processor. Process until fairly smooth. With the processor running, add the grapeseed oil in a thin, steady stream. Scrape the sides of the processor and process for another 5 seconds or so.

Scrape the aioli into a bowl. Stir in the vinegar, pepper, and Tabasco, then fold in the blue cheese. Season with salt.

Transfer to an airtight container and store in the fridge for up to 4 days.

miso-yuzu aioli

Makes about 1½ cups

Bold red miso joins the bright complexity of Japanese citrus *yuzu* for a silky aioli that's as nontraditional as it is unforgettable.

¼ cup cold water

2 Tbsp plus 1 tsp aka (red) miso

1 large egg yolk

1 Tbsp plus 1 tsp yuzu or Meyer lemon juice

½ tsp kosher salt

1 small garlic clove, finely grated on a Microplane

6 turns freshly ground black pepper

2 dashes Tabasco sauce

1 cup grapeseed oil

Combine the water, miso, egg yolk, yuzu juice, salt, garlic, pepper, and Tabasco in a small food processor. Process until fairly smooth. With the processor running, add the grapeseed oil in a thin, steady stream. Scrape the sides of the processor and process for another 5 seconds or so.

Transfer to an airtight container and store in the fridge for up to 3 days.

garlic confit aioli

Makes about 1½ cups

1½ cups peeled garlic cloves
3 rosemary sprigs
About 1½ cups olive oil
1 large egg yolk
1 Tbsp sherry vinegar
1½ tsp Dijon mustard
2 turns freshly ground
black pepper
1 dash Tabasco sauce
Kosher salt
1 tsp water

We slowly cook garlic in oil until it's sweet and smooshably soft, then use both the flavorful oil and cloves to make this aioli.

Preheat the oven to 300°F.

Combine the garlic and rosemary in a small ovenproof pot and add enough olive oil to cover the garlic by about ½ inch. (Some of the cloves might float. That's fine.) Set over medium heat. When tiny bubbles begin to break the surface of the oil, turn off the heat and transfer the pot to the center rack of the oven.

Cook until the garlic is smooshable (you should be able to crush a clove with barely any pressure from a fork), about 20 minutes. Let sit at room temperature until fully cooled. Discard the rosemary. (You can transfer the garlic and oil to an airtight container and store in the fridge for up to 1 month. Make sure the garlic is always submerged in oil, topping up with more olive oil, if necessary.)

Using a slotted spoon, remove ¼ cup of the garlic confit from the oil and add it to a small food processor along with the egg yolk, vinegar, mustard, pepper, Tabasco, and ½ tsp salt. Process until fairly smooth. With the processor running, add ½ cup of the garlic confit oil in a thin, steady stream, followed by the water, then another ¼ cup garlic confit oil. Scrape the sides of the processor and process for another 5 seconds or so. Season with salt.

Transfer to an airtight container and store in the fridge for up to 3 days.

meyer lemon kosho aioli

Makes about 1¼ cups

To bring a thrill to salmon tartare (see page 213), we turn our rendition of the Japanese condiment *yuzu kosho* into this vivid aioli, in which the aroma of Meyer lemon peel is on full display. You can certainly opt to substitute store-bought *yuzu kosho* instead; just keep in mind that it's significantly saltier and spicier than our version, so start with far less and add more gradually.

3 Tbsp Meyer Lemon Kosho (page 64)

2½ Tbsp State Bird Dashi (page 40) or water

2 tsp Meyer lemon juice, or as needed

½ tsp seeded and finely grated (on a Microplane) jalapeño chile

⅛ tsp finely grated (on a Microplane) ginger

1 small garlic clove, finely grated on a Microplane

1 large egg yolk

1 cup grapeseed oil

Kosher salt

Combine the Meyer lemon kosho, dashi, lemon juice, jalapeño, ginger, garlic, and egg yolk in a small food processor. Process until fairly smooth. With the processor running, add the grapeseed oil in a thin, steady stream. Scrape the sides of the processor and process for another 5 seconds or so. Season with salt and more lemon juice.

Transfer to an airtight container and store in the fridge for up to 3 days.

caesar aioli

Makes about 1½ cups

I have a weakness for Caesar salad. If it's on a menu, I can't *not* order it. So it had to end up on the State Bird menu in some form or another. I took the best part (the dressing) and channeled its flavors—the Parm, the pepper, the anchovy—into a thicker, richer, more intense aioli. It makes a great dip for vegetables, like romaine hearts, if you're in a classic mood, or on steak tartare toasts (see page 145), if you're not. If you have leftovers, know that a few tablespoons of water and will turn this aioli into a proper Caesar dressing.

10 high-quality oil-packed anchovy fillets, drained

1 large egg yolk

1 small garlic clove, finely grated on a Microplane

1 Tbsp plus 1 tsp red wine vinegar

2 tsp fish sauce (preferably Red Boat brand)

1 tsp Dijon mustard

½ tsp freshly ground black pepper

1 dash Tabasco sauce

1 cup grapeseed oil

1 Tbsp lemon juice

3 Tbsp finely grated (on a Microplane) Parmesan

Combine the anchovies, egg yolk, garlic, vinegar, fish sauce, mustard, pepper, and Tabasco in a small food processor. Process until fairly smooth. With the processor running, add the grapeseed oil in a thin, steady stream. Add the lemon juice and Parmesan and process until smooth. Scrape the sides of the processor and process for another 5 seconds or so.

Transfer to in an airtight container and store in the fridge for up to 3 days.

tomato aioli

Makes about 1¾ cups

In our reimagining of the Mexican dish *elote* (see page 241), the mayonnaise that's typically slathered on corn is infused with the sweetness and umami of tomatoes and aromatics cooked slowly in olive oil.

4 ripe medium Roma tomatoes, cored

2 tsp kosher salt

2 medium garlic cloves, smashed and peeled

1 tsp freshly ground black pepper

½ tsp red chile flakes

2 sprigs thyme

1 sprig rosemary, very coarsely chopped

1 cup extra-virgin olive oil, or as needed

1 large egg yolk

Preheat the oven to 200°F.

Bring a large pot of water to a boil. Cut a shallow X at the bottom of each tomato, add to the boiling water, and cook for 15 seconds. Transfer the tomatoes to a colander and rinse under cold running water. Peel off the skins.

Cut the tomatoes in half lengthwise, season all over with 1 tsp of the salt, then put them, cut side down, in a medium ovenproof sauté pan. Then, add the garlic, pepper, chile flakes, thyme, and rosemary. Add enough of the olive oil to reach halfway up the sides of the tomatoes.

Set the pan over medium-high heat and cook until you see small bubbles rising to the top, about 5 minutes. Transfer the pan to the oven and roast until the tomatoes are soft but still intact and slightly wrinkly on top, about 2 hours. Remove and reserve the tomatoes. Strain the oil, discarding the aromatics, and let cool completely.

Combine the tomatoes, egg yolk, and remaining 1 tsp salt in a small food processor and process until fairly smooth. With the processor running, add the reserved oil in a thin, steady stream. Scrape the sides and process for another 5 minutes or so.

Transfer to an airtight container and store in the fridge for up to 3 days.

mushroom aiolis

Mushroom aiolis form an important category in the State Bird larder. The combination is a synergistic one: mushrooms cooked in butter charge the aioli with umami, and the fat of the aioli amplifies the flavor of the mushrooms. The result is just one way that we attack ingredients from different angles, to make each dish we serve more interesting. You'll find three versions here—each for a type of mushroom we relish—all of which would be great accents to practically any dish using mushroom-friendly preparations, such as grilled asparagus, roasted potatoes, and steak. We, of course, have time-tested uses for each one: porcini aioli amplifies the, well, porcini-ness of porcini fried rice (see page 253); chanterelle aioli does the same for chanterelle toasts (see page 151); and black trumpet aioli matches so well with its seasonal compatriot on asparagus toasts (see page 148).

PORCINI AIOLI

Makes about 2 cups

4 Tbsp unsalted butter, cut into several pieces

1 small shallot, thinly sliced

1 medium garlic clove, smashed and peeled

8 ounces fresh porcini mushrooms, including stems, cleaned and thinly sliced

Kosher salt

Freshly ground black pepper

4 Tbsp water

1 large egg yolk

1½ tsp sherry vinegar, or as needed

1½ tsp Dijon mustard

1 dash Tabasco sauce

¼ tsp Porcini Spice Powder (page 107; optional)

1 cup grapeseed oil

Combine the butter, shallot, and garlic in a medium sauté pan. Set over high heat and let the butter melt and froth, swirling occasionally. Turn the heat to medium-high and cook, stirring and scraping often, until the shallot is translucent, about 2 minutes.

Add the mushrooms and ½ tsp salt to the pan, season with pepper, and stir well. Cook, stirring occasionally, until the mushrooms are cooked through, about 2 minutes. Pour in 2 Tbsp of the water, let the liquid come to a boil, then stir and scrape the pan until the liquid glazes the pan, about 30 seconds. Immediately transfer the pan's contents to a baking sheet and spread out to help cool quickly to room temperature.

Scrape every last bit of the mushroom mixture into a food processor. Add the egg yolk, vinegar, mustard, Tabasco, porcini spice powder (if using), 1 tsp salt, and remaining 2 Tbsp water. Process to a very coarse puree. With the processor running, add the grapeseed oil in a thin, steady stream. Scrape the sides of the processor and process for another 5 seconds or so. Season with additional salt, pepper, and vinegar.

Transfer to an airtight container and store in the fridge for up to 3 days.

CHANTERELLE AIOLI

Makes about 2½ cups

¼ cup extra-virgin olive oil

1 medium yellow onion, halved lengthwise and thinly sliced

2 medium garlic cloves, smashed and peeled

Kosher salt

Freshly ground black pepper

2 Tbsp unsalted butter

8 ounces fresh golden chanterelle mushrooms, trimmed, cleaned, and cut into bite-size pieces

1 Tbsp thyme leaves

1 large egg yolk

1 tsp sherry vinegar, or as needed

1 tsp Dijon mustard

½ cup finely grated aged pecorino (preferably Fiore Sardo) or Parmesan

1 Tbsp water (optional)

1 cup grapeseed oil

Combine the olive oil, onion, and garlic in a large sauté pan. Set over medium heat and cook, stirring occasionally, until the onion is soft and golden, 8 to 10 minutes. Sprinkle with 1 tsp salt and 5 turns pepper.

Add the butter, mushrooms, thyme, and 1 tsp salt to the pan and cook, stirring occasionally, until the mushrooms are cooked through, 5 to 8 minutes. Immediately transfer the pan's contents to a baking sheet and spread out to help cool quickly to room temperature.

Scrape every last bit of the mushroom mixture into a food processor. Add the egg yolk, vinegar, mustard, pecorino, and another 5 turns pepper. Process to a very coarse puree, stirring once or twice and gradually adding the water, if needed. With the processor running, add the grapeseed oil in a thin, steady stream. Scrape the sides of the processor and process for another 5 seconds or so. Season with additional salt, pepper, and vinegar.

Transfer to an airtight container and store in the fridge for up to 3 days.

BLACK TRUMPET AIOLI

Makes about 2 cups

3 Tbsp unsalted butter,
cut into several pieces

1 large shallot, thinly sliced

2 medium garlic cloves;
1 thinly sliced, 1 finely
grated on a Microplane

½ tsp thyme leaves

1 Tbsp rosemary leaves

8 ounces black trumpet
mushrooms, trimmed,
halved lengthwise, and
cleaned well

Kosher salt

1 tsp freshly ground
black pepper

2 large egg yolks

2 Tbsp sherry vinegar,
or as needed

3 dashes Tabasco sauce

1 cup grapeseed oil

¼ cup well-shaken
buttermilk

Combine the butter, shallot, sliced garlic, thyme, and rosemary in a large sauté pan. Set over medium heat and cook until the edges of the garlic and shallot turn golden brown, 3 to 5 minutes.

Add the mushrooms, ½ tsp salt, and ½ tsp of the pepper to the pan and cook, stirring occasionally, until softened, about 5 minutes. Immediately transfer the pan's contents to a baking sheet and spread out to help cool quickly to room temperature.

Scrape every last bit of the mushroom mixture into a food processor. Add the egg yolks, grated garlic, vinegar, Tabasco, ½ tsp salt, and remaining ½ tsp pepper. Process until fairly smooth, scraping the sides once or twice. With the processor running, add the grapeseed oil in a thin, steady stream, followed by the buttermilk. Scrape the sides of the processor once more and process for another 5 seconds or so. Season with additional salt and vinegar.

Transfer to an airtight container and store in the fridge for up to 3 days.

VINAIGRETTES
&
SAUCES

Vinaigrettes are not just for greens. While none of these dressings will disappoint when tossed with whatever lettuces grab your eye at the market, they're built for the big flavors of the State Bird kitchen. Arrayed on the pass in squirt bottles, they are used to unleash brightness and a little fat when necessary, drizzled on dishes that take full advantage of their particular makeup. The classic sharpness of sherry vinaigrette, for instance, highlights the flavor and color of the raw ripe tomatoes served with our whole-grain cheddar pancakes. The lime in our fish sauce vinaigrette, on the other hand, provides just the right jolt to a dish of rich, fatty cubes of fried pork belly and sweet plums, while the umami-rich salty-sweet quality of the dressing's namesake teams up with fresh chile and fresh herbs to evoke the dish's inspiration—those bright, spicy protein-forward Southeast Asian "salads." Once you get to know each vinaigrette, you can decide for yourself how best to apply it.

white soy sauce–lime vinaigrette

Makes about 1¾ cups

We riff on the Japanese sauce *ponzu* to make this unforgettable vinaigrette. Starting with a simple mixture of white soy sauce (more delicate and elegant than the dark kind) and lime juice (instead of ponzu's traditional yuzu), we then add bonito flakes and dried kelp, the same duo that give Japanese dashi its smokiness and umami, letting them steep until their flavors bloom. Grated ginger and garlic add extra complexity.

½ cup shiro shoyu (white soy sauce, such as Yamashin brand)

½ cup lime juice

Generous ½ cup katsuobushi (Japanese bonito flakes)

¼ ounce kombu (Japanese dried kelp), snipped into several pieces

½ tsp finely grated (on a Microplane) ginger

½ tsp finely grated (on a Microplane) garlic

¾ cup plus 2 Tbsp grapeseed oil

Combine the shiro shoyu, lime juice, katsuobushi, kombu, ginger, and garlic in a container and stir well. Let the mixture sit at room temperature for 1 hour.

Strain the mixture through a medium-mesh sieve into a clean container, pressing on the solids to extract as much liquid as possible; discard the solids. Whisk in the grapeseed oil in a slow stream until well combined.

Transfer to an airtight container and store in the fridge for up to 1 week. Whisk well before using.

carrot juice vinaigrette

Makes about ½ cup

¼ cup carrot juice

1 Tbsp lime juice

1 tsp kosher salt

¼ tsp finely grated (on a Microplane) jalapeño chile

¼ tsp finely grated (on a Microplane) ginger

⅛ tsp finely grated (on a Microplane) garlic

1 dash Tabasco sauce

¼ cup extra-virgin olive oil

Combine the carrot juice, lime juice, salt, jalapeño, ginger, garlic, and Tabasco in a medium mixing bowl and stir well. Whisk in the olive oil in a slow stream until well combined.

Transfer to an airtight container and store in the fridge for up to 2 days. Whisk well before using.

umeboshi-rosemary vinaigrette

Makes about 2½ cups

This is just one of a few members of our pantry's arsenal that pairs rosemary and *katsuobushi* (Japanese dried, cured fish; here in the form of dashi). And like the others—such as our version of dashi itself and "bo ro" (see page 73)—it showcases the smoky, woodsy combination that seems unlikely at first glance but so inevitable after your first taste. The third major player in the dressing is *umeboshi*, a type of Japanese pickled plum that provides a unique sort of puckery acidity that I can't get enough of.

1 cup rosemary sprigs, leaves stripped and stems torn into small pieces

1 cup grapeseed oil

1 cup plus 3 Tbsp State Bird Dashi (page 40)

Scant ½ cup umeboshi (Japanese pickled plum) paste

1-inch knob ginger, peeled and finely grated on a Microplane

1 small garlic clove, finely grated on a Microplane

Combine the rosemary and grapeseed oil in a very small saucepan and set over medium-low heat. When the oil begins to sizzle and the rosemary becomes a shade or two lighter, about 5 minutes, remove the pan from the heat and let the mixture cool to room temperature. Strain through a fine-mesh sieve, discarding the rosemary.

Combine the rosemary oil, dashi, umeboshi paste, ginger, and garlic in a medium mixing bowl and whisk until well combined.

Transfer to an airtight container and store in the fridge for up to 1 month. Whisk well before using.

sherry vinaigrette

Makes about 2 cups

Perfectly balanced with the high acidity and lovable oxidized quality of sherry vinegar, this one doesn't stray far from classic vinaigrette.

½ cup sherry vinegar

2 tsp Dijon mustard

1 medium garlic clove, finely grated on a Microplane

½ tsp kosher salt

1½ cups olive oil

Combine the vinegar, mustard, garlic, and salt in a medium mixing bowl and whisk until smooth. Whisk in the olive oil in a slow stream until well combined.

Transfer to an airtight container and store in the fridge for up to 4 days. Whisk well before using.

fish sauce vinaigrette

Makes about 1 cup

This simple dressing makes a big impact thanks to plenty of fish sauce and lime. But because they exist in equilibrium—along with a small dose of sugar, rare in the savory cooking at State Bird—they add bold, bright flavor without overwhelming the flavor of what's dressed.

¼ cup plus 2 Tbsp lime juice

¼ cup plus 2 Tbsp water

¼ cup fish sauce (preferably Red Boat brand)

1½ tsp granulated sugar

½-inch knob ginger, peeled and finely grated on a Microplane

1 small garlic clove, finely grated on a Microplane

¼ cup grapeseed oil

Combine the lime juice, water, fish sauce, sugar, ginger, and garlic in a medium mixing bowl and whisk until the sugar dissolves. Whisk in the grapeseed oil in a slow stream until well combined.

Transfer to an airtight container and store in the fridge for up to 1 week. Whisk well before using.

kimchi vinaigrette

Makes about ¾ cup

Although often overlooked, the spicy, flavor-packed liquid that's a product of the kimchi-making process is a worthy ingredient in its own right. Here, it provides the acidic backbone for a dressing to brighten Spicy Yuba Noodles with Kimchi, Crab, and Tomalley Butter (page 210).

½ cup kimchi liquid (see page 60)

2 tsp fish sauce (preferably Red Boat brand)

½ tsp shiro shoyu (white soy sauce, such as Yamashin brand)

½ tsp finely grated (on a Microplane) garlic

½ tsp finely grated (on a Microplane) ginger

¼ cup grapeseed oil

2 Tbsp toasted sesame oil

Combine the kimchi liquid, fish sauce, shiro shoyu, garlic, ginger, grapeseed oil, and sesame oil in a mixing bowl and whisk until well combined.

Transfer to an airtight container and store in the fridge for up to 4 days. Whisk well before using.

red chile juice–lime vinaigrette

Makes about ¾ cup

You'll be thrilled by the flavor of this dressing, not just the heat. Blending chiles and straining the solids leaves you with a sort of liquid chile extract that's perked up with lime juice, like a fresher version of my beloved Tabasco. A little oil tempers the excitement just enough.

¼ cup plus 2 Tbsp flavorful chile juice (see page 43)
2 Tbsp lime juice
2 tsp kosher salt
⅓ cup grapeseed oil

In a small bowl, combine the chile juice, lime juice, and salt and stir well. Whisk in the grapeseed oil in a slow stream until well combined.

Transfer to an airtight container and store in the fridge for up to 4 days. Whisk well before using.

eggplant vinaigrette

Makes about 1 cup

1-pound globe eggplant, halved lengthwise
3 Tbsp extra-virgin olive oil
2 tsp kosher salt
1 ripe medium tomato, halved
1 Tbsp sherry vinegar
4 turns freshly ground black pepper

Preheat the oven to 400°F. Line a baking sheet with parchment paper. Set a fine-mesh strainer over a bowl.

Toss the eggplant halves with 2 Tbsp of the olive oil in a mixing bowl until well coated. Sprinkle on 1 tsp of the salt. Put the eggplant, skin side up, on the prepared baking sheet and roast until fully soft and creamy, about 30 minutes.

Meanwhile, grate the cut sides of the tomato on the medium holes of a box grater into the prepared strainer until all that's left in your hand is the skin and core (discard them). Press on the solids in the strainer to extract as much liquid as possible. Discard the seeds. Measure out ¼ cup of the strained pulp. Reserve the rest for another purpose.

When the eggplant is ready, scoop the flesh into a food processor. Add the tomato pulp, vinegar, pepper, remaining 1 Tbsp olive oil, and remaining 1 tsp salt. Process until smooth and creamy. If necessary, thin with just enough reserved tomato pulp to achieve a pourable texture.

Transfer to an airtight container and store in the fridge for up to 1 week.

jimmy nardello vinaigrette

Makes about 1½ cups

One summer, our farm gifted us a bumper crop of Jimmy Nardello peppers, a particularly delicious sweet Italian variety brought to the United States in the nineteenth century by the man for which it's now named. Roasted hard and then pureed with olive oil and sherry vinegar, the peppers become this sort-of-vinaigrette and our answer to the abundance. The result, which brightens our cast-iron quail eggs (see page 243), is so lusciously thick that in the kitchen we nicknamed it "pud"—as in pudding.

1 pound Jimmy Nardello peppers or another long, slender red frying pepper

¾ cup extra-virgin olive oil

2 tsp kosher salt

Freshly ground black pepper

2 Tbsp sherry vinegar

⅛ tsp finely grated (on a Microplane) garlic

Position an oven rack about 6 inches from the heat source and preheat the broiler.

In a medium mixing bowl, combine the peppers, ¼ cup of the olive oil, and 1 tsp of the salt. Season with black pepper and turn until the peppers are evenly coated. Spread the peppers in a crowded layer on a baking sheet. Broil, flipping once, until the peppers blister and char and are fully tender, 5 to 7 minutes.

Transfer the peppers and any juices to a blender along with the vinegar, garlic, remaining ½ cup olive oil, and remaining 1 tsp salt and blend on high speed until smooth. Strain through a fine-mesh sieve into a container, stirring and pressing on the solids to extract as much liquid as possible; discard the solids. (If necessary, thin with just enough water to achieve a pourable texture.)

Transfer to an airtight container and store in the fridge for up to 1 week. Whisk well before using.

tahini-chile dressing

Makes about 2 cups

Tahini, the creamy paste of sesame seeds, is a common ingredient in Middle Eastern cooking, but here we take the nutty flavor in an Asian direction with the addition of soy sauce, ginger, and salted chile paste. The egg yolk acts as an emulsifier, just as it does it a classic Caesar dressing.

¼ cup plus 2 Tbsp unseasoned rice vinegar

¼ cup Japanese soy sauce or tamari

¼ cup well-stirred tahini

2 Tbsp salted chile paste, plus 1 Tbsp chile oil (see page 43)

¼ tsp finely grated (on a Microplane) ginger

⅛ tsp finely grated (on a Microplane) garlic

1 large egg yolk

¾ cup grapeseed oil

2 Tbsp water

Combine the vinegar, soy sauce, tahini, chile paste, ginger, garlic, and egg yolk in a food processor. Process until smooth, about 1 minute. Scrape the sides of the processor. With the processor running, add the chile oil in a thin, steady stream, followed by about half of the grapeseed oil, then the water and remaining grapeseed oil.

Transfer to an airtight container and store in the fridge for up to 4 days. Whisk well before using.

ravigote

Makes about 2 cups

I think of this French concoction as onion vinaigrette, or even, because it's so chunky and lively, onion salsa. Either way, it provides the same profound pleasures of other herb-packed condiments, like Italian salsa verde or Argentinian chimichurri. But in the French version, along with lots of herbs, olive oil, and vinegar, you also find capers and onions, which make a particularly fine combination—salty and sweet, soft and crunchy. We spoon ravigote over our trout chip and dip (see page 163), where it cuts the richness of trout mayo and avocado in the same way it does that of its classic partner, panfried veal brains. Try it with any meat that needs brightening, from grilled steaks to braised cheeks, or serve it with sunny-side-up eggs.

½ cup finely diced
yellow onion

½ cup finely diced red onion

½ cup rinsed and drained
capers

¼ cup plus 2 Tbsp thinly
sliced flat-leaf parsley
(thin stems and leaves)

2 Tbsp thinly sliced
tarragon leaves

2 Tbsp thinly sliced chervil
(thin stems and leaves)

2 Tbsp thinly sliced chives

1 Tbsp black peppercorns,
coarsely cracked

¾ cup extra-virgin olive oil

¼ cup sherry vinegar

1 tsp kosher salt

Combine the yellow onion, red onion, capers, parsley, tarragon, chervil, chives, and peppercorns in a medium mixing bowl and stir well. Add the olive oil, vinegar, and salt, and stir briefly but well.

Transfer to an airtight container and store at room temperature for several hours or in the fridge for up to 3 days. Stir well before using.

state bird tomato salsa

Makes about ¾ cup

This sauce is little more than exceptional preserved tomatoes—more about those in a bit—mixed with lime juice, salt, and just enough grated jalapeño to provide a tingle of heat. At home, the trick is splurging on the very best tomatoes. Jarred are great if they're especially sweet and tart, or you could go full State Bird and scout out Early Girls.

Early Girl tomatoes are special for several reasons—they ripen earlier in the summer than most, for example, hence their name—but we love them because they develop an especially sweet, concentrated tomato flavor. When we were a young restaurant, we'd stock up on fresh Early Girls when they hit the markets and preserve them in jars. That way, we could make this sauce for our trout chip and dip (see page 163) throughout winter. Then we suddenly went from busy to really, really busy, and we just couldn't keep up. Today, we buy two thousand pounds a year from Dirty Girl Produce, a farm based out of Santa Cruz that grows the gold standard for Early Girls, and have them jarred by an excellent outfit called Happy Girl Kitchen. In the Bay Area, it only takes a little sleuthing to find jars of Early Girls—sometimes sold as "dry-farmed tomatoes." If you can't find them, buy the best canned or jarred tomatoes available and consider, though it pains me to even suggest it, adding a pinch of sugar to provide the missing sweetness.

1 cup top-quality canned whole peeled tomatoes

1 Tbsp lime juice

1 tsp kosher salt

½ small garlic clove, finely grated on a Microplane

1 dash Tabasco sauce

1 tsp finely grated (on a Microplane) jalapeño chile

In a blender, puree the tomatoes on medium-low speed until they're smooth but you can still see the tomato seeds. Strain through a medium-mesh sieve into an airtight container, stirring and pressing to extract as much liquid as possible; discard the solids.

Add the lime juice, salt, garlic, Tabasco, and jalapeño to the puree. Stir well.

Cover and store in the fridge for up to 3 days.

SPRINKLES,
CRUNCHES
&
POWDERS

This section of the larder includes the most common of the many ingredients we use to provide a last-minute dose of flavor, fragrance, and texture just before a dish hits the table. Those made with sesame, a thoroughly underrated little seed, are loosely based on the Japanese condiments *gomasio* and *furikake*, both mixtures of dried seasonings (and both made with sesame). We use them liberally—virtually anything benefits from a healthy sprinkle. You'll also find two takes on fried quinoa, whose irresistible crunch takes the sprinkle concept to the next level. Then there are a few cured and/ or dehydrated ingredients that began as a way to utilize what we had on hand but have become an indispensable part of our pantry.

lamb sesame sprinkle, below

black sesame salt, opposite

sesame togarashi, page 97

lamb sesame sprinkle

Makes about ½ cup

This mixture of toasted sesame and spices is specifically designed for the moderately musky flavor of lamb—it's added, for instance, at the last minute to a sauté of lamb with squid and dates (see page 236). Yet the combination of sesame, cumin, and coriander is a friend to most meats as well as yogurt, roasted carrots or squash, and dishes with a Middle Eastern bent.

1 Tbsp coriander seeds
1½ tsp cumin seeds
1½ tsp black peppercorns
¼ cup plus 2 Tbsp sesame seeds, toasted (see page 96)

In a small pan over medium heat, toast the coriander seeds, shaking and swirling the pan constantly, until fragrant, 1 to 2 minutes. Transfer to a plate to cool. Add the cumin seeds to the pan and repeat. Transfer the cooled seeds to a mortar and grind them to a coarse powder and then transfer to a mixing bowl. Add the peppercorns to the mortar and grind to a coarse powder, then add to the bowl along with the sesame seeds. Mix until well combined.

Transfer to an airtight container and store in a cool, dry place for up to 2 weeks.

everything spice, page 97

aromatic pepper spice, page 98

arab spice, page 99

black sesame salt

Makes about ¼ cup

So many dishes benefit from a last-minute sprinkle of this State Bird larder staple. The mixture, just black sesame seeds briefly pounded with salt, looks like cracked pepper but delivers a rich, nutty flavor that anyone who's had only hulled sesame seeds will find both exotic and addictive. Just make sure to look for pretoasted black sesame seeds—unlike white sesame seeds, untoasted black sesame seeds are particularly perishable and will likely have an off taste by the time you buy them.

¼ cup pretoasted black sesame seeds

¼ tsp flaky sea salt

Combine the sesame seeds and salt in a mortar and pound until the mixture resembles coarsely ground black pepper.

Transfer to an airtight container and store in a cool, dry place for up to 2 weeks.

TOASTING SEEDS AND NUTS

Some recipes in this book call for toasting seeds or nuts to coax out their flavors and aromas. The general technique is simple but, like all cooking tasks, it's important to execute with care. In all cases, be vigilant. What's perfectly toasted one minute can be burnt the next.

Toasting Small Seeds

When a recipe calls for multiple varieties, I prefer toasting each type separately because each has its own perfect place. That said, you can successfully toast several types at the same time. Just not sesame seeds, which we insist on toasting especially slowly and in big batches because a relatively crowded pan helps draw out their oils and bring out their nutty sweetness. Toasted in abundance, they become so delicious that you'll be sure to serve them in abundance too.

For small seeds such as caraway, coriander, cumin, fennel, and poppy, put them in a small sauté pan or skillet and set over medium heat. Shake and swirl the pan constantly, until the seeds are very fragrant and a shade or two darker, 1 to 2 minutes. For best results, use within a few hours.

For sesame seeds, put them in a sauté pan that will hold them in about a ½-inch layer and set over medium-low heat. Shake and swirl the pan almost constantly, until the seeds are very fragrant, light golden, and slightly glossy, 8 to 10 minutes. Turn off the heat, toss for a minute or so, then transfer to a large plate or baking sheet and spread in a thin layer to cool. Store in an airtight container in a cool, dry place for up to 2 weeks.

Toasting Nuts and Large Seeds

Unlike smaller seeds, we toast nuts and large seeds (such as pumpkin and sunflower) in the oven, where they toast more evenly than they would in a pan on the stove top.

Preheat the oven to 300°F. Spread the nuts or seeds in a single layer on a baking sheet and toast in the oven. Rotate and shake the sheet halfway through, until the nuts or seeds are fragrant and a shade or two darker (or lighter, in the case of pumpkin seeds), about 10 minutes. For best results, use within a few hours.

sesame togarashi

Makes about ½ cup

This all-purpose sprinkle, nothing more than toasted sesame seeds and *shichimi togarashi* (a Japanese spice blend that includes dried seaweed, orange peel, chile, and ginger), brings quiet sweetness and nuttiness from the former and a complex flavor and heat from the latter.

½ cup sesame seeds, toasted (see facing page)

½ tsp shichimi togarashi (Japanese seven-spice)

Combine the sesame seeds and shichimi togarashi in an airtight container and mix well.

Store in a cool, dry place for up to 2 weeks.

everything spice

Makes about ¾ cup

Our version of the spice mixture that coats everyone's favorite kind of bagel differs slightly from the classic. We use fennel seeds instead of caraway and skip the dried onion and garlic in favor of more compelling spices such as cumin and coriander. Still, it's a fine sprinkle that goes with our bagel-inspired pancakes with smoked fish and whipped cream cheese (see page 125).

2 Tbsp fennel seeds, toasted (see facing page)

2 Tbsp cumin seeds, toasted (see facing page)

2 Tbsp coriander seeds, toasted (see facing page)

2 Tbsp poppy seeds, toasted (see facing page)

¼ cup plus 2 Tbsp sesame seeds, toasted (see facing page)

½ tsp flaky sea salt

One at a time, transfer the toasted fennel seeds, cumin seeds, and coriander seeds to a mortar and coarsely grind, then combine the ground seeds in an airtight container. Add the poppy seeds, sesame seeds, and salt and stir well.

Store in a cool, dry place for up to 2 weeks.

aromatic pepper spice

Makes a generous ½ cup

One day, I decided that Garlic Bread with Burrata (page 153) needed a good dose of pepper. To me, eating the creamy fresh cheese without pepper was almost unthinkable, but I was eager to add more than just the coarsely cracked stuff. So in a nod to the Chinese origin (yes, really!) of the fried bread we make, we created this study in pepper that combines the sting of black peppercorns, the earthiness of white, the fruity sweetness of pink, the numbing citrusy quality of Sichuan, and the spicelike complexity of dried long peppers and Africa-born dried seeds aptly called grains of paradise. Along with a little curry powder and fennel seed, they add up to an exhilarating mixture that you'll be thrilled to have in your pantry.

1 Tbsp fennel seeds

2 Tbsp finely diced shallots

1½ tsp extra-virgin olive oil

1 tsp Madras curry powder

2 Tbsp black peppercorns

1 Tbsp white peppercorns

1 Tbsp pink peppercorns

1 Tbsp Sichuan peppercorns

1 Tbsp grains of paradise

10 Indian or Indonesian long peppers

Put the fennel seeds in a small pan, set over medium heat, and cook, shaking and swirling the pan frequently, until you see small wisps of smoke and the seeds turn a shade or two darker, 3 to 4 minutes. Transfer them to a mortar and pound to a coarse powder, then transfer to a small bowl.

Combine the shallots and olive oil in the small pan, set over medium-low heat, and let sizzle. Cook, stirring occasionally, just until the shallots are soft but not colored, about 2 minutes. Add the curry powder, stir well, and cook, stirring frequently, until the curry powder smells sweet, about 1 minute. Transfer the mixture to a second small bowl and let cool.

One at a time, separately pound the black, white, and pink peppercorns to very coarse powders; pound the Sichuan peppercorns to a fairly fine powder; and pound the grains of paradise to a coarse powder so the white interior of all the grains is visible. (Transfer the spices to the bowl with the ground fennel seeds as they're done.) Finally, use the mortar to crack the long peppers and grind them to a fine powder. Pick out any large pieces. Add the ground long peppers to the bowl.

Return the mix of ground spices to the mortar and use the pestle to stir and lightly grind for 15 to 30 seconds to marry the spices. Add the spice mixture to the shallot mixture and use your fingers to mix really well, rubbing the shallots as if you were trying to get the spices to stick to them.

Transfer to an airtight container and store in the fridge for up to 2 weeks or in the freezer for up to 3 months.

arab spice

Makes about 1 cup

In the State Bird kitchen, we treat this mixture like the French *quatre épices* that I used often in my culinary school–influenced cooking. Yet not only does this blend contain more than *quatre épices* (there are double the number of spices in here), it's decidedly Arab in origin—inspired by a recipe in *The Arab Table* by May Bsisu. To this California-born, French-trained chef, it lends an exotic quality to anything from duck to lamb, shrimp to cod. This spice is supposed to be fine, so it's done in a grinder. Plus, it contains spices (star anise, cinnamon, cloves) that you wouldn't want to find as chunks.

6 Tbsp plus 2 tsp coriander seeds

¼ cup cumin seeds

3 Tbsp plus 1 tsp black peppercorns

3 Tbsp powdered ginger

1 Tbsp whole cloves

1 Tbsp plus 1 tsp freshly grated nutmeg

5 star anise

3-inch Ceylon cinnamon stick, crumbled

Combine all the ingredients in a bowl and mix well. Then, working in batches if necessary, grind the spices in a spice grinder to a fairly fine powder.

Transfer each batch to a single airtight container and stir well. Store in a cool, dry place for up to 1 month.

chicken-egg bottarga

Makes 12 cured yolks

SPECIAL EQUIPMENT

Fruitwood chips, such as apple or cherry, soaked in water for 30 minutes and drained

10¼ cups kosher salt

1¾ cups plus 2 Tbsp granulated sugar

12 large eggs

The name is a play on the Italian term for cured fish roe. After all, roe are eggs and these are cured yolks, though from fowl, not fish. After thirty days of curing, the texture of the finished product does remind me of bottarga or even Parmesan. We cold-smoke it to add flavor, then grate it over yuba noodles with kimchi and crab (see page 210) to add a rich, smoky, salty element not dissimilar from bacon. As a snack, I eat it grated over buttered toast.

Combine the salt and sugar in a large mixing bowl and stir well. Spread just enough of this salt cure in a small baking dish to make a 1-inch layer. Using the wider end of one egg, make twelve ½-inch-deep divots in the salt cure, spacing them a little bit apart.

One by one, carefully crack the eggs over a bowl and separate the yolk using your hands, letting the egg whites drip into the bowl. Gently place a yolk into each divot, reserving the whites for another purpose. Generously sprinkle the remaining salt cure over the yolks so they're completely covered. Cover the baking dish and refrigerate for 10 days.

After the 10 days, remove the yolks (they'll be firm now) from the baking sheet, brushing off most of the salt cure, and transfer them to a wire rack set over a baking sheet. Discard the remaining cure. Leave the yolks at room temperature, uncovered, for 10 days more.

After the 10 days at room temperature, rinse the yolks under running water, rubbing them gently. Pat dry, return them to the rack, and leave uncovered, for another 10 days. The yolks will be firm like hard cheese and about half their original size.

Put the soaked wood chips in an aluminum pie plate, set at the bottom of a grill, and use a blowtorch to ignite the chips. When the fire goes out, add the grill grates and transfer the rack with the yolks to the grates. Cover with the lid and close the vents. Let the yolks smoke for 30 minutes.

Transfer to an airtight container and store in the fridge for up to 1 month.

garlic chips

Makes about ¼ cup

Simmering garlic in milk tames its harshness, leaving behind a pure, sweet flavor. Frying turns the result into a crunchy garnish for cast-iron quail eggs (see page 243) and Buffalo cauliflower (see page 249). At State Bird, we prefer to use elephant garlic, because the giant cloves give you slices that are easier to work with.

2 cups whole milk

10 large garlic cloves, thinly sliced

Rice bran, vegetable, or canola oil for deep-frying

Combine the milk and garlic in a medium saucepan, set over medium-low heat, and cook, stirring occasionally, until the milk begins to simmer, about 10 minutes. Drain the garlic in a medium-mesh sieve, discarding the milk. Rinse the garlic well under running water, agitating the garlic with your hands. Transfer the garlic to a kitchen towel, pat dry with paper towels, and then transfer to a plate lined with another kitchen towel.

Line a baking sheet with paper towels.

Pour 3 inches of rice bran oil into a large heavy pot and bring to 280°F over high heat. Add the garlic and fry, stirring occasionally and adjusting the heat to maintain the temperature, until it's crispy and a pale golden color, about 5 minutes. Use a fine-mesh skimmer to transfer the garlic to the prepared baking sheet and let cool completely.

Transfer to an airtight container and store in a cool, dark place for up to 3 days.

two quinoa crunches

Makes about 6 cups

Our quinoa crunches began as the solution to the problem of leftovers. Our menu typically has a quinoa salad, and occasionally we find ourselves with a large batch of the flavorful grain remaining after service. As anyone who has ever purchased this good-for-you grain knows, quinoa is expensive. We had to find a way to make use of it all. So we decided to double down on its slightly crunchy quality—the way the grain sort of pops between your teeth—and deep-fry it. It was a revelation. Now much of the quinoa we cook is destined for hot oil.

Sometimes we toss the resulting super-crunchy quinoa with elements of the Japanese rice topper called furikake, mixing in sesame seeds, spices, and nori seaweed. Other times we incorporate nutty sesame, sunflower, and pumpkin seeds. Either way, a generous sprinkle elevates anything it touches by adding flavor and a fresh, exciting texture.

And yes, while we use two colors, both red and white, for an especially striking appearance, feel free to use just one.

cook and cool the quinoa

4 rosemary sprigs

4 medium garlic cloves, peeled

Peel from 1 Meyer lemon, cut into wide strips, white pith removed

2 Tbsp kosher salt

1 cup white quinoa, rinsed

1 cup red quinoa, rinsed

Rice bran, vegetable, or canola oil for deep-frying

Lay out two large pieces of cheesecloth. Evenly divide the rosemary, garlic, and lemon peel among the two. Gather the edges of the cheesecloth, twist the loose cloth, and tie a knot to make sachets.

Combine 8 cups water and 1 Tbsp of the kosher salt in each of two medium pots. Bring to a boil over high heat, add a sachet to each pot, and add the quinoa, one variety per pot. Lower the heat to maintain a strong simmer and cook, stirring occasionally, until the quinoa is tender with a slight pop but not mushy, about 12 minutes for the white quinoa and about 22 minutes for the red.

As each variety of quinoa finishes, drain well in a fine-mesh sieve. Spread the quinoa on large paper towel–lined baking sheets or platters in a thin layer to cool quickly and allow excess liquid to evaporate. Refrigerate, uncovered, overnight. The next day, the quinoa is ready to fry; transfer to two bowls.

Dry the baking sheets and line with paper towels.

Pour 3 inches of rice bran oil into a deep (at least 8-inch) heavy pot and bring to 300°F over high heat. Working in 2-cup batches

furikake crunch

pumpkin seed crunch

with one variety of quinoa at a time, fry the quinoa, stirring occasionally, until it is crunchy and a shade or two darker, 3 to 5 minutes.

Scoop out each batch with a fine-mesh sieve, doing your best to remove stray grains, and transfer to the prepared baking sheets in a thin layer. Let cool.

to make furikake crunch

6 nori sheets (each about 8 by 7 inches), cut into very thin 2-inch-long strips

1 cup sesame seeds, toasted (see page 96)

½ Tbsp flaky sea salt, crumbled

1 tsp shichimi togarashi (Japanese seven-spice)

Transfer the fried quinoa to a large mixing bowl and add the nori, sesame seeds, sea salt, and shichimi togarashi. Stir well.

Transfer to an airtight container and store in a cool, dry place for up to 2 weeks.

to make pumpkin seed crunch

¾ cup pumpkin seeds, toasted (see page 96)

¾ cup sunflower seeds, toasted (see page 96)

¾ cup sesame seeds, toasted (see page 96)

1 Tbsp flaky sea salt, crumbled

Transfer the fried quinoa to a large mixing bowl and add the pumpkin seeds, sunflower seeds, sesame seeds, and sea salt. Stir well.

Transfer to an airtight container and store in a cool, dry place for up to 2 weeks.

POWDERS

The food dehydrator has become as important to our food as a blender, and it's a vital part of the fun of cooking at State Bird, too. Just as a good blender lets us play with texture—corn kernels become a silky puree, the essence of chiles is extracted to make vinaigrette—a dehydrator lets us experiment with form and flavor. It also turns perishable fresh ingredients and unusable trim into shelf-stable staples of our larder. In the case of corn, we dehydrate boiled kernels left over from service for a powder with a sweet, intense corn flavor. Otherwise, they'll have turned starchy and bland the next day. Green garlic stalks typically end up in stockpots or compost piles, but thanks to the dehydrator, we turn them into a powder to make green garlic salt. Sometimes, there's no practical purpose to our experiments. Sauerkraut is already preserved and already delicious, but when it's dried to make salty sauerkraut powder, it adds another layer of tang and umami to sauerkraut pancakes (see page 113). At less than a hundred dollars for a good home-friendly dehydrator, the machine is an affordable splurge.

sauerkraut powder

Makes about ⅓ cup

4 cups very well drained sauerkraut (see page 55)

Spread the sauerkraut in a single layer on the trays of a dehydrator. Set the dehydrator to 105°F and dehydrate until the sauerkraut is completely dry all the way through, about 24 hours. It may take up to 36 hours, though note that once it's fully dried, it can remain in the dehydrator for about another 12 hours with no ill effects.

Working in batches if necessary, transfer the sauerkraut to a small food processor or spice grinder and pulse or grind to a fine powder. Sift the powder through a medium-mesh sieve into a bowl, discarding anything that doesn't pass through.

Transfer to an airtight container and store in a cool, dry place for up to 1 month.

sauerkraut powder, opposite

porcini spice powder, page 107

corn powder

Makes about ⅓ cup

Kosher salt
3 large ears corn, shucked

Bring a large pot of generously salted water to a boil, add the corn, and cook just until the kernels are crisp-tender, about 6 minutes. Meanwhile, prepare an ice bath in a large mixing bowl. When the corn is ready, use tongs to transfer the corn to the ice bath to cool. Drain, pat dry, and cut the kernels from the cobs.

Spread the kernels in a single layer on the trays of a dehydrator. Set the dehydrator to 105°F and dehydrate until the kernels are a dark golden color, slightly shrunken, and completely dry all the way through, about 12 hours. It may take up to 24 hours, though note that once it's fully dried, it can remain in the dehydrator for about another 12 hours with no ill effects.

Transfer the kernels to a small food processor or spice grinder and pulse or grind to a fine powder. Sift the powder through a medium-mesh sieve into a bowl, discarding anything that doesn't pass through.

Transfer to an airtight container and store in a cool, dry place for up to 1 month.

green garlic powder

Makes about ⅓ cup

8 ounces green garlic stalks (bulb reserved for another purpose), outer layer removed and woody tops trimmed

Turn several gas stove-top burners to medium-high, preheat a gas grill to high, or prepare a charcoal grill for high heat.

Set the green garlic stalks directly on the stove or grill grates and cook, turning occasionally, until they're charred on the outside (dark brown but not burnt), about 5 minutes. Cut the stalks into 3-inch pieces.

Spread the green garlic in a single layer on the trays of a dehydrator. Set the dehydrator to 105°F and dehydrate until the green garlic is completely dry all the way through, about 12 hours. It may take up to 24 hours, though note that once it's fully dried, it can remain in the dehydrator for about another 12 hours with no ill effects.

Working in batches if necessary, transfer the green garlic to a small food processor or spice grinder and pulse or grind to a fine powder. Sift the powder through a medium-mesh sieve into a bowl, discarding anything that doesn't pass through.

Transfer to an airtight container and store in a cool, dry place for up to 1 month.

porcini spice powder

Makes about ½ cup

Unlike the sauerkraut powder, corn powder, and green garlic powder recipes in this book, this flavor-boosting seasoning doesn't require a dehydrator. You start with already dried mushrooms, which is how most porcini are sold in the United States, and buzz them in a blender or spice grinder. A dose of allspice makes an unconventional partner for porcini but brings out a surprisingly subtle sweetness in the mushroom that makes this stuff irresistible. Once it's part of your larder, you'll find yourself adding a dusting to everything from pasta with mushrooms to scrambled eggs.

2 ounces dried
porcini mushrooms
4 allspice berries
8 white peppercorns
1½ tsp kosher salt
¾ tsp granulated sugar

In a small food processor or spice grinder, pulse or grind the mushrooms to a fine powder, occasionally stopping to stir if necessary.

Put the allspice in a mortar and pound to a fine powder. Add the peppercorns and pound to a fine powder. Add the salt and sugar and pound to a fine powder. Add the porcini powder and stir well.

Transfer to an airtight container and store in a cool, dark place for up to 1 month.

the
SAVORY
recipes

PANCAKES

When Nicole and I were catering before we opened State Bird, we hit upon a cool alternative to the typical stuff-on-a-crouton hors d'oeuvres. We borrowed the basic idea from Asia, where savory Chinese scallion pancakes, Japanese *okonomiyaki*, and Korean *pajun* vastly outnumber sweet versions and an array of fillings keep each bite interesting. At first, our pancakes were made from a simple batter with baking powder, but when we added sourdough starter, we knew we had something special. That's how the pancakes at State Bird were born.

Because we use only a little starter, it acts more as a texture enhancer than a leavener. It makes the pancakes much more interesting than the light, fluffy breakfast staple, wresting a more complex flavor from an otherwise one-dimensional flour in the batter and giving them a slight chew set off by a delicate crust.

I know I sound a little silly. After all, it's just pancake batter. But we geek out on it the way some chefs do about pizza dough. It's that good. After about five months, the menu had a critical mass of pancakes and inspired a dedicated kitchen station at State Bird, where, all night long, cooks crisp miniature pancakes in plenty of butter that has been clarified so it doesn't burn before creating a caramelized crust. And like pizza dough, our pancake batter is alive, changing with temperature and time. It's something you have to get to know in order to do well. We've learned, for instance, that after twenty-four hours in the fridge, the batter benefits from another hour or two at room temperature, which reinvigorates those helpful yeasts. And yes, you can make these recipes without the starter, but they wouldn't be nearly as delicious.

At home, these pancakes make a killer party dish or even a first course. Two of them make a nice snack (they're rich), and four or five would make a generous part of a meal.

sauerkraut, pecorino, and ricotta pancakes

Makes about 25 small
pancakes

SPECIAL EQUIPMENT
Digital kitchen scale

When Nicole and I were busy catering, we often came home
from our gigs late, hungry, and with little energy to cook.
But we needed to eat something, so we dug through our fridge.
Almost without fail, we had four things. We had pecorino
and butter. We had tortillas (typically from La Palma in the
Mission, one of my favorite places on Earth). And, since I was
in the midst of a passionate affair with fermentation, we had
sauerkraut. Occasionally, when we were living large, there
was ricotta. So we got in the habit of blistering tortillas over
the stove burner, rubbing a stick of butter on the surface, then
packing in the acidic sauerkraut, salty pecorino, and rich
ricotta. We'd fold the tortilla like a taco and eat over the sink.

This delicious snack endured after our catering business
gave way to the restaurant. The combination even inspired
the first (and to this day, my favorite) pancake to grace State
Bird's menu. If you're short on time, a tortilla is an awesome
vehicle for these flavors, but the pancake batter delivers an
incredibly airy, crumpet-like texture and even more complex
flavor thanks to Nicole's sourdough starter. Come to think of
it, between the yeasts in the batter and bacteria in the kraut,
this pancake is a living, breathing thing. That's pretty rad.

drain the ricotta

¾ cup ricotta

Line a sieve with a double layer of cheesecloth and set it over a
medium bowl. Add the ricotta, fold over the edges of the cheesecloth,
and let sit in the fridge at least 6 hours or up to overnight to drain.

make the batter

170 grams/1¼ cups
all-purpose flour

1¼ tsp kosher salt

¾ tsp baking powder

160 grams/⅔ cup
room-temperature
(70° to 80°F) water

70 grams/¼ cup plus
1 Tbsp sourdough starter
(see page 66), 8 to 12 hours
after last feeding

1 large egg

150 grams/1 cup drained
sauerkraut (see page 55),
chopped into approximately
¼-inch pieces

85 grams/¾ cup coarsely
grated aged pecorino
(preferably Fiore Sardo)

A day before you plan to serve the pancakes, whisk together the flour, kosher salt, and baking powder in a medium mixing bowl. Combine the water, sourdough starter, and egg in a separate bowl, whisk briefly, and then add to the flour mixture. Whisk until well combined, about 30 seconds. It should be fairly smooth but small lumps are okay. Cover and transfer to the fridge to proof overnight or up to 24 hours. When it's ready, the batter should be elastic, tacky, and filled with air bubbles.

The next day, add the sauerkraut and pecorino to the cold batter and stir well. Cover, let sit at room temperature for about 1 hour, and then stir briefly.

finish the dish

7 Tbsp clarified butter
(see page 38), at room
temperature

About 1 Tbsp flaky sea salt

1 Tbsp caraway seeds,
toasted (see page 96)

2 Tbsp Sauerkraut Powder
(page 104; optional)

Preheat the oven to 200°F, set a wire rack over a baking sheet, and preheat a large cast-iron skillet over medium heat.

Once the skillet is hot, add 1½ Tbsp of the clarified butter, swirl to coat the skillet, and let it smoke. In batches of six, add a heaping tablespoon of batter per pancake. Spoon a 1-tsp dollop of the ricotta onto the center of each pancake, and press the ricotta gently. Cook until bubbles form at the edges and the bottoms are golden brown, about 3 minutes. Flip the pancakes (preferably toward the edge of the skillet, where it's not as hot and the ricotta won't get too dark) and cook until the other sides are golden brown, about 3 minutes. Transfer the pancakes to the prepared rack and keep warm in the oven while you cook the rest, adding another 1½ Tbsp butter between batches and letting it smoke before adding more batter.

Arrange the pancakes on a platter or individual plates and sprinkle a pinch of sea salt and caraway seeds over each. Serve right away with the sauerkraut powder on the side for dipping.

ginger-scallion pancakes with sea urchin and soy-lime glaze

Makes about 20 small pancakes

SPECIAL EQUIPMENT
Digital kitchen scale

The sweet, briny, custard-like lobes of raw sea urchin roe we get from divers in Mendocino are the stars of this dish. The pancakes, with slivers of ginger and scallions mixed into the batter, are simply there to provide a crisp, buttery platform, while the glaze sets off the decadence of it all.

make the glaze

¼ cup water, plus 2 Tbsp

¼ cup Japanese soy sauce or tamari

2 Tbsp granulated sugar

1 Tbsp toasted sesame oil

⅛ tsp red chile flakes

1 Tbsp cornstarch

¼ cup lime juice

Combine the ¼ cup water, soy sauce, sugar, sesame oil, and chile flakes in a small saucepan, whisk well, and bring to a boil over medium-high heat.

Meanwhile, combine the cornstarch and remaining 2 Tbsp water in a small bowl and whisk until smooth.

Once the soy sauce mixture boils, gradually pour in the cornstarch mixture while whisking; let return to a boil, about 1 minute. Transfer to a container and let cool to room temperature. The mixture will thicken as it cools. Whisk in the lime juice, strain through a fine-mesh sieve, and set aside. (Makes a scant 1 cup; you'll need about ¼ cup for this recipe. The glaze keeps in an airtight container in the fridge for up to 3 days.)

make the batter

170 grams/1¼ cups
all-purpose flour

1¼ tsp kosher salt

¾ tsp baking powder

160 grams/⅔ cup
room-temperature
(70° to 80°F) water

70 grams/¼ cup plus
1 Tbsp sourdough starter
(see page 66), 8 to 12 hours
after last feeding

1 large egg

35 grams/¼ cup thinly
sliced scallion (white
and green parts)

1 Tbsp finely julienned
ginger

1 Tbsp toasted sesame oil

1 Tbsp shiro shoyu
(white soy sauce, such
as Yamashin brand)

1 tsp sambal oelek

A day before you plan to serve the pancakes, whisk together the flour, kosher salt, and baking powder in a medium mixing bowl. Combine the water, sourdough starter, and egg in a separate bowl, whisk briefly, and then add to the flour mixture. Whisk until well combined, about 30 seconds. It should be fairly smooth but small lumps are okay. Cover and transfer to the fridge to proof overnight or up to 24 hours. When it's ready, the batter should be elastic, tacky, and filled with air bubbles.

The next day, add the scallion, ginger, sesame oil, shiro shoyu, and sambal oelek to the cold batter and stir well. Cover, let sit at room temperature for about 1 hour, and then stir briefly.

finish the dish

6 Tbsp clarified butter
(see page 38)

20 lobes uni (sea urchin roe)

2 Tbsp sesame seeds,
toasted (see page 96)

1 cup lightly packed pea
shoots, chrysanthemum
leaves (also called *shungiku*),
or baby mustard greens

Preheat the oven to 200°F, set a wire rack over a baking sheet, and preheat a large cast-iron skillet over medium heat.

Once the skillet is hot, add 1½ Tbsp of the clarified butter, swirl to coat the skillet, and let it smoke. In batches of six, add a heaping tablespoon of batter per pancake. Cook until bubbles form at the edges and the bottoms are golden brown, about 3 minutes. Flip the pancakes and cook until the other sides are golden brown, about 3 minutes. Transfer the pancakes to the prepared rack and keep warm in the oven while you cook the rest, adding another 1½ Tbsp butter between batches and letting it smoke before adding more batter.

Arrange the pancakes on a platter or individual plates and top each with a lobe of uni. Drizzle the soy-lime glaze over all of the pancakes and sprinkle with the sesame seeds and pea shoots. Serve right away.

fiscalini cheddar–whole grain pancakes with heirloom tomatoes and garlic aioli

Makes about 25 small pancakes

SPECIAL EQUIPMENT
Digital kitchen scale

Our pancakes often serve as a vehicle for some of our favorite local ingredients. For this batter, for instance, we look to a whole-grain mixture devised by local bread celebrity Josey Baker (yes, that's actually his real name!), who mills flour daily for his incredible breads. Into the batter, we stir cubes of nutty aged cheddar from Fiscalini Cheese Company in Modesto, California, which turn molten as the pancakes brown in hot butter. On top of each one, we perch perfect summer tomatoes dressed with sherry vinegar. One bite and all is well with the world.

make the batter

85 grams/1½ cups plus 2 Tbsp whole-wheat flour

40 grams/¼ cup plus 2 Tbsp whole-grain (dark) rye flour

40 grams/¼ cup plus 2 Tbsp whole-grain oat flour

1 Tbsp stone-ground cornmeal (not polenta)

1 Tbsp whole millet

1 Tbsp flaxseeds

1 Tbsp hulled sunflower seeds, fairly finely chopped

1¼ tsp kosher salt

¾ tsp baking powder

175 grams/¾ cup room-temperature (70° to 80°F) water

70 grams/¼ cup plus 1 Tbsp sourdough starter (see page 66), 8 to 12 hours after last feeding

1 large egg

125 grams/1 cup diced (½-inch cubes) aged white cheddar (such as Fiscalini)

35 grams/¼ cup thinly sliced scallion (white and green parts)

A day before you plan to serve the pancakes, combine the whole-wheat flour, rye flour, oat flour, cornmeal, millet, flaxseeds, sunflower seeds, kosher salt, and baking powder in a medium mixing bowl and stir until well mixed. Combine the water, sourdough starter, and egg in a separate bowl, briefly whisk, and then add to the flour mixture. Whisk until smooth (the grains will make it look slightly lumpy). Cover and transfer to the fridge to proof overnight or up to 24 hours. The batter will be very thick.

At least 3 hours or up to 12 hours before you plan to serve the pancakes, combine the batter, cheddar, and scallion and stir well with a rubber spatula to evenly distribute the ingredients. Cover again and refrigerate for at least 3 hours or up to 12 hours. Before you cook, let the batter sit at room temperature for about 1 hour, then stir briefly.

finish the dish

7 Tbsp clarified butter
(see page 38)

1 pound medium heirloom
tomatoes, cored, quartered,
and thinly sliced

2 Tbsp sherry vinaigrette
(see page 85)

Flaky sea salt

Freshly ground black pepper

½ cup Garlic Confit Aioli
(page 75)

Preheat the oven to 200°F, set a wire rack over a baking sheet, and preheat a large cast-iron skillet over medium heat.

Once the skillet is hot, add 1½ Tbsp of the clarified butter, swirl to coat the skillet, and let it smoke. In batches of six, add a heaping tablespoon of batter per pancake. Cook until the bottoms are golden brown, about 3 minutes. Flip the pancakes, lower the heat slightly, and cook until the other sides are golden brown, about 3 minutes. Transfer the pancakes to the prepared rack and keep warm in the oven while you cook the rest, adding another 1½ Tbsp butter between batches and letting it smoke before adding more batter.

Put the tomatoes in a medium mixing bowl, add the vinaigrette, and toss gently to coat well. Season with sea salt and pepper.

Arrange the pancakes on a platter or individual plates, then top each with aioli and a tomato slice. Serve right away.

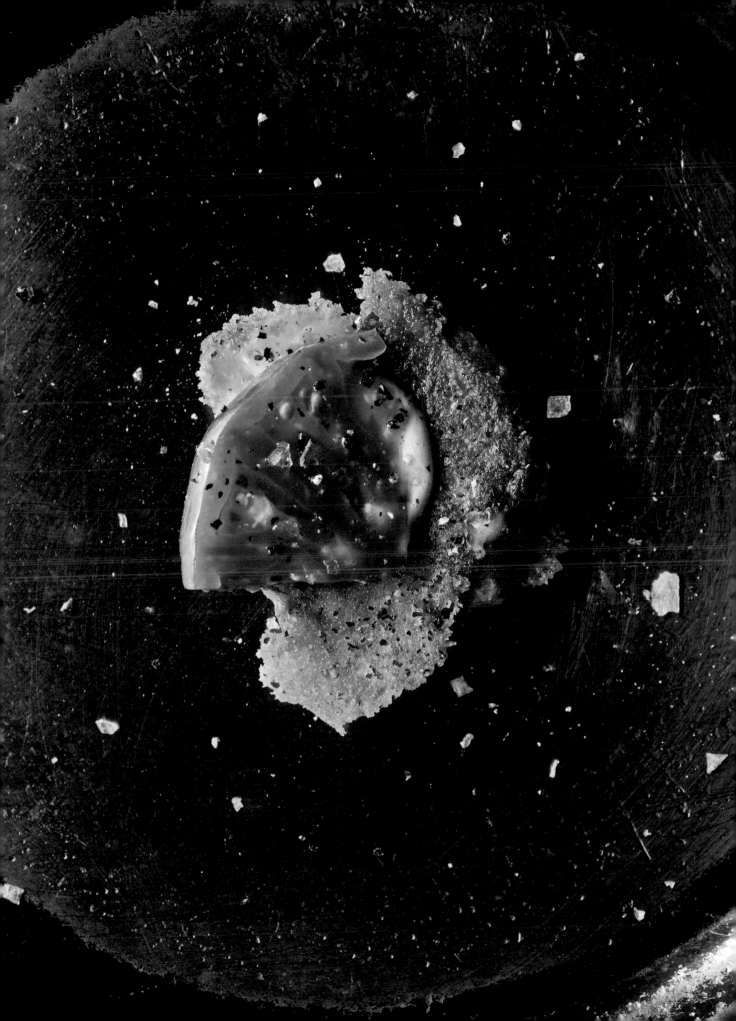

sweet corn and mt. tam cheese pancakes

Makes about 25 small
pancakes

SPECIAL EQUIPMENT
Digital kitchen scale

make the batter

170 grams/1¼ cups
all-purpose flour

¾ tsp baking powder

Kosher salt

160 grams/⅔ cup
room-temperature
(70° to 80°F) water

70 grams/¼ cup plus
1 Tbsp sourdough starter
(see page 66), 8 to 12 hours
after last feeding

1 large egg

1 medium ear corn, shucked

2 tsp thinly sliced garlic
chives or regular chives

3 tsp thinly sliced scallion
(white and green parts)

4 turns freshly ground
black pepper

2 dashes Tabasco sauce

A day before you plan to serve the pancakes, whisk together the
flour, baking powder, and 1¼ tsp salt in a medium mixing bowl.
Combine the water, sourdough starter, and egg in a separate bowl,
whisk briefly, and then add to the flour mixture. Whisk until well
combined, about 30 seconds. It should be fairly smooth but small
lumps are okay. Cover and transfer to the fridge to proof overnight
or up to 24 hours. When it's ready, the batter should be elastic,
tacky, and filled with bubbles.

At least 3 hours or up to 12 hours before you plan to serve the
pancakes, bring a medium pot of generously salted water to a
boil, add the corn, and cook just until the kernels are crisp-tender,
about 6 minutes. Meanwhile, prepare an ice bath in a large mixing
bowl. When the corn is ready, use tongs to transfer to the ice bath
and let fully cool.

Drain, pat dry, and cut the kernels off the corn cobs, doing your
best to cut close to the cob in order to keep most of the kernels
attached in large planks. Add the corn to the batter, along with
the garlic chives, scallion, pepper, Tabasco, and a generous pinch
of salt. Stir gently with a rubber spatula to evenly distribute the
ingredients. The corn planks will break up, but try to keep some
clusters of kernels intact. Cover again and refrigerate until ready
to cook.

make the corn puree

3 large ears corn, shucked

3 Tbsp whole milk

1 Tbsp unsalted butter,
at room temperature

3 or 4 dashes Tabasco sauce

⅛ tsp kosher salt

Bring another large pot of generously salted water to a boil, add
the corn, and cook just until the kernels are crisp-tender, about
6 minutes. Use tongs to remove the corn. Steady the hot corn
with a towel-wrapped hand and cut the kernels off the cob. In a
blender, combine the kernels with the milk, butter, Tabasco, and
kosher salt. Puree on low speed, gradually increasing the speed
to high, until the mixture is very smooth, about 2 minutes. Strain
the puree through a fine-mesh sieve into a small bowl, pressing
and then discarding the solids. Let cool to room temperature.

finish the dish

7 Tbsp clarified butter
(see page 38)

4 ounces triple-cream
cheese (preferably Cowgirl
Creamery Mt. Tam),
at room temperature,
cut into 25 wedges

2 Tbsp Corn Powder
(page 105; optional)

2 Tbsp thinly sliced garlic
chives or regular chives

Flaky sea salt

Freshly ground black pepper

Preheat the oven to 200°F, set a wire rack over a baking sheet,
and preheat a large cast-iron skillet over medium heat.

Once the skillet is hot, add 1½ Tbsp of the clarified butter, swirl to
coat the skillet, and let it smoke. In batches of six, add a heaping
tablespoon of batter per pancake. Cook until the bottoms are golden
brown, about 3 minutes. Flip the pancakes and cook until the other
sides are golden brown, about 3 minutes. Transfer the pancakes to
the prepared rack and keep warm in the oven while you cook the
rest, adding another 1½ Tbsp butter between batches and letting
it smoke before adding more batter.

When you've finished all of the pancakes, top each with a wedge
of cheese, and return to the oven until the cheese has melted,
about 5 minutes.

Arrange the pancakes on a platter or individual plates. Add the
corn puree, sprinkle with the corn powder (if using) and garlic
chives, and season with sea salt and pepper. Serve right away.

everything pancakes with smoked mackerel, cream cheese, and sweet-and-sour beets

Makes about 30 small
pancakes

SPECIAL EQUIPMENT
Digital kitchen scale

pickle the onions

1 pound cippolini onions,
halved through the root,
peeled, and separated into
individual layers

1½ cups water

1 cup apple cider vinegar

¼ cup granulated sugar

¼ cup kosher salt

In a small saucepan, combine the onions, water, vinegar, sugar, and salt and bring to a boil over medium heat. Turn off the heat and let the onions cool to room temperature in the liquid. Transfer to an airtight container and store in the fridge for up to 1 month.

make the beets

½ pound trimmed beets

Kosher salt

3 Tbsp aged balsamic
vinegar

2 Tbsp Japanese soy sauce
or tamari

1 Tbsp water

Put the beets in a medium saucepan, add water to cover, and season with enough salt so the water tastes salty. Bring to a boil, lower the heat to maintain a simmer, and cook until fully tender, 30 to 40 minutes. Drain the beets and let cool.

Using paper towels, rub off the beet skins, coarsely chop the beets, and then transfer to a blender. Add the vinegar, soy sauce, and water and blend until very smooth. Transfer to an airtight container and store in the fridge for up to 5 days.

make the dough

245 grams/1¾ cups
all-purpose flour

1 Tbsp granulated sugar

1 tsp kosher salt

3 Tbsp room-temperature
(70° to 80°F) water

1 Tbsp fresh yeast

2 large eggs, lightly beaten

170 grams/¾ cup
unsalted butter

70 grams/½ cup
Everything Spice (page 97)

Whisk together the flour, sugar, and salt in a medium mixing bowl and make a well in the center of the mixture. In a small mixing bowl, whisk the water and yeast until the yeast dissolves and then briefly whisk in the eggs. Add the egg mixture to the well, whisking in about a quarter of the flour mixture to make a smooth paste surrounded by loose flour.

Melt the butter in a small saucepan over low heat and then let it cool slightly so it's no longer hot but still liquid. Pour the butter into the paste and whisk until smooth. Continue to whisk, gradually incorporating the loose flour mixture to make a smooth batter (it's okay if it looks a little broken). Scrape the batter onto a baking sheet and spread to make an even, approximately ½-inch layer. Press a sheet of plastic wrap against surface of the batter to prevent a skin from forming. Refrigerate until cool, at least 1 hour or up to 4 hours. When it has cooled, it will be more like a dough than a batter.

Put the everything spice in a bowl. Roll the dough into about 30 spheres, using a mounded tablespoon of dough per ball. Add a few balls at a time to the spice mixture and toss gently to coat them. One by one, gently flatten the balls between your hands to form ½-inch-thick discs and return them to the baking sheet. Cover and refrigerate until ready to cook, at least 30 minutes or up to 4 hours.

finish the dish

Scant 1 cup clarified butter
(see page 38)

1 cup whipped cream cheese

1 pound thinly sliced smoked
mackerel (see page 45) or
store-bought smoked sable,
sturgeon, or salmon

2 Tbsp Everything Spice
(page 97)

Dill springs and pea shoots
for garnish

Preheat the oven to 200°F, set a wire rack over a baking sheet, and preheat a large cast-iron skillet over medium heat.

Once the skillet is hot, add 1½ Tbsp of the clarified butter, swirl to coat the skillet, and let it smoke. In batches of six, add the dough discs to the skillet. Cook until the pancakes have puffed up slightly and the bottoms are golden brown, 2 to 3 minutes. Flip and cook until the other sides are golden brown, another 2 to 3 minutes. Transfer the pancakes to the prepared baking sheet and keep warm in the oven while you cook the rest. Between batches, wipe out any stray seeds, add another 1½ Tbsp butter, and let it smoke before adding more discs.

Arrange the pancakes on a platter or individual plates. Spoon on dollops of the cream cheese and add the beets, pickled onions, and slices of smoked mackerel. Sprinkle with the everything spice and garnish with the dill sprigs and pea shoots. Serve right away.

buckwheat pancakes with beef tongue, giardiniera, and horseradish béchamel

Makes about 30 small pancakes

SPECIAL EQUIPMENT
Digital kitchen scale

When I returned from a trip to Chicago with a few jars of giardiniera, the lively condiment of pickled vegetables critical to any order of the Windy City specialty Italian beef, I got fixated on re-creating it. When it became an official member of our larder, my chef de cuisine at the time, Glenn Kang, dreamed up this memorable addition to our pancake repertoire. He combined other menu staples—brined and braised beef tongue, buttery pancakes that are crispy on the outside and airy inside (like a yeasted donut)—and a State Bird classic was born. Horseradish-spiked béchamel adds even more richness. And that bright, crunchy pickle offers a little relief, urging you to dive back in for another bite.

brine and cook the tongue

8 cups water

¾ cup kosher salt

¼ cup plus 1 Tbsp granulated sugar

1½ Tbsp freshly ground black pepper

2¾ tsp pink curing salt (such as Prague Powder No. 1)

3-pound beef tongue

1½ pounds yellow onions, roughly sliced

6 medium garlic cloves, smashed and peeled

2 rosemary sprigs

2 thyme sprigs

About 11 days before you plan to serve the pancakes, combine the water, kosher salt, sugar, pepper, and curing salt in a tall 4-quart container or 2-gallon resealable bag and stir until the salt and sugar have fully dissolved. Add the tongue, cover or seal, and refrigerate for 10 days.

Preheat the oven to 300°F.

Drain the tongue and transfer to a large Dutch oven along with the onions, garlic, rosemary, and thyme. Pour in enough hot (but not steaming) tap water to cover the tongue by an inch or so.

Bring to a boil over high heat, cover with a lid, and transfer to the oven. Cook until you can insert a sharp knife into the thickest part of the tongue without resistance, 3 to 3½ hours. Remove from the oven and let rest in the liquid for 1 hour. Drain the tongue, let cool completely, and then peel off and discard the outer layer. Wrap tightly with plastic wrap and refrigerate until firm, at least overnight or up to 2 days.

When you are ready to serve the pancakes, thinly slice the tongue. You'll need 30 slices for the pancakes. (Reserve any remaining tongue for another meal.)

make the dough

140 grams/1 cup
all-purpose flour

90 grams/¾ cup
buckwheat flour

1 Tbsp granulated sugar

1 tsp kosher salt

3 Tbsp room-temperature
(70° to 80°F) water

1 Tbsp fresh yeast

2 large eggs, lightly beaten

170 grams/12 Tbsp
unsalted butter

70 grams/½ cup
poppy seeds

Whisk together the all-purpose flour, buckwheat flour, sugar, and kosher salt in a medium mixing bowl and make a well in the center of the mixture. In a small mixing bowl, whisk the water and yeast until the yeast dissolves and then briefly whisk in the eggs. Add the egg mixture to the well, whisking in about a quarter of the flour mixture to make a smooth paste surrounded by loose flour.

Melt the butter in a small saucepan over low heat and then let it cool slightly so it's no longer hot but still liquid. Pour the butter into the paste and whisk until smooth. Continue to whisk, gradually incorporating the loose flour mixture to make a smooth batter (it's okay if it looks a little broken). Scrape the batter onto a baking sheet and spread to make an even, approximately ½-inch layer. Press a sheet of plastic wrap against the surface of the batter to prevent a skin from forming. Refrigerate until cool, at least 1 hour or up to 4 hours. When it has cooled, it will be more like a dough than a batter.

Put the poppy seeds in a bowl. Roll the dough into about 30 spheres, using a mounded tablespoon of dough per ball. Add a few balls at a time to the poppy seeds and toss gently to coat them. One by one, gently flatten the balls between your hands to form ½-inch-thick discs and return them to the baking sheet. Cover and refrigerate until ready to cook, at least 30 minutes or up to 4 hours.

make the béchamel

3 Tbsp unsalted butter

¼ cup all-purpose flour

½ cup heavy cream

½ cup whole milk

½ cup State Bird Chicken
Stock (page 41)

¼ cup plus 2 Tbsp
champagne vinegar

3 Tbsp finely grated
(on a Microplane)
horseradish

2 tsp kosher salt

2 turns freshly ground
black pepper

2 dashes Tabasco sauce

Melt the butter in a medium saucepan over medium heat. Add the all-purpose flour and whisk until smooth. Turn the heat to low and cook, stirring frequently, for 2 minutes.

Turn the heat to medium-high and slowly pour in the cream, milk, stock, and champagne vinegar, whisking constantly. The sauce should thicken almost immediately. Let the mixture come to a boil, whisking frequently, then lower the heat to cook at a gentle simmer for 2 minutes just to meld the flavors. Remove the pan from the heat and stir in the horseradish, kosher salt, pepper, and Tabasco. Keep in a warm place, like near the oven, until ready to use.

finish the dish

About 1¼ cups clarified
butter (see page 38)

1 cup giardiniera
(see page 65)

2 Tbsp thinly sliced chives

Preheat the oven to 200°F, set a wire rack over a baking sheet, and preheat a large cast-iron skillet over medium heat.

Once the skillet is hot, add 1½ Tbsp of the clarified butter, swirl to coat the skillet, and let it smoke. In batches of six, add the dough discs to the skillet. Cook until the pancakes have puffed up slightly and the bottoms are golden brown, 2 to 3 minutes. Flip and cook until the other sides are golden brown, another 2 to 3 minutes. Transfer the pancakes to the prepared baking sheet and keep warm in the oven while you cook the rest. Between batches, wipe out any stray seeds, add another 1½ Tbsp butter, and let it smoke before adding more discs.

Once you've cooked all the pancakes, wipe out the skillet and set over medium heat. Add 2 Tbsp clarified butter, swirl to coat the skillet, and let it smoke. Cook the tongue slices in batches, flipping once and adding more butter as necessary, until lightly browned on both sides and hot throughout, 1 to 2 minutes.

Arrange the pancakes on a platter or individual plates. Add 1 Tbsp of the béchamel, a slice of tongue, and about ½ Tbsp of the giardiniera. Garnish with the chives. Serve right away.

TOASTS
&
BREADS

$9

Well into the Avocado Toast Explosion, when every restaurant in America seemed to be serving a variation on the theme, we discovered pancakes provided a delicious way to be different. Everything we had ever considered putting on a slice of bread became fair game to be worked into pancakes, but then we topped one with pickled anchovies and realized that some things *are* better with bread. And so our toasts category was born. Ours typically follow a formula—slather on something lush and fatty (yogurt butter, chanterelle aioli) and top it with something worth celebrating.

tomato toasts with lime-pickled anchovies

Makes about 20 toasts

The first toast we put on our menu is also the simplest—just bread toasted in butter, rubbed with garlic, and topped with tomato and pickled anchovy. Of course, it's the details that make it amazing. We bake the bread, grate the best tomatoes we can find, and suspend the fresh anchovies in time with a bright brine, just hours after they come out of the water.

1 pound soft-ripe heirloom tomatoes, halved

¼ cup extra-virgin olive oil

½ tsp kosher salt

Freshly ground black pepper

About 6 Tbsp clarified butter (see page 38)

Twenty ½-inch-thick slices Sesame Bread (page 156) or store-bought sesame-topped semolina bread

1 large garlic clove, peeled and halved crosswise

20 Lime-Pickled Anchovies (page 136)

Flaky sea salt

Grate the cut sides of the tomatoes on the large holes of a box grater set over a bowl, until all that's left in your hand is the skin and core (discard them). Add the olive oil, kosher salt, and 6 turns pepper and stir well.

Warm 2 to 3 Tbsp of the butter in a large heavy skillet over medium heat. Add the bread slices, working in batches to avoid crowding the pan and adding more butter as necessary, and cook, flipping once, until light golden on both sides, about 2 minutes per side. Transfer to paper towels and immediately rub the cut sides of the garlic back and forth on one side of each slice.

Spoon a generous tablespoon of the tomato mixture over each toast. Lay the anchovies over the tomato, sprinkle with some sea salt, and add a turn or two of pepper. Serve right away.

LIME-PICKLED ANCHOVIES

Makes about 60 anchovies

Of all the recipes in this book, it's this relatively simple preparation that might be the most challenging to re-create at home. While it requires only a handful of ingredients and a little patience, it is dependent on having anchovies that are just hours out of the water. I don't say this to discourage you but to emphasize how fresh the fish must be to withstand this preparation without going to pieces in your fingers. (If you live in the Bay Area, stroll down Pier 47, near Fisherman's Wharf, to J&P Bait between April and October, and before 9 a.m., to pick some up.) I didn't include the recipe to frustrate you but to share one of my proudest accomplishments at State Bird.

Every good cook has his counterpart to the anchovies at State Bird, those nonnegotiable ingredients or processes that no matter the price, time commitment, effort, or impracticality, he refuses to compromise on. Of course, not every ingredient we use meets this standard. I only wish our plums, green beans, and corn could be in our hands minutes after they're picked. But keeping some things sacred reminds us that we can always be better.

My hope is that this idea inspires you as you cook, perhaps even to seek out unbelievably fresh anchovies so you can experience this elegant pickle at home. After we carefully gut and scale the anchovies, we drop them into brine, which firms the fatty flesh and infuses it with flavor, amplifying its best qualities. Then we carefully remove the backbones and lay the fish on crème fraîche–dolloped sesame pancakes or tomato pulp–topped toast, but it might be best consumed in the style of my seven-year-old son, Jasper, who eats them in one bite, like a little seal. Barking noises are optional.

1¾ cups water

¾ cup plus 2 Tbsp lime juice

6 Tbsp kosher salt

1 medium garlic clove, thinly sliced

1 medium jalapeño chile (including seeds), thinly sliced

10 basil leaves

1 pound exceptionally fresh anchovies (each 3 to 4 inches long)

About ¼ cup grapeseed oil

Combine the water, lime juice, and salt in a straight-sided 1-quart container and stir until the salt dissolves. Add the garlic, jalapeño, and basil and stir briefly. Keep this brine in the fridge while you prepare the anchovies.

Set the anchovies on a bed of crushed ice to keep them cold as you work. Working with one anchovy at a time, use a sharp knife to cut just behind the gills to remove the head. Insert the tip of the knife into the opening and nudge out the reddish black blob (the guts).

Starting from the opening, slit open the belly, stopping just before the small fin about 1 inch from the tail. Use the sharp edge of the knife blade to gently scrape one side of the exposed rib cage to remove the red viscera, then slice off the thin band of flesh you've pulled from the belly to create a straight edge. Flip the fish and do the same to the other side of the rib cage. Put the anchovy back on the bed of ice and repeat with the remaining anchovies.

Fill a large mixing bowl with water and add a tray of ice cubes. One by one, hold the anchovies under the water, use your thumb to gently rub the skin in the direction of the head to dislodge the scales, and gently rub the open belly to remove any lingering viscera. When the water gets murky, drain it and replace with fresh water and more ice cubes. Remove the anchovies from the water, shake gently, and add them to the brine. Cover with plastic wrap pressed against the surface of the brine and refrigerate for 2 days.

One by one, remove the anchovies from the brine. Hold each anchovy with your thumb against the belly and your forefinger against the back and very gently pinch along the length of the fish just to help the backbone release from the flesh. Gently open the fish like a book, grab the backbone at the top, and lift it to remove it and the tail in one piece. Put the anchovy, flesh side down, in a small, flat airtight container in which all will fit snugly (approximately 4 by 4 by 1½ inches), stacking them in several layers. Pour in just enough of the grapeseed oil to cover.

If not serving immediately, store in the fridge for up to 1 week.

THE
RELIGION
OF
ANCHOVIES

When anchovies arrive at State Bird, six cooks stop what they're doing. Carlos puts down his knives. Christina puts guinea hen butchery on hold. And four others pause to greet the ten-pound crate heaped with small silvery fish. For the next six hours, these six cooks will work quickly and quietly, their heads bowed like monks, to painstakingly head, gut, and scale each anchovy and drop them into a vat of brine. Two days later, these six cooks will tenderly remove the backbones of each fish and immerse the fillets in oil. Through this ritual, we're able to capture qualities that anchovies rarely have the chance to flaunt, turning a cheap, often overlooked fish into what tastes like a luxury.

Most of us know anchovies as a canned or jarred product that's been preserved with salt. These can be wonderful, with an aggressive briny flavor that's used sparingly to provide a backbone of umami to compound butters, sauces, and Caesar dressing— the magic potion I learned to make as a sixteen-year-old cook that changed me from a kid wary of the cartoonish, stinky pizza topping to an anchovy devotee. Since then, I've adored the anchovy and respected its place at the bottom of the food chain—it's a healthful, sustainable fish that reproduces so rapidly that it's nearly impossible to overfish. The revelation that led to the almost religious anchovy fanaticism at State Bird came fifteen years later, and it began with a mistake.

In the past, whenever I ordered fresh anchovies from my supplier, each delivery was a mixed bag—pristine fish mingled with others whose delicate flesh had begun to break down around the belly, coming apart with even the gentlest touch, like a newspaper that had been left out in the rain. This, I assumed, was inevitable, a messy end for a fragile creature.

Then one day, every last anchovy that arrived was perfect—every tiny eye clear, the flesh so firm that when I held one fish sideways by the tail, the body didn't droop but instead defied gravity by curving upward. I called the supplier to ask what had changed. Thinking I was complaining, they apologized and explained that they had been too busy that week to do what they typically did: buy forty or so pounds of anchovies from a fisherman on Tuesday, store them, and then sell them to restaurants like mine on Wednesday. This time, they had rushed the process, picking up the fish from the fisherman that morning and hustling them straight to me. Their mistake was actually a windfall. And I've never again worked with a supplier who lets anchovies spend more than a few hours out of the water.

At State Bird, this level of freshness lets us execute a particular preparation. With day-old anchovies, I'd have to pack them in salt. In a month or so they were lovely but had the strong, iron-laden flavor, in part from the guts, that many people find distasteful. But because today our anchovies are so fresh, their flesh is still rigid from rigor mortis and our cooks can scale and gut them without the fish falling to bits in their hands. We're left with flawless fish, plump flesh and glittering silvery skin intact. The brief brining preserves the freshness we value so highly, lightly pickles the flesh, and heightens the flavor with acid and salt, so that the anchovies make converts out of even professed anchovy haters. Everyone who tastes them is blown away by how unfishy they are. They taste the way you want all great fish to taste—not like the sea itself but like *being* at the sea, if you know what I mean. Each bite evokes not a mouthful of seawater but that feeling of walking along the beach and taking in the salty breeze.

Our stunning anchovies come from J&P Bait, an operation run by Erik Sandquist. I call him The Anchovy Guy, because he's the only anchovy fisherman who sells them for live bait or to restaurants in and around San Francisco. They're not his sole catch—he crabs for a month in the winter—but they occupy a special place in his heart (he named his dog Anchovy). If they didn't, there would be little reason to work so hard to catch fish that sell for only $3 a pound, when salmon command three or four times that.

Erik has been fishing for anchovies professionally for almost a decade, much longer if you count his childhood. He grew up on the water in San Rafael, a town about 25 miles north of San Francisco. When he was about six years old, he launched the bayside town's equivalent of a lemonade stand, selling the mudsuckers, bull heads, and shiners he caught just behind his home to the local bait and tackle. At fourteen, he worked as a deckhand on charter boats. At eighteen, he was running boats as the captain and got hooked.

Now, during anchovy season—from April to October—he and his crew of three head out on two boats as early as 1 a.m. They either fish the ocean along the coast, from Half Moon Bay to Stinson Beach, where the anchovies swim freely, or they comb the bay, where big tides push the anchovies and where they're confined by the currents. While larger operations might use helicopters to scout their catch, Erik and his crew use simple sonar and look for a congregation of seabirds, who are likely hovering over a school of fish.

They fish using a purse seine, or large net—in their case, about six hundred feet around and fifty feet deep—with openings at the top and bottom. A line made of cork threads the opening at the top, so it floats on the surface of the water. A line made of lead, called the purse line, threads the bottom opening, so it sinks. Once they locate a school of anchovies, they go rod-and-reel fishing, throwing in a line with a dozen or so gold hooks attached. Gold hooks attract anchovies, which they yank out of the water for a size check. They're looking for anchovies that are 4 to 5 inches long, but sometimes, smaller ones are all they can find. If they're happy with the size of the fish, the boat drags the cork line to encircle the school. Then, they pull the purse line, which acts like a drawstring, closing the bottom opening to prevent the anchovies from escaping by swimming downward. Then they pull up the net and dump the fish into live wells onboard.

They return to Fisherman's Wharf, Pier 47, with their catch. The good news for Erik is he won't have to go back out to sea until he needs a refill, in a few days. He and his crew deposit the anchovies into netted pens in the bay. Here they'll live happily, almost constantly swimming laps in unison, until wholesalers, beach fishermen, and fishing boats come to buy them. Then the nets are raised to bring the anchovies to the surface of the water to be scooped out with other nets into the suppliers' crates, fishermen's buckets, or boats' live wells. The operation is simple. It's low tech. And it works.

Although these anchovies are one of the products I'm proudest to serve at State Bird, close to 90 percent of Erik's catch never makes it to the dinner table but rather serves as live bait for striped bass, halibut, ling and rock cod, salmon, and other fish caught in the bay and off the coast. I understand why. Preparing them is laborious and impractical. We take $30 of fish and put about $180 of labor into getting them onto the plate. But to us, it's worth it.

radish toasts with yogurt butter and fish floss

Makes about 20 toasts

Very few combinations are more delicious—or more French—than crunchy, tongue-nipping radishes and soft, salty butter. Bread, another friend to butter, makes an obvious vehicle. Of course, at State Bird we add our own twist. Yogurt brings its lactic tang, and instead of salt, we look to a sprinkle of smoky, umami-rich fish floss, a compelling ingredient in the Chinese larder that has become part of ours.

make the yogurt butter

8 Tbsp unsalted butter, at room temperature

¾ cup full-fat yogurt, at room temperature

Put the butter in a medium bowl, add ¼ cup of the yogurt, and whisk until smooth. Gradually whisk in the remaining ½ cup yogurt. Keep at room temperature until ready to use or transfer to an airtight container and store in the fridge for up to 1 week.

finish the dish

About 6 Tbsp clarified butter (see page 38)

Twenty ½-inch-thick slices Sesame Bread (page 156) or store-bought sesame-topped semolina bread

Flaky sea salt

Extra-virgin olive oil for drizzling

Freshly ground black pepper

6 medium mixed radishes (such as red, black, and watermelon), thinly sliced on a mandoline

About 2 cups Fish Floss (page 144)

2 Tbsp thinly sliced chives

Warm 2 to 3 Tbsp of the butter in a large heavy skillet over medium heat. Add the bread slices, working in batches to avoid crowding the pan and adding more butter as necessary, and cook, flipping once, until light golden on both sides, about 2 minutes per side. Transfer to paper towels.

Spread the yogurt butter over each toast. Sprinkle with a pinch of sea salt, drizzle on a little olive oil, and add a few turns of pepper. Lay five or six radish slices over each toast and drizzle with a little more olive oil. Sprinkle a generous tablespoon of fish floss down the center. Add another sprinkle of salt, a turn or two of pepper, and a pinch of chives. Serve right away.

FISH FLOSS

Makes about 2⅓ cups

SPECIAL EQUIPMENT

Fruitwood chips, such as apple or cherry, soaked in water for 30 minutes and drained

Food dehydrator

I love being surprised by food. It reminds me that even after twenty-plus years of cooking, I still know very little, and that's an exciting idea. I felt this way when I first confronted a desiccated, finely shredded pile of *something* at a Chinese restaurant. Sweet and salty with a fluffy texture that evaporated as it hit my tongue, like a strange sort of cotton candy. When I found out it was called "pork floss," I had more questions than answers. Since then, I've managed to fill in at least a few of the blanks. We make floss today not from pork but from the odds and ends of fish like tuna, swordfish, and black cod; curing, hot-smoking, dehydrating, and finally grinding the fish into this weird and wonderful flavor enhancer. You can find fish floss at well-stocked Chinese markets, but ambitious cooks, at restaurants and at home, will get a kick out of making it themselves. Home cooking doesn't typically leave you with a pound of fish trim, so ask a friendly fishmonger if he'll sell you meaty trim.

1¼ tsp kosher salt

½ tsp granulated sugar

Scant ¼ tsp freshly ground black pepper

1 pound boneless albacore tuna, swordfish, and/or black cod ends and scraps, cut into ¾-inch pieces

1 Tbsp extra-virgin olive oil

1 tsp smoked sweet paprika

In a medium mixing bowl, combine the salt, sugar, and pepper; add the tuna; and toss to coat well. Spread the tuna in a single layer on a baking sheet, spacing the pieces a little bit apart, and let it cure, uncovered, in the fridge for 2 days.

After 2 days, put the soaked wood chips in an aluminum pie plate, set at the bottom of a grill, and use a blowtorch to ignite the chips. When the fire goes out, add the grill grates and transfer the baking sheet with the fish to the grates. Cover with the lid and close the vents. Let the fish smoke for 30 minutes.

Spread the fish in a single layer on the trays of a dehydrator. Set the dehydrator to 105°F and dehydrate until the fish is firm but not hard, 4 to 6 hours.

Transfer to a food processor, add the olive oil, and pulse until all of the tuna has become a tangle of fluffy filaments. Sprinkle with the paprika and mix well.

Transfer to an airtight container and store in the fridge for up to 2 weeks.

steak tartare toasts with green garlic and caesar aioli

Makes about 20 toasts

Steak tartare and Caesar dressing, both old-school culinary masterworks, often share a restaurant table, but they don't often share a plate. Despite raising eyebrows at first glance, the combination makes sense on closer inspection, since classic tartare includes anchovy and egg yolk and the two are in full force in my Caesar dressing-turned-aioli. From there, it's the little details that turn a good idea into a good dish. Letting the beef air out in the fridge overnight, which brightens its color and firms its texture. Using (or even better, making) good bread. And adding a judicious drizzle of fragrant lemon olive oil—a truly special product extracted from olives ground with citrus rinds in the same press.

make the tartare

1 pound boneless lean beef (such as fillet or strip loin)

4 small green garlic stalks (bulb and tender stem), roots and woody tops trimmed, outermost layer removed

½ cup capers, briefly rinsed, drained well, and minced

¼ cup extra-virgin olive oil

Kosher salt

Freshly ground black pepper

½ cup thinly sliced parsley (thin stems and leaves)

1 tsp lemon olive oil (preferably Asaro brand)

1 tsp flaky sea salt

Generous squeeze of lemon juice

Pat the beef dry. Set a small wire rack over a plate, add the beef to the rack, and refrigerate, uncovered, overnight.

The next day, thinly slice the green garlic stalks. Bring a small pot of lightly salted water to a boil, add the green garlic, and cook for 30 seconds. Drain, rinse under cold water, then drain well again.

Put the capers in a medium mixing bowl. Combine the garlic with the olive oil, a generous pinch of kosher salt, and several turns of pepper in a small skillet and set over medium-high heat. Cook just until the garlic sizzles, about 2 minutes, and then pour the mixture over the capers and stir well.

Remove the beef from the fridge. Using a very sharp chef's knife, cut the beef against the grain into ¼-inch slices. Cut each slice into ¼-inch-thick strips, then line them up and slice crosswise into ¼-inch cubes. Coarsely chop the cubes, running your knife through them several times. Add the mixture to the caper mixture and then add the parsley, lemon oil, sea salt, 12 turns pepper, and just enough lemon juice to brighten the flavors.

finish the dish

About 6 Tbsp clarified
butter (see page 38)

Twenty ½-inch-thick slices
Sesame Bread (page 156) or
store-bought sesame-topped
semolina bread

1½ cups Caesar Aioli
(page 77)

4 ounces aged pecorino
(preferably Fiore Sardo)

Flaky sea salt

Green Garlic Powder
(page 106; optional)
for sprinkling

Small handful baby
watercress for serving

Warm 2 to 3 Tbsp of the butter in a large heavy skillet over medium heat. Add the bread slices, working in batches to avoid crowding the pan and adding more butter as necessary, and cook, flipping once, until light golden on both sides, about 2 minutes per side. Transfer to paper towels.

Spread the aioli over each toast, then top with the tartare. Use a vegetable peeler to shave thin, wide slices of the pecorino over the toasts. Sprinkle with a pinch of sea salt, a pinch of green garlic powder, and a little baby watercress. Serve right away.

asparagus toasts with black trumpet aioli

Makes about 20 toasts

At State Bird, it's a given that we cook according to the season. But this dish is especially cool because as winter tails off and spring begins, there's this magical moment when dark, earthy black trumpet mushrooms still grace the markets even as bright green stalks of asparagus start to appear. This brief period of coming-and-going inspired one of my favorite toasts, slathered with an aioli infused with the flavor of these wintry mushrooms and then topped with sautéed asparagus.

About 6 Tbsp clarified butter (see page 38)

Twenty ½-inch-thick slices Sesame Bread (page 156) or store-bought sesame-topped semolina bread

2 Tbsp extra-virgin olive oil, plus more for drizzling

20 thick asparagus spears, trimmed of woody bottoms and peeled

1½ cups Black Trumpet Aioli (page 81)

Flaky sea salt

Freshly ground black pepper

4 ounces cave-aged Gruyére

1 Tbsp thinly sliced chives

Warm 2 to 3 Tbsp of the butter in a large heavy skillet over medium heat. Add the bread slices, working in batches to avoid crowding the pan and adding more butter as necessary, and cook, flipping once, until light golden on both sides, about 2 minutes per side. Transfer to paper towels.

Warm 1 Tbsp of the olive oil in a large sauté pan over medium-high heat until you see wisps of smoke. Add half the asparagus and cook, flipping once, until each side is charred but the spears are still crunchy, 4 to 6 minutes. Repeat with the remaining olive oil and asparagus. Cut the asparagus into 1½-inch pieces.

Spread the aioli over each toast. Sprinkle with a pinch of sea salt, drizzle on a little olive oil, and add a few turns pepper. Top each toast with three or four pieces of asparagus. Add another sprinkle of salt and a turn or two of pepper. Grate on the Gruyére and sprinkle with the chives. Serve right away.

marinated chanterelle toasts with chanterelle aioli

Makes about 20 toasts

marinate the mushrooms

½ cup extra-virgin olive oil

3 large shallots, thinly sliced

3 medium garlic cloves, smashed and peeled

7 thyme sprigs

2 tsp kosher salt

Freshly ground black pepper

12 ounces fresh golden chanterelle mushrooms, trimmed and cleaned; small ones halved through the stem, large ones quartered

1 Tbsp sherry vinegar

1 Tbsp thinly sliced flat-leaf parsley

1 tsp thinly sliced tarragon

1 tsp thinly sliced chervil

1 tsp thinly sliced chives

1 tsp flaky sea salt

1 large ripe tomato

Combine ¼ cup of the olive oil, the shallots, garlic, thyme, 1 tsp of the kosher salt, and 5 turns pepper in a medium saucepan and set over medium-low heat. Cook until the oil bubbles slightly and the ingredients begin to soften, about 2 minutes. Stir in the mushrooms, remaining 1 tsp kosher salt, and another 5 turns pepper and continue cooking until the oil bubbles again and the mushrooms release their liquid, about 2 minutes. Continue to cook until the mushrooms are fully cooked, 4 to 5 minutes more.

Transfer the mixture to a bowl and let cool to room temperature. Remove and discard the thyme sprigs and any large pieces of garlic. Add the remaining ¼ cup olive oil, the vinegar, parsley, tarragon, chervil, chives, and sea salt.

Slice about ⅛ inch from the bottom of the tomato. Grate the tomato, starting with the cut bottom, on the medium holes of a box grater set over the bowl of mushrooms, until all that's left in your hand is the skin and core (discard them). Stir the mushroom mixture well, then cover and let marinate for at least 15 minutes or up to 2 hours.

finish the dish

About 6 Tbsp clarified butter (see page 38)

Twenty ½-inch-thick slices Sesame Bread (page 156) or store-bought sesame-topped semolina bread

1¾ cups Chanterelle Aioli (page 80)

Flaky sea salt

Extra-virgin olive oil for drizzling

Freshly ground black pepper

2 ounces aged pecorino (preferably Fiore Sardo) or Parmesan

Warm 2 to 3 Tbsp of the butter in a large heavy skillet over medium heat. Add the bread slices, working in batches to avoid crowding the pan and adding more butter as necessary, and cook, flipping once, until light golden on both sides, about 2 minutes per side. Transfer to paper towels.

Spread the aioli over each toast. Sprinkle with a pinch of sea salt, drizzle on a little olive oil, and add a few turns of pepper. Spoon about 2 Tbsp of the mushroom mixture onto each toast. Add another sprinkle of sea salt and a turn or two of pepper. Using a peeler, gently shave a few pieces of the pecorino over the toasts. Serve right away.

garlic bread with burrata

Serves 8

SPECIAL EQUIPMENT
Digital kitchen scale

Dim sum is a fantastic blur of food. Carts crammed with dishes and stacked with bamboo steamers roam the restaurant. Servers wield tongs to pass out hot plates and pull out scissors to snip food into portions. Between the dumplings, noodles, buns, and chicken feet, nothing stands out because everything sort of does. Yet there's one item that has always caught my eye across the dining room: a golden-brown orb coated in sesame seeds. The realization that the carts at State Bird needed their own version of the sesame ball led to the creation of this eye-catcher—garlicky bread puffed in hot oil and crowned with creamy burrata, like a mountain erupting with cheese.

It has become one of a handful of dishes that never leave the menu. We make simple dough with sourdough starter, which gives the resulting bread an irresistible tang and springy texture. We apply a sweet garlic puree twice, brushing it on as we form the dough and then again after it's fried. To finish, we add what looks like ash on this dairy volcano—a dusting of rosemary salt and a sprinkle of an aromatic blend of peppercorns and spices, Sichuan peppercorns, dried long pepper, and curry powder. It adds a subtle but surprising quality to the otherwise familiar flavors. It's a little disorienting, just like your first time eating dim sum.

make the dough

60 grams/¼ cup sourdough starter (see page 66), 8 to 12 hours after last feeding

240 grams/1 cup room-temperature (70° to 80°F) water

190 grams/1½ cups bread flour

190 grams/1½ cups all-purpose flour

2 tsp Aromatic Pepper Spice (page 98)

1 tsp baking powder

1¾ tsp kosher salt

1 Tbsp extra-virgin olive oil

1 Tbsp plus 1 tsp Sweet Garlic Puree (page 39)

About ½ tsp flaky sea salt

A day before you plan to serve the garlic bread, combine the sourdough starter and water in a medium bowl and give it a good, brief stir. Put the bread flour, all-purpose flour, pepper spice, baking powder, and salt in the bowl of a stand mixer fitted with the paddle attachment and mix on low speed, just until well combined.

Add the starter mixture to the flour mixture and mix just until the dough comes together, 2 to 3 minutes. Transfer to a medium mixing bowl, cover, and refrigerate for 8 to 12 hours to proof. The dough will rise slightly.

Line a 13 by 18-inch baking sheet with a silicone baking mat.

Turn the dough out onto a work surface and divide into eight equal portions. Working with one piece of dough at a time, flatten the portion into a disc. Fold and tuck the edges of the disc underneath to form a smooth ball. Put each ball, rounded side up, on the prepared baking sheet. Rub the top of each ball with about ¼ tsp of the olive oil and cover loosely with plastic wrap. Return to the refrigerator to proof for at least 12 or up to 24 hours.

In a small bowl, mix the garlic puree with the remaining 1 tsp olive oil.

Gently pat each ball of dough into an approximately 4-inch circle and transfer to a work surface. Spread ½ tsp of the garlic puree onto each round and then sprinkle each with a pinch of the sea salt, crumbling the salt as you sprinkle.

Fold each round into a loose, approximately 1½-inch-wide log. Working with one at a time, gently and evenly stretch each log to a length of 9 inches. Cut each log in half crosswise and stack the two halves on top of each other on the baking sheet so the cut ends face opposite directions, pressing lightly so that the halves stick together. Proceed to the next step, or cover and refrigerate the dough for up to 3 hours.

finish the dish

Rice bran, vegetable, or canola oil for deep-frying

8 Tbsp unsalted butter, melted

2 Tbsp Sweet Garlic Puree (page 39)

2 tsp flaky sea salt

1 tsp finely chopped rosemary leaves

1 pound burrata

2 tsp Aromatic Pepper Spice (page 98)

3 Tbsp extra-virgin olive oil

½ ounce Parmesan

Let the dough proof in a warm spot for 45 minutes (or 60 minutes if it has been in the fridge).

Meanwhile, pour 3 inches of rice bran oil into a large heavy pot and bring to 350°F over high heat. Set a wire rack over a baking sheet.

In a small bowl, combine the melted butter and garlic puree and stir until well mixed. In another small bowl, combine the sea salt and rosemary and stir well.

Lift one of the dough pieces, hold it at both ends, and evenly stretch it to an approximately 9-inch length. Still holding the dough, twist one of the ends once, then connect the short edges so they overlap by about 2 inches to form a ring, pressing lightly so the edges adhere. Fold the length of connected dough onto itself and toward the center of the ring, then pinch firmly. Gently stretch it to make a slightly larger ring, and return it to the baking sheet. Repeat with the remaining dough.

Working in batches to avoid crowding, add the dough twists to the oil and fry, flipping once, until puffed and pale golden brown, 4 to 5 minutes. Transfer to the prepared rack as they're done and immediately brush their tops generously with the butter mixture.

Transfer the warm breads to plates or a platter. Scoop a big dollop of the burrata onto each bread. Sprinkle on the rosemary salt and pepper spice, drizzle with the olive oil, and use a Microplane to grate the Parmesan on top. Serve right away.

sesame bread

Makes 2 loaves

SPECIAL EQUIPMENT
Digital kitchen scale

1¼ tsp fresh yeast

340 grams/1½ cups
room-temperature
(70° to 80°F) water

170 grams/¾ cup sourdough
starter (see page 66), 8 to
12 hours after last feeding

385 grams/2¾ cups
unbleached bread flour

170 grams/¾ cup
whole-wheat flour

2 Tbsp plus ¼ tsp
kosher salt

3½ Tbsp extra-virgin
olive oil

95 grams/⅔ cup sesame
seeds, toasted (see page 96)

When Stuart decided to devote a section of the State Bird menu to toasts, he came to me to design the perfect bread. So I came up with a list of qualities that would help the delicious things he put on top shine. The ideal toast bread would be tasty but not so flavorful that it distracted from those delicious things. It would need a nice tight structure so none of those goodies would fall through the large holes that pock the crumb of breads made with lots of water. It would need a delicate crust that didn't take effort to chew, toppling the toppings whenever anyone took a bite. After much experimentation, this bread was born. It's an easy bread, coated with sesame seeds and baked in a pan, but if you must, you can substitute Italian semolina loaf from a good bakery.

Combine the yeast, water, sourdough starter, bread flour, and whole-wheat flour in the bowl of a stand mixer fitted with the hook attachment. Mix on low speed until all of the flour is incorporated, about 1 minute. Add the salt and continue for 2 minutes. Turn the speed to medium and mix for 3 minutes. Turn the speed to low and add 1½ Tbsp of the olive oil and mix until the oil is incorporated, 4 to 5 minutes.

Lightly oil a large mixing bowl, add the dough, and flip and pat the dough to lightly coat in the oil. Cover and transfer to the fridge to proof until it doubles in size, 8 to 12 hours.

Generously oil two 9 by 5-inch loaf pans. Put the sesame seeds on a baking sheet.

Turn the dough out onto a lightly floured work surface and divide in half. Working with one half of the dough at a time, pat out into a 7 by 6-inch rectangle of even thickness. Fold the rectangle lengthwise into thirds like a letter, pressing gently to seal. Then, still lengthwise, fold the dough in half, pressing firmly to seal the edge (you will have a long tube-like shape).

Lightly spray the dough all over with water and then transfer to the baking sheet with the sesame seeds, seam side down. Push the seeds up the sides and on top, patting gently so that a generous amount adhere. Transfer the dough, seam side down, to one of the prepared loaf pans. Repeat with the other half of dough.

Cover the pans and proof in a warm spot until the dough fills the bottom of the pans and puffs up slightly, about 3 hours.

Meanwhile, preheat the oven to 375°F.

Evenly drizzle the remaining 2 Tbsp olive oil over the tops of the loaves. Bake, rotating the pans halfway through, until the tops are light golden brown and tapping the tops produces a hollow sound (the centers should register 200°F on a thermometer), 30 to 40 minutes. Flip the loaves onto a wire rack to cool.

Store, uncovered, at room temperature for up to 8 hours, or tightly wrapped in plastic wrap for up to 2 days.

CHIP
&
DIP

This is one of my favorite categories of food at State Bird, and rarely if ever does the menu not include at least one dish that takes this form. It came about after I started catering, when my food veered away from fancy and fussy and toward fun. Nicole and I were serving what amounted to really good party food, and what's better at a party than chips and something scoopable? When we opened State Bird, I took the concept and ran with it, using the chip-plus-dip idea as a lens to help me focus my creative impulses. It was a great way to remind customers that they weren't at a fine-dining establishment, and it had the added benefit of inspiring some truly delicious eats.

cure-it-yourself trout roe with potato chips and horseradish crème fraîche

Serves 4 to 6

SPECIAL EQUIPMENT
Digital kitchen scale

This is chip and dip at its simplest and, maybe, its best. I recommend seeking out whole roe sacs and curing the eggs yourself. It's a cool technique—easier than you might think and less expensive than buying it jarred. Look for whole roe sacs at seafood markets (especially those that cater to Russians) or ask if a friendly fishmonger can order them for you.

cure the roe

1 pound trout roe sacs

Kosher salt

⅛ tsp finely grated (on a Microplane) Meyer lemon zest

Fill a large bowl with warm water, add the roe sacs, and soak for 30 seconds to help loosen the eggs. Drain well.

Set a crosswire rack over a medium mixing bowl. One at a time, put the roe sacs, open side down, on the rack. Steady the sac with one hand. Using firm but gentle pressure, run the index finger of your other hand back and forth along the top of the sac to dislodge the eggs from the membrane, letting them fall through the rack's openings and into the bowl. Discard the membrane.

Fill the bowl with enough warm water to cover the eggs. Use your hands to gently agitate the eggs in the water, then quickly but carefully tip the bowl to pour off the now murky water and any debris, using your hand to keep the eggs from sliding out of the bowl. Repeat once with warm water, then again with cold water. Drain the roe well in a fine-mesh sieve.

Weigh the prepared roe; 2 percent of this weight is the amount of salt you'll need. You'll probably have about 350 grams roe, which requires about 7 grams salt. Transfer the roe to a medium bowl. Add the salt and lemon zest and stir gently but well. Cover and cure in the refrigerator for at least 20 minutes or up to 2 hours.

finish the dish

¾ cup crème fraîche

½-inch piece horseradish, peeled

3 turns freshly ground black pepper

1 tsp thinly sliced chives

Your favorite salted potato chips

Use a whisk to whip the crème fraîche to soft peaks in a medium mixing bowl, about 2 minutes. Transfer to a serving bowl, use a Microplane to grate the horseradish over the crème fraîche, and sprinkle with the pepper and chives. Serve right away with potato chips and the roe alongside.

smoked trout dip and avocado with tomato salsa and ravigote

Serves 6 to 8

This dish is our ode to Midwestern smoked whitefish pâté, which Nicole and I ate during our Michigan days. Like so many State Bird dishes, it started small. We'd began by serving a dish of red trout, crusting fillets with rice powder, crisping the skin in a skillet, and dousing the fish with a mixture of brown butter and fish sauce. In the course of breaking down those stunning trout to yield plate-perfect fillets, our cooks naturally left behind bits of imperfect flesh. Throwing out this kind of trim, whether flesh or bone, and even this relatively small amount, would be a waste of a beautiful ingredient, not to mention a crime against a restaurant's bottom line. So we briefly smoked the flesh and folded it into aioli. We divided the rich, smoky mixture into half a dozen little bowls beside dollops of guacamole. We spooned on a simple tomato salsa and an herby vinaigrette thick with capers and onions. We added some potato chips for scooping. We set out the bowls on one of the carts that roam the restaurant, and in a few minutes the dish was gone. Today, it is our most popular dish by far, and we buy lots of whole trout just to keep up with demand. What started as a way to use up trim now generates plenty of trim of its own.

make the trout mayo

1¼ pounds smoked trout (see page 44)

1 large egg yolk

2 Tbsp sherry vinegar

1 Tbsp Dijon mustard

2 dashes Tabasco sauce

Kosher salt

Freshly ground black pepper

1 cup grapeseed oil

Combine 1 cup of the trout, the egg yolk, vinegar, mustard, Tabasco, ¼ tsp salt, and several turns of pepper in a food processor. Process to a coarse puree. With the processor running, add the grapeseed oil in a thin, steady stream. Scrape the sides of the processor and process for another 5 seconds or so.

Transfer the mixture to a medium mixing bowl. Fold in the remaining trout until well distributed, keeping it in large pieces. Gently stir in more salt and pepper to taste. If not using immediately, transfer to an airtight container and store in the fridge for up to 3 days.

finish the dish

4 ripe Hass avocados, pitted, peeled, and cut into ¼-inch cubes

1 Tbsp plus 1 tsp Sweet Garlic Puree (page 39)

1 Tbsp plus 1 tsp lemon juice, or as needed

Kosher salt

Freshly ground black pepper

4 dashes Tabasco sauce

¾ cup Ravigote (page 90)

¾ cup State Bird Tomato Salsa (page 91)

Your favorite salted potato chips

Combine the avocados, garlic puree, lemon juice, 2 tsp salt, ¼ tsp pepper, and Tabasco in a medium mixing bowl. Stir roughly and well until you have a very chunky mixture bound by creamy mashed avocado. Season with more lemon juice, salt, and pepper—it should taste bright but not acidic, like avocado but better.

Add equal dollops of the trout mayo and avocado mixture to several small bowls. Stir the ravigote and spoon it into each bowl. Divide the tomato salsa among the bowls, pouring it around the sides. Serve right away with potato chips.

dungeness crab salsa with serrano crema and corn tortilla chips

Serves 4

cook the crab

2-pound live
Dungeness crab

Put the crab in the freezer for 15 minutes or so to dull its senses. Bring a large pot of generously salted water to a rolling boil. Carefully drop in the crab and cook, adjusting the heat if necessary to maintain a strong simmer, for 13 minutes. Meanwhile, prepare an ice bath in a very large mixing bowl. When the crab is cooked, use tongs to transfer the crab to the ice bath to cool.

Put the crab, bottom side up, on a cutting board and use your fingers to remove the triangular flap. Turn over the crab. Grab the top shell firmly and lift to remove. Collect any juices and scoop out the tomalley (which resembles soft scrambled eggs) and reserve for another purpose. Remove and discard the gills and other loose stuff from the sides of the exposed body.

Twist the legs and claws from the body. Use sturdy kitchen shears to cut the shell of the legs and claws, then remove the meat in large pieces with your fingers or a small fork. Press down gently on the body until you crack through the cartilage. Cut the body in half and use a small spoon or your fingers to remove the meat. Pick through the meat for any lingering pieces of shell. Discard the shells. Transfer to an airtight container and store in the fridge for up to 1 day.

make the crema

1 serrano chile, seeded

¾ tsp kosher salt

¼ cup well-shaken buttermilk

1 tsp lemon juice

2½ Tbsp crème fraîche

Mince the serrano on a cutting board, then sprinkle on a good pinch of the kosher salt and use the flat of a chef's knife to crush the chile and salt to a paste. Combine the chile paste, buttermilk, lemon juice, and remaining kosher salt in a small bowl and stir. Add the crème fraîche and stir until well combined. Transfer to an airtight container and store in the fridge for up to 1 day.

finish the dish

½ cup State Bird Tomato Salsa (page 91)

4 ounces thin-skinned cucumbers (such as Japanese, Persian, or English), peeled and cut into irregular ½-inch pieces

4 French breakfast radishes, quartered lengthwise

2 scallions (white and green parts), thinly sliced

2 Tbsp thinly sliced cilantro (thin stems and leaves)

1 Tbsp extra-virgin olive oil

Flaky sea salt

Freshly ground black pepper

¼ cup mixed radish sprouts and bolted cilantro fronds (optional)

1 Tbsp very thinly sliced serrano chile

Good-quality tortilla chips or fried tortillas for serving

In a medium mixing bowl, combine the crab, tomato salsa, cucumbers, radishes, scallions, and cilantro and then toss gently but well. Pour the crema onto a serving plate and then spoon on the crab mixture. Drizzle with the olive oil, season with sea salt and pepper, and sprinkle with the radish sprouts and cilantro fronds and serrano. Serve right away with tortilla chips.

spiced pork ciccioli with buttermilk–cacao nib crackers

Serves 8 to 12

The composition of *ciccioli* seems to differ by region, but as far as I can tell, most versions of the Italian product are some delicious combination of pork scraps transformed from trash into treasure. Our take is made by cooking pork and aromatics together slowly until the lard renders to submerge the meat and turn it spoon-tender. That fat, now infused with the flavor of decidedly nontraditional spices that nod to the Middle East and Asia, joins the meat to make a spreadable (or this case, dippable) treat, similar in appearance to the more recognizable French pork rilletes. Nicole's cacao nib crackers and blistered summer vegetables add textural balance and cut the pate's richness.

make the ciccioli

1½ pounds pork shoulder, cut into 2-inch pieces

½ pound pork fatback, cut into 2-inch pieces

3 Tbsp orange juice, plus 3 strips orange peel (each about 3 by 1 inch), white pith removed

¼ cup Arab Spice (page 99)

1 Tbsp kosher salt

2 tsp red chile flakes

4 whole cloves

3 allspice berries

2 medium garlic cloves, smashed and peeled

2 dried Indian or Indonesian long peppers

1 star anise

1 small rosemary sprig

1 small thyme sprig

Two days before you plan to serve the ciccioli, combine all of the ciccioli ingredients in a large mixing bowl and mix well with your hands. Cover and let the pork marinate in the fridge for at least 12 hours or up to 24 hours.

The next day, preheat the oven to 300°F.

Transfer the pork and marinade to a large baking dish (with a lid) wide enough to fit the pork in two snug layers. Cover the surface of the pork with a sheet of parchment paper, top with the lid, and bake, without stirring, until very tender and nearly falling apart, 2½ to 3 hours. The fat will have rendered to mostly submerge the pork. Let cool to room temperature.

Discard any visible aromatics and spices. Using a slotted spoon, transfer the pork to the bowl of a stand mixer fitted with the paddle attachment, reserving the fat left behind. Use your hands to shred the pork into small pieces. Mix the shredded pork on medium-low speed and add the reserved fat in a thin, steady stream. Continue to mix until the mixture has a coarse but spreadable texture, about 1 minute.

Transfer the pork to a container and press a sheet of plastic wrap against the surface of the meat. Cover with a lid or more plastic wrap and refrigerate overnight to let the flavors meld. Store in the fridge for up to 2 weeks.

finish the dish

Kosher salt

2 Tbsp grapeseed oil

12 cherry tomatoes

10 Jimmy Nardello peppers

10 shishito or Padrón peppers

Several basil sprigs

12 ripe fresh figs, quartered

A few large grape clusters

Handful of baby mustard greens

1 recipe Buttermilk–Cacao Nib Crackers (facing page)

About 2 hours before serving, take the pork out of the fridge and let come to room temperature. Season with salt.

Working in batches to avoid crowding, pour the grapeseed oil into a large skillet and set over medium-high heat. When you see wisps of smoke, add the tomatoes, Jimmy Nardellos, and shishitos. Season lightly with salt and cook, stirring once, until the peppers are well blistered and charred, 1 or 2 minutes. Add the basil, stir, and remove the pan from the heat.

Divide the pork, figs, grapes, tomatoes, mustard greens, and peppers among individual plates. Serve right away with the crackers.

BUTTERMILK–CACAO NIB CRACKERS

Makes about 8 servings

SPECIAL EQUIPMENT
Digital kitchen scale

105 grams/¾ cup
pastry flour

105 grams/¾ cup
all-purpose flour, plus
more for dusting

1 Tbsp granulated sugar

30 grams/¼ cup cacao nibs

½ tsp baking powder

½ tsp kosher salt

70 grams/5 Tbsp
unsalted butter, cold,
cut into ¼-inch pieces

140 grams/½ cup plus 1 Tbsp
well-shaken buttermilk

3 Tbsp extra-virgin olive oil

1 Tbsp flaky sea salt

Combine the pastry flour, all-purpose flour, sugar, cacao nibs, baking powder, and kosher salt in a stand mixer fitted with the paddle attachment. Mix on low speed for 30 seconds to combine, then add the butter and continue to mix until the butter is in pea-size pieces, about 2 minutes. With the mixer running, gradually pour in the buttermilk and mix just until combined, about 30 seconds. Stop the mixer and knead a few times by hand to incorporate any dry ingredients not yet in the dough.

Cut the dough into three equal pieces, shape each into an even rectangle, wrap tightly in plastic wrap, and refrigerate for at least 3 hours or up to overnight.

Clear space in your freezer. Working with one piece of dough at a time, remove it from the fridge and roll it out into an approximately 9 by 12-inch rectangle on a lightly floured piece of parchment paper. Transfer the rectangle and parchment to a 13 by 18-inch baking sheet, cover with another sheet of parchment paper, and then immediately transfer to the freezer. Repeat with the remaining two pieces of dough, adding the rectangles and parchment to the baking sheet in the freezer, and chill for 10 minutes. (If not baking immediately, wrap the baking sheet entirely in plastic wrap and store in the freezer for up to 1 month.)

Preheat the oven to 350°F.

Remove the dough and parchment from the freezer and put them on three 13 by 18-inch baking sheets. Immediately brush all three rectangles with the olive oil and sprinkle with the sea salt. Use a fork to poke holes in the dough, all the way to the baking sheet, at approximately ½-inch intervals.

Bake, rotating the pans occasionally and using a fork to pop any bubbles, until golden brown, 10 to 12 minutes. Let cool to room temperature on the sheets, then crack into 3-inch shards.

Transfer to an airtight container and store at room temperature for up to 3 days.

SALADS

It's no accident that the dishes in this chapter don't have lettuce. I wanted to underscore our expansive definition of the category. It channels the just-call-it-a-salad inclusiveness with which English speakers welcome virtually any dish that's either not served hot or features something resembling a dressing. That's why you'll find our take on tabbouleh (a Middle Eastern "salad," I suppose, though here reimagined with Japanese elements) and crunchy pork belly, fruit, and herbs with fish sauce vinaigrette, a salad in the vein of Thai *yam*. Like all salads, conventional and not, these look more enticing on a plate, not in a bowl.

quinoa tabbouleh with marinated tuna, shiitakes, and bonito-rosemary aioli

Serves 4 to 6

cook and cool the quinoa

4 rosemary sprigs

4 medium garlic cloves, peeled

Peel from 1 Meyer lemon, cut into wide strips, white pith removed

2 Tbsp kosher salt

½ cup white quinoa, rinsed

½ cup red quinoa, rinsed

Lay out two large pieces of cheesecloth. Evenly divide the rosemary, garlic, and lemon peel among the two. Gather the edges of the cheesecloth, twist the loose cloth, and tie a knot to make sachets.

Combine 8 cups water and 1 Tbsp of the salt in each of two medium pots. Bring to a boil over high heat, add a sachet to each pot, and add the quinoa, one variety per pot. Lower the heat to maintain a strong simmer and cook, stirring occasionally, until the quinoa is tender with a slight pop but not mushy, about 12 minutes for the white quinoa and about 22 minutes for the red.

As each variety of quinoa finishes, drain well in a fine-mesh sieve. Spread the quinoa on a large baking sheet or platter in a thin layer to cool quickly and allow excess liquid to evaporate.

finish the dish

1 cup thinly sliced stemmed shiitake mushrooms

1 cup State Bird Dashi (page 40)

1 tsp kosher salt

1 cup chrysanthemum leaves (also called *shungiku*), thick stems removed, plus micro leaves for garnish

8 ounces ahi tuna steaks, cut into ⅓-inch cubes

½ cup White Soy Sauce–Lime Vinaigrette (page 84)

½ cup thinly sliced flat-leaf parsley (thin stems and leaves)

¼ cup Bonito-Rosemary Aioli (page 73)

Generous ¼ cup quinoa–pumpkin seed crunch (see page 102)

Prepare an ice bath in a medium mixing bowl.

Combine the mushrooms, dashi, and salt in a small saucepan and bring to a gentle boil over medium heat. Add the chrysanthemum leaves, stir, and cook for 30 seconds more. Pour the pan's contents into a small mixing bowl and set it in the ice bath, stirring until cool. When it has cooled fully, strain the mushrooms and chrysanthemum, reserving the dashi for another purpose.

Ten minutes before serving, combine the tuna and ¼ cup of the vinaigrette in a small bowl and toss to coat well.

Combine the white and red quinoa, parsley, and remaining ¼ cup vinaigrette in a medium mixing bowl and toss well. Transfer the quinoa mixture to a serving platter, then arrange the tuna mixture and little piles of the mushroom mixture on top. Spoon on the aioli, sprinkle on the crunch, and garnish with micro leaves. Serve right away.

eggplant tonkatsu with miso-yuzu aioli, pickled ginger, and pickled okra

Serves 6

When you get your start cooking at an Italian American joint and go on to become obsessed with Japanese cuisine, this is where you end up. You love *tonkatsu*, the deep-fried pork cutlets so good they've spawned dedicated restaurants throughout Japan, and you can't help applying the technique to eggplant. But instead of going the marinara-mozzarella route, you stay in the Asian mode, employing aioli spiked with miso and perking up the richness with pickled ginger and okra. Traditional *tonkatsu* typically comes with crunchy cabbage salad, so ours does too. Don't let all the components throw you—this dish is achievable at home with a little advance preparation. That said, if you skipped everything but the eggplant and aioli, your friends would still be happy.

bread the eggplant

1 cup all-purpose flour

3 large eggs, lightly beaten

2½ cups coarse fresh bread crumbs

1 large globe eggplant, cut into about twelve ¼-inch-thick rounds

Set a wire rack over a baking sheet. Put the flour, beaten eggs, and bread crumbs in separate bowls.

Working with a few slices at a time, dredge the eggplant rounds in the flour and then the eggs, turning to coat them well. Add the eggplant rounds to the bread crumbs and use your hands to firmly pat and press the bread crumbs so each round is completely covered. Put the rounds on the prepared rack as they're breaded and repeat with the remaining eggplant. (If not frying immediately, refrigerate, uncovered, for up to 2 hours.)

finish the dish

Rice bran, vegetable, or canola oil for deep-frying

Kosher salt

1 cup thinly sliced cabbage (preferably Arrowhead)

8 cherry tomatoes, halved

¼ cup thinly sliced Japanese cucumber

2 Tbsp White Soy Sauce–Lime Vinaigrette (page 84)

1 recipe Pickled Ginger (page 62)

1 recipe Pickled Okra (page 62)

1 Tbsp grapeseed oil

½ cup Miso-Yuzu Aioli (page 74)

Small handful of New Zealand spinach (optional)

Generous pinch radish microgreens or micro basil (optional)

Generous pinch shichimi togarashi (Japanese seven-spice)

Set a wire rack over a baking sheet. Pour 3 inches of rice bran oil into a large heavy pot and bring to 350°F over high heat.

Add the eggplant slices to the oil, in several batches to avoid crowding the pan, and fry until the eggplant is golden brown and crispy, about 5 minutes. As it's fried, transfer the eggplant to the prepared rack and immediately season generously with salt.

In a large mixing bowl, toss the cabbage, tomatoes, and cucumber with the vinaigrette and a pinch of salt.

Just before serving, drain the ginger. Drain the okra and halve each pod lengthwise. Warm the grapeseed oil in a large skillet over medium-high heat until you see wisps of smoke. Add the okra and cook, flipping once, until slightly charred, 2 to 3 minutes.

Quarter each eggplant slice and arrange on plates or a platter and add the aioli in dollops. Top with the cabbage salad and sprinkle on the spinach, microgreens, shichimi togarashi, pickled okra, and pickled ginger. Serve right away.

grilled beef and brussels sprouts salad with shiso and umeboshi

Serves 4

marinate the beef

½ cup Japanese soy sauce or tamari

¼ cup plus 3 Tbsp granulated sugar

1 small garlic clove, finely grated on a Microplane

2 Tbsp grapeseed oil

10 ounces strip, tri-tip, or your favorite grilling steak (preferably about 1½ inches thick)

Combine the soy sauce, sugar, and garlic in a mixing bowl and whisk until the sugar dissolves. Add the grapeseed oil and whisk until well combined.

Put the steak in a resealable bag and pour in all but about ¼ cup of the soy sauce mixture, reserving the rest. Force the air out of the bag, seal, and massage the steak to make sure it's well coated in the marinade. Refrigerate for at least 4 hours or up to 6 hours.

finish the dish

3 ounces Brussels sprouts, ends trimmed, outer leaves removed, separated into individual leaves

6 scallions, trimmed

2 Tbsp grapeseed oil

6 ounces fresh maitake (hen-of-the-woods) mushrooms, trimmed, cleaned, and torn into bite-size pieces

Kosher salt

¼ cup Umeboshi-Rosemary Vinaigrette (page 85), plus 2 Tbsp

Generous ¼ cup katsuobushi (Japanese bonito flakes)

3 small Japanese turnips, trimmed and thinly sliced on a mandoline

3 green shiso leaves, torn into several pieces at the last minute

½ tsp sesame seeds, toasted (see page 96)

Rinse the Brussels sprout leaves, drain well, and refrigerate for about 30 minutes.

Meanwhile, separate the white scallion bulbs from the greens. Halve the bulbs lengthwise, cut most of the greens into 2- to 3-inch lengths, and thinly slice some greens for garnish.

Prepare a grill (or preheat a grill pan or wide heavy skillet) to medium-high heat. Oil the grill grates or add enough oil to the grill pan or skillet to very thinly cover the surface.

Pour the reserved soy sauce mixture onto a plate. Remove the steak from the bag and shake off any excess marinade. Grill the steak, turning occasionally, until it's golden brown all over but the meat is still rare, 5 to 7 minutes. Transfer the steak to the plate and turn to coat in the soy sauce mixture. Let rest.

Set a large skillet over high heat and add the 2 Tbsp grapeseed oil. When the oil just begins to smoke, add the mushrooms and a generous sprinkle of salt and cook, flipping once, until lightly golden, about 3 minutes. Add the scallion bulbs and green lengths and cook, stirring once or twice, until tender but not mushy, about 2 minutes. Add the Brussels sprouts and cook, shaking the pan, just until warm and lightly golden but still raw and bright, about 15 seconds. Transfer the mushroom mixture to a large mixing bowl.

Slice the steak against the grain into ¼-inch-thick slices and add them to the mushroom mixture. Add the ¼ cup vinaigrette, toss well, and arrange in a shallow bowl. Top with the katsuobushi, turnips, shiso, and sesame seeds. Sprinkle on the reserved scallion greens and drizzle on the remaining 2 Tbsp vinaigrette. Serve right away.

fried pork belly with plum, fish sauce, herbs, and long pepper

Serves 6 to 8

I returned from a trip to Vietnam and a visit to the Red Boat Fish Sauce operation obsessed with the golden, umami-fueled elixir. And because successful dishes so often rely on the excitement produced by contrast, I paired the fermented product with ingredients that were, in some ways, its polar opposite; from classic partners like herbs, chiles, and lime to peak-season fruit. These fresh elements also happened to enhance rich ones, so we incorporated the luscious braised pork belly in our larder, dusted in cornstarch and fried to give a crisp crust to the meltingly tender meat and fat. The salad became one of the rare year-round State Bird staples, the fruit changing along with the season—grapes in the fall, citrus in the winter, and stone fruit like plums and apriums when the weather warmed and they abound in farmers' markets—like wild anchovies in the waters of Phu Quoc.

Rice bran, vegetable, or canola oil for deep-frying

2 pounds Braised Pork Belly (page 46), cut into approximately 1½ inch cubes, chilled

2 cups cornstarch

Kosher salt

2 pounds firm, ripe plums, halved lengthwise, pitted, and cut into bite-size pieces

1 medium jalapeño chile (including seeds), very thinly sliced

1½ cups lightly packed mixed fresh herbs (such as mint, Thai basil, cilantro, and bronze fennel fronds)

1 cup Fish Sauce Vinaigrette (page 86)

2 dried Indian or Indonesian long peppers (optional)

Line a baking sheet with layers of paper towels. Pour 3 inches of rice bran oil into a large heavy pot and bring to 335°F over high heat.

Combine the pork belly and cornstarch in a large mixing bowl and toss to coat the cubes well.

In several batches to avoid crowding the pot, add the pork to the oil and fry until the belly is golden brown and crispy, 5 to 8 minutes per batch. As it's fried, transfer the pork to the prepared baking sheet and immediately season lightly with salt.

Arrange the pork belly and plums on a large plate. Sprinkle with the jalapeño and mixed herbs, then douse with the vinaigrette. If desired, use a Microplane to finely grate the long peppers evenly over the salad. Serve right away.

fresh hawaiian heart of palm salad with tahini-chile dressing

Serves 4

I've always had a special place in my heart for Chinese chicken salad. The jumble of chicken, iceberg, and a spicy sesame dressing is one of those Americanized riffs that bares little resemblance to the Asian dish it's probably based on. My homage skips the chicken but keeps the crunch in the form of fresh hearts of palm. We get ours from Lesley Hill and Michael Crowell of Wailea Agricultural Group, a farm on Hawaii's Big Island I've worked with for almost twenty years. (It's also where Nicole and I got married.) Hearts of palm are admittedly hard to come by on the mainland, so while there is no true substitute, you could use fennel or kohlrabi to a different but delicious effect.

2 cups baby kale

5 ounces yuba (preferably Hodo Soy brand), sheets unfolded and sliced into 3 by 1-inch strips

8 ounces fresh hearts of palm, cut into bite-size pieces

4 ounces small Japanese turnips, trimmed and thinly sliced

2 cups citrus segments (from pomelo, grapefruit, blood orange, or a mixture)

¼ tsp kosher salt

8 turns freshly ground black pepper

¼ cup White Soy Sauce–Lime Vinaigrette (page 84)

½ cup Tahini-Chile Dressing (page 89)

2½ cups mixed herbs and micro greens (such as mint leaves, bronze fennel fronds, and micro shiso)

¼ cup quinoa–pumpkin seed crunch (see page 102)

Combine the kale, yuba, hearts of palm, turnips, and citrus in a large mixing bowl. Sprinkle with the salt and pepper, add the vinaigrette, and toss gently to coat.

Arrange the hearts of palm mixture on a platter, spoon on the tahini-chile dressing, and sprinkle with the herbs and quinoa crunch. Serve right away.

STAB
&
DRAG

Unlike many of the categories on the menu, this one revealed itself long *after* most of its archetypes were born. As I watched from the open kitchen, I noticed that certain dishes required the same action from customers—before a bite started its mouth-bound trajectory, a diner had to spear a delicious something and then drag it through a saucy something. This might not count as a revelation—for some cooks, it might seem as obvious as pointing out that soup is a category of slurpable liquids—but seeing it for the first time inspired a blueprint that has shaped many dishes since. And because dinner at State Bird is far from a formal affair—forks often become optional—some of these recipes (like Duck Liver Mousse with Warm Duck-Fat Financiers) might more accurately be described as "grab and drags."

nectarines with whipped crescenza cheese, basil oil, and pink pepper

Serves 4

When the season brings nectarines that have a great balance between sweetness and acidity, I grab some, before Nicole hoards them all, and look to this simple preparation: a drizzle of basil oil, a sprinkle of pink peppercorn salt, and a shmear of creamy Crescenza (a soft-ripened, rindless cheese from Bellwether Farms in Petaluma, California, that is essentially just a puddle of buttery delight).

make the basil oil

2 cups lightly packed basil leaves

1 cup grapeseed oil

Bring a large pot of water to a boil over high heat, add the basil, and cook until wilted, about 10 seconds. Drain the basil in a sieve, then rinse under cold running water. Squeeze out excess water, coarsely chop the basil, transfer to a bowl, and put in the freezer, uncovered, for 5 minutes.

Line a sieve with a coffee filter or cheesecloth and set it over a small bowl.

Remove the basil from the freezer, transfer to a blender, and add the grapeseed oil. Blend on high speed for 2 minutes. Immediately transfer to the prepared sieve and let drain for 1 hour, gently stirring occasionally; do not press on or squeeze the basil. Discard the solids. Transfer to an airtight container and store in the fridge for up to 1 week.

prepare the cheese

8 ounces Crescenza cheese (also called Stracchino)

1 Tbsp Sweet Garlic Puree (page 39)

1 tsp kosher salt

5 turns freshly ground black pepper

Combine the cheese, garlic puree, salt, and black pepper in a small food processor and process until well combined with a spreadable texture. Transfer to an airtight container and store in the fridge for up to 5 days. Let it come to room temperature before serving.

finish the dish

1¾ tsp kosher salt

½ tsp pink peppercorns, coarsely cracked in a mortar

1 Tbsp white balsamic vinegar

2 turns freshly ground black pepper

1 dash Tabasco sauce

3 Tbsp olive oil

4 large ripe yellow nectarines, halved lengthwise, pitted, and cut into bite-size chunks

Small basil leaves or red sorrel leaves for garnish

In a small bowl, combine 1½ tsp of the salt and the pink peppercorns, stir well, and set aside.

In a medium mixing bowl, combine the vinegar, black pepper, Tabasco, and remaining ¼ tsp salt. Whisk well, then slowly stream in the olive oil while whisking until well combined.

Spoon the cheese onto a serving dish or individual dishes and spread to form a low mound. Add the nectarines to the vinaigrette and toss gently but well. Spoon the nectarines on and around the cheese, drizzle with 2 Tbsp of the basil oil, sprinkle with the pink peppercorn salt, and garnish with the basil. Serve right away.

persimmons with kinako dressing and black sesame salt

Serves 4 to 6

When fall comes and persimmons hit the markets, plates at State Bird become a canvas for the fruit. We turn it into a sauce, the fruit's heady sweetness taming the richness of duck confit. Nicole turns the Hachiya variety, whose flesh becomes pulpy when ripe, into cold, delicate granita. And it's during the fall that we make *hoshigaki*, an elegant Japanese preparation that requires hanging peeled persimmons from strings for weeks and massaging them daily with your fingertips until they're fully dried, intensely flavored, and have a remarkable chew.

Yet it's our simplest treatment of the fruit that I wanted to share with you here: Wedges of the raw Fuyu variety sprinkled with cracked black sesame seeds and set on a cool sauce made from *kinako*, ground roasted soybeans (available at Japanese markets or online) that have a buttery, toasty quality. In the summer, substitute crunchy cucumbers for the persimmons. In spring, swap in cherries, pitted and then warmed in brown butter.

½ cup kinako (roasted soybean flour), plus more for sprinkling

1 tsp kosher salt

¼ tsp ground ginger

¼ cup plus 1 Tbsp grapeseed oil

¼ cup plus 1 Tbsp toasted sesame oil

2 Tbsp unseasoned rice vinegar

6 ripe Fuyu persimmons, peeled and cut into 8 wedges

2 Tbsp Black Sesame Salt (page 95)

Combine the kinako, kosher salt, and ground ginger in a medium mixing bowl and stir well. Slowly pour in the grapeseed oil, sesame oil, and vinegar, whisking constantly until the dressing is well combined.

Pour the dressing in shallow serving bowls, arrange the persimmons on top, and sprinkle on the black sesame salt and a generous pinch of kinako. Serve right away.

duck liver mousse with warm duck-fat financiers

Serves 4 to 6

SPECIAL EQUIPMENT
Digital kitchen scale

For Nicole's first attempt at financiers, little French almond cakes, she followed a recipe from a cookbook whose author called for cream and honey, and that unconventional rendition became her tradition. It stuck with her even after she eventually came across the classic version in Claudia Fleming's *The Last Course* (spoiler alert: no cream, no honey). Since Nicole's financiers were already deliciously wacky, she decided to take the fun one step further, substituting the brown butter with duck fat. In one of the earliest collaborations between the savory and pastry sides of the State Bird kitchen, we paired the sweet cake with an unexpected French friend: duck liver mousse.

Both components are simpler than you might think. For the financiers, you mix a simple batter in a bowl and bake it in little molds. For the mousse, you make a duck liver milk shake (that's how we think of it), bake it, then blend in lots of butter. When you swipe a warm financier through the satiny mousse, each bite makes the same delicious sense as buttered cornbread (more so if the mousse is smeared on top with a sprinkle of sea salt and pepper). The mousse makes more than you need at one serving. It keeps in an airtight container in the fridge for up to 3 days.

make the mousse

½ pound duck livers, trimmed of stringy white membrane

1 cup heavy cream

1 Tbsp dry Madeira, plus ½ tsp

1 Tbsp tawny port, plus ½ tsp

1 large egg

1 tsp kosher salt

2 turns freshly ground black pepper

2 dashes Tabasco sauce

Generous ¼ tsp freshly grated nutmeg

12 Tbsp unsalted butter, cut into 1-inch cubes, at room temperature

Preheat the oven to 350°F.

Combine the duck livers, cream, 1 Tbsp Madeira, 1 Tbsp port, egg, salt, pepper, Tabasco, and nutmeg in a blender. Puree until very smooth, then strain the mixture through a fine-mesh sieve into a small ovenproof pot, stirring the solids to extract as much liquid as possible. Discard the solids.

Put the pot with the duck mixture in a baking dish or roasting pan and transfer to the oven. Pour enough steaming hot water into the baking dish to reach the same level as the duck liver mixture. Tightly cover the pot with aluminum foil and bake in the water bath until the mixture has mostly set but the center still jiggles when you shake the pot, 30 to 35 minutes. You may see some cracks on the surface—that's nothing to worry about.

Combine the hot duck mixture and butter in a blender and blend until smooth. Add the remaining ½ tsp Madeira and ½ tsp port and blend briefly to mix well.

Let the mixture cool to room temperature, then transfer to a container, cover, and refrigerate until chilled and thickened to a creamy consistency, at least 4 hours or up to 3 days.

make the financiers

55 grams/⅓ cup plus 1 Tbsp all-purpose flour

25 grams/¼ cup confectioners' sugar

½ tsp kosher salt

60 grams/⅔ cup almond meal

60 grams/¼ cup heavy cream, at room temperature

2 Tbsp orange blossom or wildflower honey

4 large egg whites, at room temperature

65 grams/¼ cup plus 2 tsp rendered duck fat, warm

Flaky sea salt

Freshly ground black pepper

Sift the flour, confectioners' sugar, and kosher salt into a small mixing bowl. Add the almond meal and stir well.

In a medium mixing bowl, combine the cream, honey, and egg whites and whisk until the honey dissolves. Add the flour mixture to the cream mixture and whisk until completely smooth. About a third at a time, whisk in the warm duck fat. Cover and refrigerate for at least 30 minutes or up to 4 days.

Preheat the oven to 400°F. Coat two silicone molds (see Note) with nonstick cooking spray and put them on a large baking sheet.

Evenly divide the batter among each mold, stopping just below the rim.

Bake until the financiers are golden brown and rise slightly above the rim of the molds, about 20 minutes, rotating the baking sheet halfway through. Remove from the oven and let cool slightly.

Remove the financiers from the molds, transfer to a platter, and top with a shmear of mousse. Crumble on the sea salt and sprinkle with pepper. Serve right away.

Note: The silicone molds you'll need for these financiers are available at good restaurant supply stores and via online suppliers such as JB Prince. Look for 12 by 7-inch (quarter-sheet-pan size) molds labeled "15 half rounds"—that is, each mold has 15 hemispherical forms, which are about 1½ inches in diameter and hold ½ ounce of batter.

duck croquettes with wagon wheel cheese and raisin verjus

Serves 4 to 8

Crisp croquettes of duck confit would be a pleasure all by themselves, but we don't stop there. We sneak a big chunk of cheese into each one, which spills out as your fork crashes through the golden crust. We like Cowgirl Creamery's Wagon Wheel because it melts beautifully but still has character. All that richness aches for some contrast, so we look to raisins—no Francophile will be surprised to hear that duck matches beautifully with dried fruit—to make a bracing sweet-tart sauce. Any high-quality raisins work, but if you can find the Red Flame variety, your sauce will have a striking purplish color.

cure and confit the duck

3 Tbsp kosher salt

1 Tbsp plus 2 tsp granulated sugar

1½ tsp freshly ground black pepper

3 pounds skin-on duck legs

9 thyme sprigs

3 rosemary sprigs

6 medium garlic cloves, smashed and peeled

1 large shallot, coarsely sliced

About 4 cups rendered duck fat (just enough to cover the duck legs)

At least 2 days before you plan to make the croquettes, stir together the salt, sugar, and pepper in a small bowl and then sprinkle the mixture evenly all over the duck legs. Scatter the thyme, rosemary, garlic, and shallot evenly on a large plate. Put the duck legs, skin side up, on top, cover with a piece of parchment paper, add another plate, and top with about 8 pounds of weight (a gallon jug of water or several large cans of beans will do the trick). Refrigerate to cure for 2 days.

After curing, preheat the oven to 300°F.

Rinse the duck legs briefly under running water and pat dry. Discard the aromatics.

In a Dutch oven just wide enough to fit the duck legs in one snug layer, melt the duck fat over medium heat. Add the duck legs so that they're completely submerged and cook until the fat is just barely bubbling. Cover with the lid and transfer the pot to the oven. Cook, rotating the pot once or twice, until the meat pulls from the bone with a gentle tug in more or less one piece but before it starts to fall off the bone, about 2½ hours. Remove the pot from the oven and let cool to room temperature, about 1 hour (the meat will continue to cook during this time). If not using immediately, cover and refrigerate for up to 1 week.

make the raisin verjus

1 cup raisins (preferably Red Flame)

1 cup red verjus

¼ cup red wine

¼ cup water

1 Tbsp grapeseed oil

1 tsp kosher salt

4 turns freshly ground black pepper

Combine the raisins, verjus, and wine in a small saucepan and bring to a simmer over medium heat. Transfer the mixture to a blender, add the water, grapeseed oil, salt, and pepper and blend on high speed until completely smooth. If not using immediately, transfer to an airtight container and store in the fridge for up to 3 days.

finish the dish

3 large eggs

1½ Tbsp minced thyme

Freshly ground black pepper

5½ ounces Cowgirl Creamery Wagon Wheel cheese or young Fontina, provolone, or Comté cheese, cut into twenty-five ¾-inch cubes

1 cup fairly fine dried bread crumbs

½ cup all-purpose flour

Rice bran, vegetable, or canola oil for deep-frying

Kosher salt

½ cup thinly sliced scallions (white and green parts)

Remove the duck legs from the fat and remove and discard the skin. Pull the meat from the bones (discarding the bones) and pick into approximately ¾-inch pieces. Place in a large mixing bowl. Strain the fat through a fine-mesh sieve into a bowl. Slowly pour the fat into an airtight container, leaving behind any opaque liquid (duck juices!).

Add the duck juices, ¼ cup of the fat, 1 egg, thyme, and 4 turns pepper to the meat. Use your hands to mix well, shredding some of the meat. Cover and refrigerate for about 30 minutes.

Form the duck mixture into about 25 balls, using about 2 Tbsp of the mixture per ball. One by one, stuff each ball with a cube of cheese, enclose the cheese in the mixture, and roll into a neat ball.

Set a wire rack over a baking sheet. Put the bread crumbs and flour in separate bowls. Crack the remaining 2 eggs into a bowl and beat lightly. One by one, dredge the duck balls in the flour and then the eggs, coating them well. Add the balls to the bread crumbs, using your hands to gently press the crumbs so each ball is completely covered. Transfer the duck croquettes to the rack as they're breaded.

Line a baking sheet with paper towels. Pour 3 inches of rice bran oil into a large heavy pot and bring to 325°F over high heat.

Working in several batches to avoid crowding the pot, add the croquettes to the oil and fry, stirring occasionally, until golden brown and crispy, 3 to 4 minutes per batch. Use a slotted spoon to transfer the croquettes to the prepared baking sheet and season with salt.

Spoon the raisin verjus onto plates and top with the croquettes and a sprinkling of scallions and pepper. Serve right away.

black butter–balsamic figs with basil and fontina fondue

Serves 4

make the fondue

⅓ cup heavy cream

⅔ cup shredded Fontina Val d'Aosta or Cowgirl Creamery Wagon Wheel cheese

1 large egg yolk, at room temperature

⅛ tsp kosher salt

3 turns freshly ground black pepper

2 dashes Tabasco sauce

2 Tbsp crème fraîche

Bring the cream to a simmer in a small saucepan over medium-high heat. Immediately turn the heat to very low to keep warm.

Pour an inch or so of water in a second small saucepan and bring to a boil. Put the cheese in a heatproof mixing bowl that will fit in the saucepan without touching the water. Set the bowl in the pan and turn the heat to medium-low. When the cheese begins to melt, about 30 seconds, pour in the warm cream. Continue to cook the cheese mixture, stirring constantly with a wooden spoon, until the cheese has fully melted, 1 to 2 minutes.

Stir the egg yolk, salt, pepper, and Tabasco into the cheese until well combined. Turn off the heat, remove the bowl, and stir in the crème fraîche until well combined. Cover and keep warm for up to 1 hour.

finish the dish

2 Tbsp unsalted butter

8 large ripe fresh figs (preferably Black Mission or Kadota), halved lengthwise

5 thyme sprigs

⅛ tsp kosher salt

½ tsp freshly ground black pepper

3 Tbsp balsamic vinegar

1 Tbsp thinly sliced scallion (white and green parts)

Micro basil leaves or torn basil leaves for garnish

Melt the butter in a large sauté pan over high heat. Let it bubble and crackle, swirling the pan occasionally, until it stops crackling and turns golden brown, about 1 minute. Continue to cook, swirling constantly, until the butter smokes and turns a blackish color, about 30 seconds more.

Put the figs, cut side down, in the pan, turn the heat to medium, and cook without stirring until golden brown, about 1 minute. Add the thyme and sprinkle on the salt and pepper. Toss well and continue to cook, tossing occasionally and making sure to brown the round sides, until the figs are deep golden brown and soft but not falling apart, about 2 minutes.

Add the vinegar to the pan, turn the heat to high, and cook, swirling and tossing constantly, just until it reduces slightly to glaze the figs, about 30 seconds.

Drizzle about ½ cup of the fondue on a large plate, top with the figs and glaze, and sprinkle on the scallion and basil. Serve right away.

SEAFOOD

hog island oysters with
kohlrabi kraut, toasted sesame,
and togarashi oil **203**

dashi-potato porridge with shellfish salsa
and pickled seaweed **205**

clam-kimchi stew with pork belly and tofu **209**

spicy yuba noodles with kimchi,
crab, and tomalley butter **210**

salmon tartare with fermented turnips
and meyer lemon kosho aioli **213**

deep-fried sweet soy-marinated fish parts **215**

rice-crusted trout with garum,
brown butter, hazelnuts,
and mandarin **217**

When we feature the bounty of the sea at State Bird, we try to strike a balance between transformation and celebration. On the one hand, we love to incorporate the bold flavors and textures that define our food. On the other, we aim to honor the perfection of the ingredients we work hard to procure—and that fishermen work far harder to raise or catch.

hog island oysters with kohlrabi kraut, toasted sesame, and togarashi oil

Makes 24 oysters

Contrasts are what keep great food interesting and lure you back for another bite. At State Bird, we take advantage of less conventional but equally exciting *fresh* and *fermented*. We pair raw, unadulterated bivalves, just hours out of the water and still alive, with kohlrabi that's been fermenting for weeks though also technically alive. The acidic, funky, slightly crunchy kraut acts like mignonette, balancing the oysters' richness and brininess. A splash of dashi accentuates the sea flavor. The result is not the pure pleasure of oyster but something even more compelling.

make the togarashi oil

1 cup grapeseed oil

¼ cup shichimi togarashi (Japanese seven-spice)

Combine the grapeseed oil and shichimi togarashi in a small saucepan, set over low heat, and bring to 180°F, 10 to 15 minutes. Do not rush the process with higher heat. Turn off the heat, let the mixture sit for 4 hours, then strain through a fine-mesh sieve into an airtight container. Discard the solids. (It makes about 1 cup; you'll need about 2 Tbsp for this recipe. Store in the fridge for up to 2 weeks.)

finish the dish

1 cup well-stirred Kohlrabi Kraut (page 56)

¾ cup State Bird Dashi (page 40)

½ Meyer lemon

Kosher salt

24 Hog Island Sweetwaters or other medium briny, minerally raw oysters (such as Kusshi or Beau Soleil)

Shaved ice

¼ cup Sesame Togarashi (page 97)

Combine the kraut and dashi in a medium mixing bowl. Use a Microplane to zest the ½ lemon directly into the bowl. Stir well.

Starting with a pinch of salt, gradually season the kraut mixture, not to make it taste salty but to balance the acidity of the kraut and bring out the oceanic flavor of the dashi.

Put the oysters in a large bowl and cover with shaved ice to keep them cold. If you'd like, fill a large platter with shaved ice.

One at a time, shuck the oysters and then use a knife to slice through the adductor muscle, releasing the oyster from the shell. Take care not to spill the delicious oyster liquor. Arrange the oysters on the half shell on the platter.

Stirring well before each addition, add a heaping teaspoon of the kraut mixture to the wide end of each shell without obscuring the oyster. Drizzle about ¼ tsp of the togarashi oil over the kraut and top with about ½ tsp of the sesame seeds. Serve right away.

dashi-potato porridge with shellfish salsa and pickled seaweed

Serves 4 to 6

You never know when you'll learn something. One morning, I dragged out leftovers from the fridge—a Japanese dashi-based soup made with braised pork, potatoes, and seaweed from dinner at a friend's restaurant—and was in a rush, so I didn't warm it up. It definitely wasn't the kind of romantic moment when culinary revelations are made.

But when I bit into a cold chunk of potato, I was floored. The night before, the rich soup had tasted of pork, and the dashi contributed only a background of umami. Now the smoky sea flavor of the stock was front and center. Striking, too, was the way this flavor interacted with that of the potato, an ingredient that, as a French-trained chef, I associated with butter and rosemary, not fish and kelp. When I got to State Bird, I explored the unfamiliar pairing, simmering Yukon golds in dashi and tweaking the result with acid in the form of pickled seaweed— an homage to the original dish but also a nod to my love of cucumber pickles in a classic American potato salad.

Like most of our dishes, this one has morphed over the years. Today we serve it with a sort of seafood salsa, which accentuates the dashi flavor and drives home the dish's land-and-sea vibe. Each bite of the cold porridge is earthy and briny, bright and rich, satisfying and exciting.

make the pickled seaweed

½ ounce dried wakame seaweed

1 cup liquid from Fermented Turnips (page 57)

½ cup State Bird Dashi (page 40)

About 4 hours before you plan to serve the porridge, put the seaweed in a mason jar. Bring the fermented turnip liquid and dashi to a boil in a medium pot over high heat and pour it over the seaweed. Let sit at room temperature for at least 1 hour or up to 4 hours. Set a fine-mesh sieve over a bowl, then strain the seaweed, reserving the liquid for another pickling project. Coarsely chop the seaweed into approximately 1-inch pieces.

make the porridge

Peel from 1 Meyer lemon, cut into wide strips, white pith removed; 1 Tbsp plus 1 tsp Meyer lemon juice; plus ½ Meyer lemon

3 rosemary sprigs

1 tsp black peppercorns

1 pound Yukon gold potatoes, peeled and cut into ¾-inch cubes

8 cups State Bird Dashi (page 40)

6 Tbsp extra-virgin olive oil

3½ Tbsp shiro shoyu (white soy sauce, such as Yamashin brand)

2 Tbsp thinly sliced scallion (green parts only)

⅛ tsp shichimi togarashi (Japanese seven-spice)

⅛ tsp kosher salt

Lay out a large piece of cheesecloth and put the strips of lemon peel, rosemary, and peppercorns on it. Gather the edges, twist the loose cloth, and tie a knot to make a sachet.

Combine the potatoes and dashi in a medium pot, add the sachet, and bring to a gentle simmer over high heat. Lower the heat to maintain a simmer and cook until the potatoes are fully tender and slightly crumbly at the edges but not falling apart, 15 to 20 minutes. Remove from the heat and let the potatoes cool in the dashi.

Strain the potatoes and measure out 1¼ cups of the dashi, reserving the rest for another purpose (such as making soup).

Combine the potatoes and ½ cup of the dashi in a large mixing bowl. Using a small whisk, gently strike the potatoes to knock off some of their edges. Your goal is to achieve large chunks of potatoes lightly bound by thick, starchy liquid. Add the olive oil, shiro shoyu, scallion, lemon juice, shichimi togarashi, and salt. Use a Microplane to finely grate the zest from the remaining ½ Meyer lemon into the bowl. Use a rubber spatula to mix the ingredients gently but well, then stir in just enough of the remaining dashi to achieve the consistency of a porridge. Cover and refrigerate until chilled, at least 1 hour or up to 4 hours.

make the shellfish salsa

8 mussels, scrubbed, debearded, and rinsed well

8 littleneck clams, soaked in salty water for 1 hour and then drained and rinsed

2 cups State Bird Dashi (page 40) or water

4 ounces cleaned squid, bodies slit open and cut into 1-inch pieces, tentacle clusters halved

3 Tbsp White Soy Sauce–Lime Vinaigrette (page 84)

2 Tbsp extra-virgin olive oil

Combine the mussels and clams in a small pot and cover with a lid. Set over medium heat and cook, gently jostling the pot from time to time, just until the shellfish pop open, 5 to 7 minutes. Transfer the mussels, clams, and their juices to a medium mixing bowl. Remove the meat, discarding the shells, and set aside.

In the same pot, add the dashi and bring to a gentle simmer over medium heat. Add the squid and cook, stirring occasionally, until just opaque and tender, about 1 minute. Drain the squid well, discarding the dashi, and then add it to the shellfish.

Add the pickled seaweed, vinaigrette, and olive oil to the bowl and stir to coat the seafood.

finish the dish

4 Fermented Turnips (page 57), thinly sliced

1 small watermelon radish, quartered and thinly sliced

¼ cup quinoa-furikake crunch (see page 102)

Ladle the potato porridge into individual serving bowls. Top with the fermented turnips and radish, spoon on the shellfish salsa, and sprinkle on the crunch. Serve right away.

clam-kimchi stew with pork belly and tofu

Serves 4

I'd eaten the Korean soup called *jigae* many times but never made it myself, until one chilly night, a month or so before State Bird opened. I had gotten home late and was hungry, so I went digging through the refrigerator and spotted an old jar of kimchi that I'd made during my at-home fermenting adventures. As kimchi hangs around in your fridge, it slowly transforms, getting a little funkier every day. This one had been around for several months, so it had developed a particularly bold flavor, just the thing for *jigae*. What I dreamed up that night, then refined over the years and ultimately added to the menu, was a mash-up of all the *jigaes* I'd eaten. Spicy and funky from fermented cabbage, rich from slowly braised pork belly, and briny and fresh from briefly cooked clams, it had the same spirit as the real thing, even though it was as authentic as a San Francisco night is balmy. A giant bowl of it warmed and relaxed me, at least until the next day.

8 ounces Braised Pork Belly (page 46), chilled, plus 2 cups flavorful liquid

1 tsp unsalted butter, plus 1 Tbsp

1 tsp kosher salt

2 tsp toasted sesame oil

1 Tbsp julienned ginger

¾ cup drained kimchi (see page 60), chopped into 1-inch pieces, plus 5 Tbsp kimchi juice

8 ounces drained medium-firm tofu (preferably Hodo Soy brand), cut into 1-inch cubes

8 littleneck clams, soaked in salty water for 1 hour and then drained and rinsed

2 heads baby bok choy, trimmed and separated

2 Tbsp thinly sliced scallions

Line a plate with paper towels.

Cut the pork belly across the grain into ½-inch-thick slices, then cut the slices into 1½-inch pieces.

Warm the 1 tsp butter in a medium sauté pan over medium heat until it melts and froths. Add the pork belly and cook, flipping occasionally, until the pieces are golden brown on both sides, 5 to 7 minutes. Transfer the pork belly to the prepared plate, leaving the fat in the pan, and season the pork with the salt. Set aside.

Pour out all but 1 Tbsp of the fat, reserving it for another use. Add 1 tsp of the sesame oil and set over medium-high heat until the fat shimmers. Add the ginger and cook, stirring constantly, until fragrant but not colored, about 30 seconds. Add the kimchi and cook, stirring constantly, until fragrant, about 1 minute.

Add the flavorful braised pork belly liquid and the kimchi juice to the pan and let come to a gentle simmer. Lower the heat to maintain a simmer and cook for 15 minutes, just to let the flavors meld. Add the tofu, clams, bok choy, and reserved pork belly; cover the pan; and cook, lightly shaking the pan once or twice, just until the clams have opened, about 4 minutes.

Remove the pan from the heat, stir in the remaining 1 Tbsp butter and 1 tsp sesame oil, and sprinkle with scallions. Serve right away.

spicy yuba noodles with kimchi, crab, and tomalley butter

Serves 4

prepare the crab and tomalley butter

One 2-pound Dungeness crab, cooked (see page 165), meat picked and tomalley reserved

2 Tbsp unsalted butter, at room temperature

Combine the tomalley and butter in a small saucepan, set over low heat, and cook, stirring occasionally, until the butter melts and the mixture is just warm. Remove the pan from the heat and stir vigorously until well combined. Transfer the butter and crabmeat to separate airtight containers and store in the fridge for up to 4 hours.

finish the dish

8 ounces yuba (preferably Hodo Soy brand), sheets unfolded and sliced into 6 by 1-inch strips

1 Tbsp unsalted butter

1 Tbsp julienned ginger

1 tsp toasted sesame oil

1 tsp sambal oelek

1 cup kimchi (see page 60), chopped into approximately 1-inch pieces

1 tsp kosher salt

3 scallions, trimmed and cut into 3-inch lengths, plus 2 Tbsp thinly sliced (white and green parts)

¼ cup Kimchi Vinaigrette (page 87)

2 Tbsp finely grated (on a Microplane) Chicken-Egg Bottarga (page 100)

2 tsp sesame seeds, toasted (see page 96)

Rinse and drain the yuba, gently squeezing to remove any excess liquid.

Combine the unsalted butter, ginger, sesame oil, and sambal oelek in a medium sauté pan; set over high heat; and cook until the butter has melted and the ginger is fragrant but not colored, about 3 minutes.

Add the kimchi, yuba, and salt to the pan and cook, stirring constantly, until the surface of the sauté pan takes on a light brown hue, 2 to 3 minutes. Add the scallion lengths and cook, stirring, until they're tender, 1 to 2 minutes more. Remove the pan from the heat and gently stir in the crabmeat and crab butter.

Transfer the contents of the pan to a plate. Sprinkle with the sliced scallions, drizzle with the vinaigrette, and top with the bottarga and sesame seeds. Serve right away.

salmon tartare with fermented turnips and meyer lemon kosho aioli

Serves 4

We start with wild king salmon—caught the day we serve it, the buttery flesh begging to be eaten raw—and apply the same elements of acid and fat, freshness and crispness that a French chef would to beef tenderloin. Only we use the ingredients particular to our larder. Instead of capers, parsley, and shallots, we use fermented turnips, scallion, and cucumber. Instead of dashes of Worcestershire, we look to white soy sauce and dashi, which coax out the oceanic qualities of the fish. Aioli spiked with bright but funky *yuzu kosho* stands in for traditional raw egg, and a shower of Japanese-spiced fried quinoa provides an irresistible crunch.

8 ounces skinless, sushi-grade salmon fillets, pin bones removed if necessary

3 Tbsp thinly sliced crosswise Fermented Turnips (page 57)

3 Tbsp thinly sliced scallion (white and green parts)

2½ Tbsp White Soy Sauce–Lime Vinaigrette (page 84)

1 Tbsp extra-virgin olive oil

2 tsp State Bird Dashi (page 40)

1 tsp shiro shoyu (white soy sauce, such as Yamashin brand)

¼ tsp shichimi togarashi (Japanese seven-spice)

10 ounces thin-skinned cucumbers (preferably Japanese), cut into irregular bite-size pieces

3 Tbsp Meyer Lemon Kosho Aioli (page 76)

½ cup quinoa-furikake crunch (see page 102)

Using a very sharp chef's knife, slice the salmon horizontally into ⅛-inch-thick planks. Slice each plank into long ⅛-inch-thick strips, then line them up and slice crosswise into ⅛-inch cubes. Chop about a third of the cubes until they're the texture of coarsely ground meat.

Combine the sliced and chopped salmon in a medium mixing bowl and use your hands to mix thoroughly. Add the fermented turnips, scallion, vinaigrette, olive oil, dashi, shiro shoyu, and ⅛ tsp of the shichimi togarashi and use a spoon to mix the tartare until the ingredients are very well distributed, about 30 seconds.

Put the cucumbers in individual serving bowls, add the salmon, dollop the aioli on the side, and sprinkle with the remaining ⅛ tsp shichimi togarashi. Sprinkle the crunch over the salmon. Serve right away.

deep-fried sweet soy–marinated fish parts

Serves 4 to 6

Part of the fun of opening State Bird was finally having the freedom to experiment and give in to our culinary whims. We could now dream up a dish minutes before service and prepare enough for just six portions. Once we did, the ideas flowed.

Sometimes, we found ourselves with trout tails or salmon collars. These tasty, often neglected parts are great for nibbling and require little more than a simple marinade and quick trip in hot oil. Having a surplus of fish collar might not be a problem you typically face at home, but the spirit applies wherever you are—have fun, try new things, and experiment on your friends.

marinate the fish

½ cup Japanese soy sauce or tamari

¼ cup granulated sugar

2 Tbsp mirin (sweet rice wine)

½ tsp finely grated (on a Microplane) ginger

¼ tsp finely grated (on a Microplane) garlic

2 pounds fish tails, collars, and bellies (from salmon, black cod, and/or red trout)

Combine the soy sauce, sugar, mirin, ginger, and garlic in a medium mixing bowl and stir until the sugar has fully dissolved. Divide the fish among large resealable bags so they fit comfortably, then divide the soy sauce mixture among the bags. Seal the bags, forcing out as much of the air as you can, and use your hands to distribute the marinade all over the fish. Marinate in the fridge for 2 days.

finish the dish

Rice bran, vegetable, or canola oil for deep-frying

3 Tbsp thinly sliced scallion (green parts only)

1 Tbsp sesame seeds, toasted (see page 96)

4 lemon wedges

Remove the fish from the marinade and pat dry. Transfer the marinade to a small saucepan, bring to a simmer over medium heat, and cook until it has thickened slightly, about 5 minutes. Set aside.

Line a large baking sheet with paper towels. Pour 3 inches of rice bran oil into a large heavy pot and bring to 335°F over high heat.

In two batches to avoid crowding the pot, add the fish to the oil and fry until golden brown and crispy on the outside and just cooked through, 3 to 8 minutes per batch, depending on the size of the fish parts. As it's fried, transfer the fish to the prepared baking sheet. Brush the fish all over with the thickened marinade.

Arrange the fish on a platter, sprinkle on the scallion and sesame seeds, and put the lemon wedges on the side. Serve right away.

rice-crusted trout with garum, brown butter, hazelnuts, and mandarin

Serves 4

Often it just seems like we're creating something new at State Bird when, on closer inspection, we're simply tweaking time-honored flavor combinations. This preparation is a great example: it's essentially a reimagining of trout *à la grenobloise*, one of my favorite French fish dishes. The ingredients might be altered but the fundamental elements that make the dish such a pleasure remain intact. Instead of capers, lemon segments, and parsley tossed with brown butter, the salty element comes from spiced fish sauce, the citrus is sweet-tart mandarins, and the herbs are cilantro and mint. Slivers of ginger underscore the Asian orientation. Hazelnuts add texture and nod to the almonds in the similar (and similarly tasty) preparation *à la almandine*. Respecting tradition is what allows us to successfully break with it.

1 cup jasmine rice

8 Tbsp unsalted butter

Four 4-ounce skin-on red trout, sea trout, or arctic char fillets

Kosher salt

Freshly ground black pepper

2 Tbsp grapeseed oil

1 Tbsp State Bird Garum (page 42)

1 Tbsp julienned ginger

2 mandarin oranges, segmented and white pith removed, plus 2 tsp mandarin orange juice

16 hazelnuts, toasted (see page 96), and halved

20 mint leaves

8 cilantro sprigs, thick stems discarded, picked into a few delicate clusters of leaves

1 cup baby mustard greens

Grind the jasmine rice to a fine powder in a spice grinder. Pour the rice powder through a fine-mesh sieve into a small skillet, set over medium-high heat, and cook, shaking and tossing constantly, until the rice powder is very aromatic and just begins to smoke, about 5 minutes. Transfer to a plate and let cool.

Melt the butter in a small light-colored skillet over medium-low heat. Let it froth and bubble, occasionally stirring and pushing the froth aside to check on the color, until the butter turns a caramel hue, 6 to 8 minutes. Set aside.

Pat the fillets dry and season both sides with salt and pepper. One by one, add the fillets, skin side down, to the rice powder, pressing lightly to help the rice powder adhere.

Warm the grapeseed oil in a heavy skillet (wide enough to hold the fillets with room to spare) over high heat until you see wisps of smoke. Add the fillets, skin side down, and cook for 1 minute. Turn the heat to medium and continue to cook until the skin is light golden brown and crispy, about 4 minutes. Carefully flip the fillets, cook for 30 seconds more, and transfer, skin side up, to a platter.

Add the garum, ginger, mandarin segments, mandarin juice, and hazelnuts to the brown butter and set over high heat. Cook, swirling the skillet, just until the mixture comes to a simmer, about 30 seconds. Remove from the heat, add the mint and cilantro, swirl again, and spoon the mixture over the fish. Top with the mustard greens. Serve right away.

MEAT

spiced guinea hen dumplings
with garlic chives and aromatic broth 225

roasted bone marrow with chanterelles,
pink peppercorns, and cider vinegar 229

pork ribs glazed in their own juices 233

cumin lamb with squid, dates,
shishito peppers, and thai basil 235

WOLFE
RANCH
QUAIL

For better or worse, we tend to do things the hard way at State Bird, and we're drawn to producers who take a similarly rough road to quality. That's one reason I spent a solid three years courting a quail farmer named Brent Wolfe.

In California culinary circles and beyond, Brent is a legend, renowned for raising the finest quail in the country, and possibly the world. His affection for the bird began at age eleven, the day his mom dropped him off at a chicken show and he left with a crate of quail chicks, gifted by a breeder. And that's what Brent ultimately became, selectively breeding to develop what I like to think of as a "special blend" that tastes better than anything else I've tried.

His commitment to and fascination with the quirky ground bird propelled him past the many challenges of raising them. Quails, for instance, have a relatively low hatch rate. It's a niche product, far less meaty than chicken, duck, and partridge. And you don't see a group of yellow jackets teaming up to carry off larger birds, as Brent has seen them do to tiny quail chicks. Yet there is no logic when it comes to love.

Since we opened, we've served quail fried and perched on sweet-and-sour stewed onions, and for nearly as long I'd been trying to convince Brent to supply the several hundred we need each week to keep up with demand. And for years, Brent demurred. A perfectionist, he was famous around town for not delivering his quail (a task he still does himself) on the day you requested but often a few days later, when the birds had plumped enough to meet his high standards. If committing to a tall weekly order meant sacrificing quality, he just couldn't do it.

Still, we kept in touch, and when I learned he had increased his production, ever so gradually, we decided to commit to each other. To seal the deal, we offered to take whole birds and debone them ourselves. With Brent's quail, my costs doubled and our workload increased. But we've never looked back.

spiced guinea hen dumplings with garlic chives and aromatic broth

Serves 8

SPECIAL EQUIPMENT
Digital kitchen scale

We couldn't serve our food dim sum–style without including dumplings in the mix. And while many versions have made it onto the menu, only one never left. Making these at home requires ambition—you must cure and confit guinea hen, make pho-inspired broth, and roll out dumpling dough. But it's worth the effort to experience the delightfully disorienting flavors— preserved lemons, brown butter, charred ginger!—that are pure State Bird.

confit the guinea hen and make the filling

2 Tbsp Arab Spice (page 99), plus 1 tsp

¼ cup plus ½ Tbsp kosher salt

2 Tbsp granulated sugar

2 tsp freshly ground black pepper

6 guinea hen legs

4 cups rendered duck fat

4 Tbsp unsalted butter, at room temperature

3 cups thinly sliced fresh shiitake mushroom caps

Rind from 2 preserved lemons (see page 63), rinsed and finely diced, plus 1 tsp pulp

½ small garlic clove, finely grated on a Microplane

¼ tsp finely grated (on a Microplane) ginger

½ cup thinly sliced cilantro (thin stems and leaves)

⅓ cup thinly sliced scallions (white and green parts)

At least 3 days before you plan to make the dumplings, combine the 2 Tbsp Arab spice, salt, sugar, and pepper in a bowl and stir well. Sprinkle the mixture all over the guinea hen legs. Put the legs, skin side down, on a baking sheet so that they are snug but not overlapping. Cover and refrigerate to cure for 2 days.

After curing, preheat the oven to 300°F.

In a Dutch oven just wide enough to fit the hen legs in one snug layer, melt the duck fat over medium heat. Add the legs so that they're completely submerged and cook until the fat is just barely bubbling, then cover with the lid and transfer the pot to the oven. Cook, rotating the pot once or twice, until the meat is fork tender and begins to pull away from the bone, about 1½ hours. Remove from the oven and let cool to room temperature, about 1½ hours (the meat will continue to cook during this time). Cover and refrigerate overnight or up to 1 week.

When ready to use, remove the legs from the fat. Set aside ¼ cup of the fat for the broth, reserving the rest for another purpose. Remove the meat from the bone and cut into approximately ½-inch chunks, discarding the bones and cartilage but keeping the skin. Then, go digging for the deep-brown deposits of what I call "guinea hen gold"—the concentrated, flavorful juices from the meat that have become gelatinous. Set aside whatever you've got for the broth.

Melt the butter in a large light-colored skillet over medium-low heat. Let it froth and bubble, occasionally stirring and pushing the froth aside to check on the color, until the butter turns a caramel hue, about 6 minutes. Add the mushrooms and cook, stirring occasionally, until soft, about 8 minutes. Add the 1 tsp Arab spice and cook, stirring, for 30 seconds, then add the guinea hen meat and cook just until warmed through, about 1 minute. Scrape the mixture into a large bowl and set aside to cool.

Add the preserved lemon rind and pulp, garlic, and ginger to the bowl and mix well, leaving most of the meat in chunks. Add the cilantro and scallions and mix gently but thoroughly.

Line a baking sheet with parchment paper.

Roll the hen mixture into about 50 small balls, using 1 Tbsp of mixture per ball, and put them on the prepared baking sheet. Cover and refrigerate at least 1 hour or up to 2 days.

make the broth

2-inch knob unpeeled ginger, plus 1-inch knob, peeled

3 medium garlic cloves; 1 peeled

1 medium yellow onion, halved lengthwise and thinly sliced

2½ ounces fresh shiitake mushrooms (caps and stems), bottoms trimmed, cleaned, and thinly sliced

¼ cup reserved fat from the guinea hen confit

1 star anise

3 whole cloves

1 small rosemary sprig

8 cups State Bird Chicken Stock (page 41)

¼ cup fish sauce (preferably Red Boat brand), or to taste

Handful of cilantro stems, very coarsely chopped

Handful of mint sprigs, very coarsely chopped

1 Tbsp plus 2 tsp Meyer lemon juice, or to taste

Set a crosswire heatproof rack over a burner on the stove top and then turn the burner to medium-high. Put the unpeeled ginger and unpeeled garlic on the rack directly over the flame. Cook, turning occasionally, until the skins are completely blackened, about 3 minutes for the garlic and 5 minutes for the ginger.

Transfer the blackened ginger and garlic to a cutting board. Scrape off most of the char with a chef's knife, smash them with the flat of the knife, and put in a large pot. Add the onion, mushrooms, ¼ cup fat, star anise, cloves, and rosemary. Set the pot over medium heat, wait for the fat to sizzle, and cook, stirring once or twice, for about 3 minutes, just to aromatize the vegetables.

Add the chicken stock and fish sauce (and any guinea hen gold). Increase the heat to bring the liquid to a strong simmer and cook for 20 minutes to infuse the stock with the flavor of the aromatics, then turn off the heat.

Smash the peeled ginger and peeled garlic with the flat of a chef's knife. Add to the pot along with the cilantro and mint. Let steep for 5 minutes, then strain through a fine-mesh sieve into another pot, firmly pressing the solids to extract as much liquid as possible. Stir in the lemon juice, then taste and season with more fish sauce or lemon juice. Transfer to an airtight container and store in the fridge for up to 2 days. Skim the fat before using.

make the dough and form the dumplings

615 grams/5 cups plus
2 Tbsp all-purpose flour,
plus more for dusting

475 grams/2 cups water

1 tsp kosher salt

1 large egg beaten with a
splash of water

Put the flour in the bowl of a stand mixer fitted with the paddle attachment. Combine the water and salt in a small saucepan and bring to a boil over high heat, stirring to dissolve the salt. Measure 415 grams/1¾ cups of the hot water. Start the mixer on medium speed and pour in the hot water in a thin, steady stream. Mix until clumps form, then increase the speed slightly and mix until a very rough dough forms and separates from the sides of the bowl, about 3 minutes. If necessary, add more hot water, 1 tsp at a time, just until the dough comes together. The dough should be soft but not sticky.

Transfer the dough to a clean work surface and knead and roll until fairly smooth, about 1 minute. Gather the dough into a ball, cover, and refrigerate at least 1 hour or up to 6 hours.

Set up a pasta roller. Generously dust a work surface with flour. Cut the dough in quarters. Working with one quarter, use a rolling pin to roll out into a ¼-inch-thick rectangle, just narrow enough to fit through the pasta roller (if necessary, trim the dough slightly to adjust the width or shape).

Dust the dough with flour and roll through the pasta roller at the widest setting. Adjust the pasta roller to the next setting and roll the dough through again. Repeat, adjusting the setting each time and dusting with flour as necessary, until the dough is just less than 2 millimeters thick. You should just barely be able to see the color of your finger through the dough. Repeat with the other quarters of the dough.

Lay out one length of the dough with the long side facing you and brush the surface with the egg. Arrange the balls of filling along the center of the dough, spacing them about 1½ inches apart. Fold the long sides of the dough over the filling, bringing the edges together and gently pinching so they adhere. Carefully rotate the tube of dough forward so that the pinched edge lies flat on the work surface. Cut the dough between each ball of filling. Pinch the cut edges together to seal, forcing out any air inside to form the dumplings. Trim the edges of each dumpling to create an approximately ¼-inch unfilled border around the filling.

finish the dish

Kosher salt

About 5 Tbsp grapeseed oil

⅓ cup thinly sliced
garlic chives or scallion
(green parts only)

1 tsp Arab Spice (page 99)

⅓ cup lemon olive oil
(preferably Asaro brand)

Gently heat the broth in a medium pot over low heat and cover to keep warm. Line two large baking sheets with parchment paper.

Bring a large pot of water to a boil over high heat and add enough salt to make it taste nearly as salty as the ocean. Working in several batches to avoid crowding the pot, add the dumplings and cook until the wrappers are fully cooked but not mushy, 1½ to 2 minutes. As the dumplings finish cooking, use a skimmer to carefully transfer them to the prepared baking sheets.

Meanwhile, warm a large nonstick pan over medium-high heat. Add 1 Tbsp of the grapeseed oil and swirl to coat the pan. Working in several batches to avoid crowding the pan, add the dumplings and cook, flipping once, until very light golden in spots on both sides, about 1 minute, adding a bit more oil between batches as necessary.

Divide the dumplings among eight serving bowls. Add a generous pinch of garlic chives and Arab spice to each bowl, pour in 1 cup of the broth, and drizzle on about 2 tsp of the lemon olive oil. Serve right away.

GUINEA HEN GOLD

I call the by-product of guinea hen confit "gold" not just for its color but for its value. We search the depths of confit pans, mining the meat and fat to extract deposits of concentrated guinea hen juices. Gelatinous when cold and gleaming like uncut gemstones, this is precious stuff, one of the many surprise treasures that cooking provides. We add it to the aromatic broth that accompanies our guinea hen dumplings. We apply the same concept when we confit duck, incorporating duck gold into croquettes (see page 195) to enhance the flavor. It's as much an ingredient in our larder as it is a reminder to always seek as you cook. You never know when you might strike gold.

roasted bone marrow with chanterelles, pink peppercorns, and cider vinegar

Serves 6

prep the marrow bones

Kosher salt

Three 7-inch pieces center-cut beef marrow bones, halved lengthwise by a butcher

Ice cubes

Two days before you plan to serve the bone marrow, pour about 6 inches of water into a container big enough to hold the bones. Salt the water generously and stir until the salt dissolves. Add the bones, then empty a tray of ice cubes into the water, transfer to the fridge, and let soak for 1 day.

The next day, drain the bones and cover again with generously salted ice water. Soak in the fridge for 1 day more.

make the sauce

5 Tbsp finely chopped shallots

3 Tbsp unsalted butter, plus 4 Tbsp cold and cut into 1-inch cubes

1 tsp kosher salt

3 turns freshly ground black pepper

½ cup apple cider vinegar

¼ cup State Bird Chicken Stock (page 41) or water

¼ cup thinly sliced flat-leaf parsley (thin stems and leaves)

1 Tbsp pink peppercorns

Combine the shallots and 3 Tbsp butter in a small skillet, set over medium heat, and let the butter melt and froth, swirling the pan occasionally. Season with ½ tsp of the kosher salt and the black pepper and continue to cook, stirring occasionally, until the shallot is translucent but not colored, about 3 minutes.

Add the vinegar to the skillet, raise the heat slightly, and gently simmer until reduced by half, 4 to 6 minutes. Add the chicken stock and remaining ½ tsp kosher salt and continue to simmer for 1 minute more. Add the remaining 4 Tbsp cold butter and swirl the pan or whisk aggressively until the butter has completely melted, about 30 seconds. Remove the pan from the heat and stir in the parsley and pink peppercorns. Season with salt. Cover and keep warm for up to 30 minutes. Reheat over low heat, if necessary, just before serving.

finish the dish

2 medium garlic cloves, peeled and halved crosswise

1 Tbsp kosher salt, plus 1 tsp

12 turns freshly ground black pepper

¾ tsp thyme leaves

2 Tbsp grapeseed oil

8 ounces fresh golden chanterelle mushrooms, trimmed, cleaned, and cut through the stem into bite-size pieces

6 large, thick slices crusty bread, cut into thirds

Extra-virgin olive oil for brushing

Generous pinch flaky sea salt

Preheat the oven to 400°F. Set a wire rack over a baking sheet.

Drain the marrow bones well and pat dry. Arrange the bones, cut side up, on the prepared rack. Lightly rub the exposed marrow in each bone with the garlic, then evenly season with the 1 Tbsp kosher salt and the black pepper and sprinkle with the thyme leaves. Roast until the bones have browned slightly and the marrow is spreadable and soft but not melted, about 18 minutes, rotating the baking sheet halfway through.

Meanwhile, heat 1 Tbsp of the grapeseed oil in a large skillet over medium-high heat until you see wisps of smoke. Add half the mushrooms to the skillet, spreading them in a single layer. Season with ½ tsp kosher salt and cook, stirring occasionally, until lightly golden, about 5 minutes. Transfer to a plate. Repeat with the remaining grapeseed oil, mushrooms, and ½ tsp kosher salt. Return the first batch to the pan, remove the pan from the heat, cover, and set aside.

Heat a grill pan or griddle over medium-high heat. Brush the bread slices on both sides with olive oil and cook, flipping once, until toasted and brown in spots, about 5 minutes. Sprinkle with sea salt.

Arrange the marrow bones on a large platter, spoon on the mushrooms, and spoon about 2 Tbsp of the sauce over each bone. Serve right away with the grilled bread on the side.

pork ribs glazed in their own juices

Serves 6 to 8

For a restaurant dish, these ribs are remarkably friendly to the home cook, with approximately zero concessions to convenience. Cooked slowly in foil with garlic, rosemary, and lemon, they steam in their own juices, which you later use to make a glaze, refreshed at the last minute with those same aromatics. A dusting of the Japanese spice mixture called *shichimi togarashi* provides a little heat and even more complexity without any added effort. The flavors are as sophisticated as the process is uncomplicated. If only every restaurant-quality dish were this simple.

2 equal-size racks pork spare ribs (2 to 2½ pounds each), preferably St. Louis–cut

2 Tbsp kosher salt

1½ tsp freshly ground black pepper

5 medium garlic cloves; 4 thinly sliced, 1 smashed and peeled

2 lemons, top and bottom trimmed, cut into ¼-inch rounds, plus 1½ Tbsp lemon juice, or as needed

1 large rosemary sprig, leaves only, plus 1 small sprig, torn in half

1½ Tbsp cornstarch

1 Tbsp water

1 tsp shichimi togarashi (Japanese seven-spice)

¼ cup thinly sliced scallions (white and green parts)

Preheat the oven to 350°F.

On a work surface, lay out a sheet of aluminum foil that is about 4 inches longer than the rib racks, then lay a piece of parchment paper that's about 3 inches longer than the racks in the center of the foil.

Season the rib racks on both sides with the salt and pepper. Lay one rack, meaty side down, on the parchment paper. Scatter the sliced garlic on the rack, tile it with the lemon rounds, and scatter on the rosemary leaves. Lay the other rack, meaty side up, on top of the first rack.

Wrap the racks snugly in the parchment, tucking the short sides under to create a neat package. Next, do the same with the aluminum foil, sealing the edges well to make sure no steam or juices escape during the cooking process.

Put the foil package on a baking sheet and bake until the meat is very tender but not falling off the bone, about 2 hours, rotating once halfway through. Remove from the oven and let the ribs rest at room temperature for 1 hour.

Open the package and scrape out and discard the lemon, garlic, and rosemary. Carefully transfer the racks to a cutting board and cut into individual ribs. Pour the juices from the package into a small saucepan. Do not skim the fat. Add the smashed garlic and torn rosemary sprig to the saucepan, set over high heat, and bring to a simmer.

In a small bowl, stir together the cornstarch and water until smooth. Gradually pour the cornstarch mixture into the pan, let come to a boil, and cook, stirring frequently, just until the glaze is thick enough to coat the back of a spoon, 1 to 2 minutes. Remove from the heat. (You can cover and set aside for up to 3 hours. Re-warm in a small saucepan over low heat until it comes to a simmer, then remove from the heat.) Stir in the lemon juice (to taste), season with salt, and then strain the glaze through a fine-mesh sieve into a mixing bowl, discarding the solids.

Prepare a grill (or preheat a grill pan or wide heavy skillet) to cook over high heat. Oil the grill grates (or add enough oil to the grill pan or skillet to very thinly cover the surface). Add the ribs and grill, turning occasionally, until they're browned all over, 3 to 5 minutes.

As the ribs are browned, brush them generously with the glaze. Transfer the ribs to a platter and sprinkle with the shichimi togarashi and scallions. Serve right away.

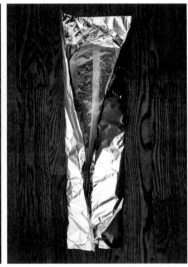

cumin lamb with squid, dates, shishito peppers, and thai basil

Serves 4

I was just a few bites into dinner at Z&Y, a restaurant in San Francisco's Chinatown, when I found myself daydreaming about a new dish for State Bird. I was blown away by their cumin lamb, an exhilarating pile of juicy meat encased in a crisp, intensely flavored crust. I was also happily bewildered by the presence of its namesake spice, which I'd always associated with the food of India and the Middle East, on a tableful of dishes fragrant from soy sauce and rice wine. Back in my kitchen, I aimed to re-create what I liked best about the dish but also to make it my own. For me, the combination of cumin and lamb brought to mind the food of North Africa and the Middle East—where cumin was likely born, millennia before it came to northern China by way of the Silk Road—so I looked to other North African flavors for elements of sweetness, in this case dates and orange juice. Briefly cooked vegetables added freshness and adorned the milk-fed lamb we get from farmer Don Watson's small herd. And I couldn't resist tossing in squid—lamb and cephalopods make an unlikely but compelling match. The result is a State Bird classic, a dish you'd find nowhere else but here.

make the glaze

2 cups lamb stock
(see page 41)

¾ cup orange juice

¼ cup Japanese soy sauce
or tamari

3 Tbsp fish sauce (preferably
Red Boat brand)

3 strips orange peel
(each about 3 by 1 inch),
white pith removed

1-inch knob ginger,
peeled and smashed

1 small jalapeño chile,
thinly sliced

1 medium garlic clove,
smashed and peeled

2 Tbsp potato starch

2 Tbsp water

Combine the lamb stock, orange juice, soy sauce, fish sauce, orange peel, ginger, jalapeño, and garlic in a small pot and bring to a boil over high heat.

Meanwhile, in a small bowl, whisk together the potato starch and water until smooth.

Once the stock mixture comes to a boil, whisk in the potato starch mixture in a thin stream. Let the mixture return to a boil, whisking constantly, until it thickens enough to coat the back of a spoon, about 5 seconds. Lower the heat to medium and simmer, whisking, for 30 seconds. Strain the glaze through a medium-mesh sieve into a heatproof measuring cup. Reserve ½ cup for this dish, cover, and keep warm for up to 1 hour. (Freeze the rest in ½-cup batches for the next time you make the dish.)

finish the dish

12 shishito or Padrón peppers

10 wax beans, trimmed

4 thin scallions, cut into 2-inch lengths

1 head baby bok choy, trimmed and separated

2 ounces zucchini, cut into bite-size slices

1 Tbsp cumin seeds

1 Tbsp coriander seeds

1 tsp black peppercorns

½ cup potato starch

2 ounces boneless lamb leg or loin, cut into 2-inch-wide, ¼-inch-thick slices

Kosher salt

1 Tbsp toasted sesame oil

1 Tbsp unsalted butter

½ tsp sambal oelek

4 ounces cleaned squid, bodies sliced into ¼-inch rings, tentacle clusters kept whole

2 ounces yuba (preferably Hodo Soy brand), sheet unfolded and sliced into 3 by 1-inch strips

4 dried dates (preferably Deglet Noor), quartered lengthwise and pitted

½ cup Thai basil leaves

Pea sprouts for topping

1 Tbsp Lamb Sesame Sprinkle (page 94)

Combine the peppers, wax beans, scallions, bok choy, and zucchini in a medium mixing bowl and set aside.

Toast the cumin seeds and coriander seeds in a small pan over high heat, shaking and swirling the pan constantly, until fragrant, 1 to 2 minutes. Transfer to a mortar and grind to a fine powder, then transfer to a small bowl. Add the peppercorns to the mortar and grind to a fine powder. Add the ground pepper and the potato starch to the bowl, and mix until well combined.

Lightly season the lamb slices on one side with salt. Combine the lamb and the potato starch mixture in a medium mixing bowl and toss well to coat each slice. Shake off any excess and transfer the lamb to a plate.

Combine the sesame oil and butter in a large sauté pan and set over high heat. When the butter melts and bubbles, add the lamb in a single layer and cook until the bottom is golden brown, about 2 minutes. Flip the lamb and add the sambal oelek and the vegetables. Season with ¼ tsp salt, stir well to combine, and cook until the zucchini and shishitos start to brown, about 1 minute.

Add the squid and yuba to the pan, stir well to combine, and cook, stirring once, until the yuba crisps at the edges, about 1 minute.

Add the dates to the pan and cook, stirring occasionally, until the surface of the pan develops a golden-brown coating, about 30 seconds. Add the reserved lamb glaze, stir well, and cook, scraping the pan, until the glaze reduces by half and looks glossy, about 1 minute more. Stir in the basil.

Transfer the contents of the pan to a plate and top with the pea sprouts and sesame sprinkle. Serve right away.

VEGETABLES

polenta "elote" with corn salad,
tomato aioli, and queso fresco **241**

cast-iron quail eggs with summer vegetable condiments
and garlic chips **243**

carrot mochi with pickled carrots, carrot vinaigrette,
and pistachio dukkah **247**

buffalo cauliflower with blue cheese
and garlic chips **249**

porcini fried rice with balsamic spring onions,
ramps, and porcini aioli **253**

yuba "all'amatriciana" with fresh tomatoes
and chanterelle mushrooms **255**

polenta "elote" with corn salad, tomato aioli, and queso fresco

Serves 6 to 8

For someone like me, who's more jazzed about corn's flavor than its aggressive sweetness, *elote* represents the height of corn cookery. The Mexican street staple, which I first tried in Chicago as an impressionable recent culinary school grad, features grilled ears of corn slathered with mayo, coated in salty cotija cheese, dusted with chile powder, and finished with a squeeze of lime. The curbside cook who provided my introduction used sweet corn, not the starchy field corn common in Mexico, and each addition seemed designed to tame the vegetable's sugary quality. I was sold.

When we take on the dish at State Bird, we use corn in two forms. We fry polenta in slabs, add a slick of mayonnaise invigorated by slow-cooked tomato, then top it with sweet kernels dressed with lime. We keep the dish firmly in savory territory, just where I like it.

make the polenta

2⅓ cups whole milk

2⅓ cups water

5 Tbsp unsalted butter

1 tsp kosher salt

1 cup stone-ground polenta

5 turns freshly ground black pepper

3 dashes Tabasco sauce

Combine the milk, water, butter, and salt in a medium pot and bring to a boil over medium-high heat. Add the polenta in a steady stream, whisking constantly. Turn the heat to very low and cook at a bare simmer, stirring occasionally, until the polenta is tender and thickened but still pourable, 30 to 45 minutes. Stir in the pepper and Tabasco. Pour the polenta into a 9 by 13-inch baking pan, spread to an even 1-inch-thick layer, and let cool slightly. Then, transfer to the fridge to chill completely, 1 to 2 hours.

finish the dish

24 quail eggs

1 Tbsp clarified butter
(see page 38), melted

¼ cup Jimmy Nardello
Vinaigrette (page 88)

¼ cup Eggplant Vinaigrette
(page 87)

1 recipe Garlic Chips
(page 101)

1 cup lightly packed mixed
edible flowers, microgreens,
and microherbs (optional)

Flaky sea salt

One by one, hold each quail egg over a medium bowl and use a paring knife to poke a hole through each eggshell about ¼ inch from the top of the egg's narrow end. With the blade against the hole, carefully saw most of the way through the top of the egg shell. Use the knife to pry off the top of the shell and pour the egg into the bowl.

Warm an 8-inch well-seasoned cast-iron pan over medium heat for 2 minutes. Dab a paper towel with the clarified butter and rub the surface and sides of the pan to coat well. Carefully pour in the eggs, quickly but gently shaking and swirling the pan so the eggs cover the surface in a single layer but the yolks don't break. Cook until the whites have set but the yolks are still runny, about 3 minutes.

Remove the pan from the heat. Dollop both the Jimmy Nardello and eggplant vinaigrettes around the eggs and spoon on the creoja in little piles. Sprinkle on the garlic chips and the mixture of flowers, greens, and herbs (if using) and season with sea salt. Serve right away.

carrot mochi with pickled carrots, carrot vinaigrette, and pistachio dukkah

Serves 4

Carrots appear in four forms in this salad, dreamed up by our incredibly talented chef de cuisine Gaby Maeda. She turns the root vegetable into lively, crunchy pickles. She roasts it until it's sweet and tender. She concocts a vinaigrette using its juice. And, most unusual, she turns it into balls of the Japanese rice cake called *mochi*, which has a chewy, slightly springy quality that I just love. Part Japanese, Gaby grew up in Hawaii, where her grandmother would crisp mochi in oil, then top it with soy sauce and nori. She also ate a popular Hawaiian dish called mochiko chicken, the meat dredged in glutinous rice flour and fried. Recalling this gave her an idea. Gaby thought of mixing rice flour with an intensely carroty puree to make mochi dough. This dish is a perfect example of how our cooks shape our food.

make the carrot mochi

8 ounces large carrots, peeled and cut into 1-inch dice

½ cup plus 2 Tbsp carrot juice

¼ tsp kosher salt

1 cup mochiko-style sweet rice flour, plus more as needed

1 Tbsp extra-virgin olive oil

Combine the carrots, ½ cup of the carrot juice, and kosher salt in a small saucepan and bring to a boil over medium-high heat. Cook, skimming the foam on the surface as often as necessary, until all but ⅓ inch or so of the liquid has evaporated, about 10 minutes. Lower the heat to maintain a simmer and cook just until the liquid has completely evaporated and the carrots are fully tender, about 10 minutes more.

Transfer the carrots to a blender and puree on high speed until very smooth, adding up to 2 Tbsp of the remaining carrot juice if necessary to blend. Transfer to a bowl and stir in the flour until a smooth dough forms, gradually adding more flour as needed just until the tacky dough no longer sticks to your hands. Roll the dough into 1½-inch balls.

Prepare an ice bath in a medium mixing bowl.

Bring a pot of generously salted water to a boil. Add the mochi balls and boil, stirring occasionally, until they're no longer grainy in the center (cut one in half and taste it), 6 to 8 minutes. Use a slotted spoon to transfer the mochi to the ice bath to cool, then drain well in a colander. Drizzle with the olive oil and toss to coat. (If not using immediately, transfer to an airtight container and store in the fridge for up to 24 hours. Bring to room temperature before using.)

finish the dish

Rice bran, vegetable, or
canola oil for deep-frying

½ cup celery leaves

½ cup Red Chile Juice–Lime
Vinaigrette (page 87)

2 Tbsp unsalted butter

1 Tbsp Everything Spice
(page 97)

Kosher salt

½ cup Blue Cheese Aioli
(page 74)

⅓ cup coarsely crumbled
dense, creamy blue cheese
(such as Bayley Hazen)

1 recipe Garlic Chips
(page 101)

Delicate baby mustard
greens for garnish

Line two baking sheets with paper towels.

Pour 3 inches of rice bran oil into a large heavy pot and bring
to 335°F over high heat. Standing back from the pot, carefully
add the celery leaves (they'll bubble and spit) and fry, stirring
occasionally, until pale yellow and crispy, about 30 seconds. Use
the spider skimmer to transfer the leaves to a prepared baking
sheet and immediately season with salt.

Working in several batches to avoid crowding the pot, add the
breaded cauliflower to the oil and fry until it is golden brown
and crispy, about 3 minutes per batch. As it's fried, use the
skimmer to transfer the cauliflower to the prepared baking
sheets and immediately season with salt. While it's still hot,
put the fried cauliflower into a large mixing bowl, add the
vinaigrette and toss well.

Drain the pickled cauliflower.

Melt the butter in a small sauté pan over medium-high heat. Let it
bubble and crackle, swirling the pan occasionally, until the butter
stops crackling and turns golden brown, about 3 minutes. Remove
the pan from the heat, add the everything spice and pickled
cauliflower, and swirl to mix well.

Spoon the aioli onto a platter. Arrange the cauliflower on the
platter and garnish with the pickled cauliflower, fried celery
leaves, blue cheese, and garlic chips. Garnish with mustard
greens. Serve right away.

porcini fried rice with balsamic spring onions, ramps, and porcini aioli

Serves 4

The magic of fried rice is not just that the grains are resurrected by a little hot oil but, if you ask me, that they're improved as they're infused with flavor and crisped in spots. The general technique aside, this dish detours through the rice-loving country of Italy, celebrating the glory of porcini mushrooms in three forms—sauteed, raw, and as rich aioli.

cook the rice

1 cup short-grain white rice

The day before you plan to serve the fried rice, put the rice in a large mixing bowl and add enough water to cover by 1 inch. Use your hands to stir the rice, then empty the water, fill the bowl again, and repeat the process until the fresh water looks clear after stirring, about three times. Drain the rice well in a fine-mesh sieve, letting it sit in the sieve for about 10 minutes.

Combine the rinsed rice and 1 cup plus 2 Tbsp water in a rice cooker and cook according to the manufacturer's directions. When the rice is cooked, use a spoon to fluff it in the rice cooker, allowing steam to escape. Transfer the rice to a small baking sheet, spread it out in a thin, even layer, and let cool. Store, uncovered, in the fridge overnight. If the rice dries out now, it will end up fluffier and less clumpy later.

cook the onions and ramps

3 Tbsp extra-virgin olive oil

2 red spring onion bulbs (about 1 inch thick), greens trimmed and bulbs cut through root end into 8 wedges

6 large ramps, bulbs halved lengthwise, greens reserved

½ tsp kosher salt

10 turns freshly ground black pepper

8 thyme sprigs

½ cup balsamic vinegar

Warm the olive oil in a sauté pan over high heat until you see wisps of smoke. Add the onions and ramp bulbs to the pan, sprinkle with the salt and pepper, and cook, stirring frequently, until the onions color and soften slightly, about 2 minutes. Add the thyme and cook, stirring occasionally, until the onions are golden brown in spots, another 2 minutes. Add the balsamic vinegar and let it bubble, stirring occasionally, just until most of the liquid has evaporated, about 2 minutes more. Set aside until ready to use, or let cool and store in an airtight container in the fridge for up to 4 days.

finish the dish

2 Tbsp plus 2 tsp State Bird Dashi (page 40)

1 tsp shiro shoyu (white soy sauce, such as Yamashin brand)

1 tsp sherry vinegar

3 Tbsp grapeseed oil

4 ounces fresh porcini mushrooms, including stems, cleaned and thinly sliced, plus several very thin slices

Kosher salt

Generous 1 Tbsp Porcini Aioli (page 79)

1 Tbsp finely grated (on a Microplane) Parmesan

Generous pinch Porcini Spice Powder (page 107)

Small handful of sunflower sprouts or pea shoots

In a small bowl, stir together the dashi, shiro shoyu, and sherry vinegar. Set aside.

Warm 1 Tbsp of the grapeseed oil in a large heavy skillet over high heat until you see wisps of smoke. Add the 4 ounces porcinis, sprinkle with ½ tsp salt, and cook, stirring occasionally, until the porcinis soften and just begin to brown, about 2 minutes.

Add the rice and remaining 2 Tbsp grapeseed oil, sprinkle with ½ tsp salt, and stir everything together, breaking up any clumps of rice. Cook, stirring occasionally, until the rice is heated through, fluffy, and slightly crispy in spots, 4 to 5 minutes. Add the ramp greens, stir well, and cook just until they wilt, about 30 seconds.

Add about half of the dashi mixture, stir well, and cook for 30 seconds more. Remove the skillet from the heat and stir in the remaining dashi mixture. Season with salt.

Transfer the fried rice to a serving dish. Top with a few of the onions and ramp bulbs, reserving the rest for another purpose. Add the aioli in a few dollops. Sprinkle with the Parmesan, porcini powder, sprouts, and the very thinly sliced porcini. Serve right away.

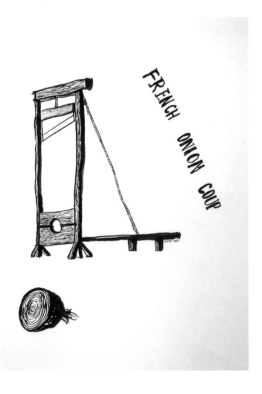

yuba "all'amatriciana" with fresh tomatoes and chanterelle mushrooms

Serves 4

My riff on bucatini all'amatriciana would be laughed out of Rome. The components of the hallowed Roman pasta dish are sacrosanct. The noodle is long and hollow. The sauce contains canned tomatoes, garlic, onion, chile, and the porky complexity of guanciale—cured pig jowl. The cheese dusted on top is Pecorino Romano. If using rigatoni would raise eyebrows, I don't even want to know what they'd think of tofu skin.

But State Bird isn't the place for a traditional plate of pasta, even if it's one of my favorites. Our sauce is made from grated fresh tomatoes spiked with sherry vinegar. Earthy chanterelles, sweet basil leaves, and fresh cherry tomatoes provide exciting texture and color. And most blasphemous of all, instead of pasta I look to yuba, the chewy skin that forms when you simmer soy milk to make tofu.

make the tomato sauce

1 pound sweet-tart heirloom tomatoes (such as Brandywine or Purple Cherokee), halved

1 Tbsp extra-virgin olive oil

1 Tbsp sherry vinegar

1 tsp kosher salt

5 turns freshly ground black pepper

Grate the cut sides of the tomatoes on the large holes of a box grater set over a bowl, until all that's left in your hand is the skin and core (discard them). Add the olive oil, vinegar, salt, and pepper to the bowl and stir well. Set aside.

finish the dish

8 ounces yuba (preferably Hodo Soy brand), sheets unfolded and sliced into 6 by ½-inch strips

2 ounces thinly sliced guanciale, cut into 1-inch pieces

3 Tbsp unsalted butter, cut into 3 pieces

1 medium garlic clove, thinly sliced

4 ounces fresh golden chanterelle mushrooms, trimmed, cleaned, and cut into ¼-inch slices

¼ tsp red chile flakes

10 turns freshly ground black pepper

Kosher salt

3 ounces aged pecorino (preferably Fiore Sardo), finely grated, plus more for garnish

12 large basil leaves

10 cherry and grape tomatoes, preferably a variety of colors and shapes, halved

1 Tbsp extra-virgin olive oil

Rinse and drain the yuba, gently squeezing to remove any excess liquid.

Combine the guanciale, 1 Tbsp of the butter, and the garlic in a large sauté pan, set over medium-high heat, and cook, stirring occasionally, until the guanciale has rendered some of its fat and just begun to brown at the edges, about 3 minutes. Add the mushrooms, chile flakes, and 5 turns pepper and cook, stirring occasionally, until the mushrooms have softened, 1 to 2 minutes.

Add the yuba, 1 Tbsp butter, and 1 tsp salt and cook, stirring constantly, until the edges of the yuba brown slightly, about 3 minutes. Add the tomato sauce and remaining 1 Tbsp butter and cook, stirring frequently, until the sauce reduces and coats the noodles but the mixture is still slightly saucy, 30 to 60 seconds. Sprinkle with the pecorino and ½ tsp salt, stir well, and cook for 30 seconds more.

Remove the pan from the heat, season with salt, and stir in the basil. Sprinkle with the cherry tomatoes and remaining 5 turns pepper, drizzle with the olive oil, and garnish with more pecorino. Serve right away.

LIFE OF BROCCOLI

peanut
muscovado
MILK

Peanut Muscovado Milk—or, as we call it at State Bird, *World Peace*—is a simple, intense infusion: peanuts steeped in milk and cream, then sweetened with anisey muscovado sugar. It got its nickname because of the "now I want to give you a hug" reaction it inspires. It also marks the very first time a creation of legendary French chef Michel Bras (hazelnut milk punch) has been crossed with something from a San Francisco health food store (a hippie-style peanut milk, made without dairy). In Chinese medicine, nut milks are said to provide a sense of well-being. As a not-so-secret hippie, I agree. It is a chilled, sippable dessert designed for the State Bird experience. It embodies so many of my quirks as a pastry chef.

As a kid growing up in Los Gatos, just north of Santa Cruz, I spent a lot of time at the health food store. While my friends were raiding 7-Eleven aisles and shoving hand pies in their faces, I was wandering the aisles of the Campbell Co-op with my mom, the shelves full of tempeh, nutritional yeast, and flaxseeds.

My mom prohibited the eating of pretty much all processed foods, and like the good girl I was, I never broke the rules, even when no one was watching. I thought she'd be able to smell an It's-It on my breath. For sweets, I had to settle for Panda brand black licorice and my mom's carob pudding. What made this deprivation bearable was the occasional treat—the plums and apricots that grew in our neighbor's backyard and the once-a-year root beer float that my dad okayed. I know teenagers are supposed to rebel, but in high school, I became an even pickier eater than my mom. I learned to cook after I decided I wanted to be a vegetarian, and my mom told me that was fine as long as she didn't have to make my broccoli stir-fries.

Way before I was a pastry chef, I was an art student who baked bread. Practically every morning in my late teens, I made challah dough, leaving it on the counter to rise while I took photography classes at De Anza College in Cupertino (where I met a handsome fellow named Stuart Brioza). When I got home, I'd braid and bake, then set up Joel-Peter Witkin–esque still lifes—the bread arranged with dead flowers and fish bones. Yikes. Fortunately, Stuart seemed to like them. He even bought me my first bread book, *Secrets of a Jewish Baker*.

When I got into the School of the Art Institute of Chicago, I moved to the Windy City. And when I needed a job to pay for school, I found a little bakery in Wicker Park called Red Hen Bread. It had just opened two days earlier when I waltzed in and asked for work. Three weeks into my time there, I realized that getting paid to do something I loved beat paying to learn something I wasn't even sure I liked. When Red Hen's owner and head baker, Nancy Carey, told me she was a recovering fine artist who found her way into a life of wheat and yeast, her path became a model for mine. Only instead of an artist turned baker, I became an art school dropout turned baker's apprentice.

For the next three and a half years, I was covered in flour by 3 a.m. each morning and aching when I clocked out each evening at the end of my sixteen-hour shift. I watched Nancy make the same doughs over and over again, and then I made those same doughs over and over again. To some of you, this might seem like the definition of torture. But I couldn't get enough.

I loved it all. The glowing, quiet mornings, when it felt like no one else in the world was awake. The physical exertion of heaving giant bags of flour and kneading dough that became more resistant by the minute, like some sort of low-tech exercise machine. The day I got to operate the humongous mixer to make fifty pounds of cookie dough, like adult Play-Doh. The secret society of oddballs who gathered before dawn to perform rituals that turned water, flour, and yeast into hundreds of baguettes, ciabatta, and rye loaves.

Even though we made the same breads every morning, the work never felt mindless, because you never master bread. It has rules—and I love rules!—but still challenges you every day with its moods and quirks. It requires listening. Watching Nancy, I learned to plunge my hands into dough and try to hear what it was telling me. To this day, unpredictability is one of the most satisfying aspects of baking. It also drives me nuts. By the time I left Chicago, I knew that I wanted to be a baker forever.

I joined Stuart in Ellsworth, Michigan, at Tapawingo, an amazing restaurant where he had been hired, at just twenty-five years old, to be executive chef. I was the twenty-three-year-old baking the restaurant's bread and helping the pastry chef, Adam Bolt, make his lemon tarts and profiteroles. When Adam moved on, I got a surprise promotion.

For a while, I stuck with the old-school desserts we'd been making, but I got antsy and decided to create a few myself. It was strange—on the one hand, I was head pastry chef, and on the other, I was a culinary student, an utterly amateur cook who learned as I went. Fortunately, I had help. Thanks to a stack of cookbooks, I studied under mentors I'd never met, exploring the food of the greats through their written recipes. François Payard showed me how to make frozen parfait. Alice Waters gave me a crash course on sabayon. Charlie Trotter helped me appreciate the minimalist approach. I formed a special relationship with Claudia Fleming. She taught me how to make ganache and anglaise and financier, but I realized she and I shared a profound spiritual connection when I came upon her recipe for an ice cream flavored with melted Panda-brand black licorice. It felt like a sign.

Along with my cookbooks, I was also lucky to have a huge kitchen stocked with great equipment, an incredible Amish dairy up the road, and access to some of the best local fruit in the country. And because it was essentially just me in that kitchen, I also had the freedom to mess up. So I did. A lot. When my chocolate didn't temper or my cakes fell or my caramel crystallized, I had to figure out why by trying again and again. Every time I did, I got better.

And of course, I had Stuart. We talked often about food, dreaming out loud of the wacky restaurants we'd open together—including an *insane* idea for a place where all the food went around on carts, like dim sum!—and bluntly critiquing each other's creations like art professors at a workshopping session. We ate great food together, treating the long Michigan winters, during which Tapawingo shut down, as really fun research trips and traveling to some of the best restaurants in New York.

I had the pleasure of not just tasting Stuart's food but watching him create it. He didn't stop at a good idea but kept exploring until it had reached another plane of deliciousness. I tried to do the same, starting with some memorable flavor embedded in my palate or a favorite cookbook recipe, then relentlessly searching for ways to take the obvious appeal of butter, sugar, caramel, and fruit in strange, exhilarating directions. I enjoyed the process of discovering the elements that would complete a dish, preferably something unexpected (peppery olive oil! shaved fennel!) so it could both make an already great dessert better as well as make you wonder. Pardon the pun, but this is what I think of as the sweet spot. You know you've hit it when a bite of a dessert gives you the food version of that feeling you get when you're so excited you want to punch something or when you see an animal so cute you want to squeeze it. Inventing was the opposite of the comforting repetition I'd loved about baking, but just as addictive.

When Stuart and I were hired at Rubicon, in San Francisco, I found a new collaborator: Sara Cox, who was technically my assistant but who in many ways knew more than her accidental-pastry-chef boss. She and I worked through every dish together, sharing ideas and helping each other to make them better. She also taught me the pain and pleasure of making true French macarons, which I would end up bastardizing years later for State Bird's ice cream sandwiches.

When Sara moved on, my right-hand lady became Mikiko Yui, who, thank goodness, followed me to State Bird. Stuart might be my partner in life, but Mikiko is my partner in pastry. We clicked almost immediately and quickly achieved full mind-meld, recognizing at the same moment when a dish is finally right. As I write this, she is planning to move back to Japan. Nothing will be the same without her.

When we opened State Bird, I was excited to embrace a new kind of freedom. The idea was to take inspiration whenever and from wherever it came, to evolve constantly. And this spontaneity gave the restaurant a vitality it might not have had otherwise. But I'm a baker at heart—all that lawlessness freaked me out. So after much tinkering, Mikiko and I settled on a few stable concepts that came to define our desserts. Every night, there would be three options: an ice cream sandwich, a bowl of granita, and what I call a crunch-and-dip (shards of crackly chocolate to be dunked in various creamy concoctions and fruity dollops). We could still be creative, the flavors and garnishes and textural elements morphing as the seasons changed and as ideas struck. We could also be both the exciting restaurant whose food never stayed the same *and* the kind of homey place where your favorite dish never left the menu. Later, I added a fourth "wild card" dessert that follows no blueprint—a girl's gotta have her fun.

Speaking of fun, from Day One we served Peanut Muscovado Milk. I like desserts that aren't too sugary and I occasionally sneak in hippie ingredients, and peanut milk employs the slight bitter edge of brown rice syrup to rein in sweetness. I have a thing for nostalgic flavors, and the peanut milk reminds me of peanut butter cookies dipped in milk. I also like the element of the unexpected, and for so many people the pleasure of peanut milk is a complete *huh?* until their first taste.

It also reflects the idiosyncrasies of State Bird itself. Peanut milk is my coming to terms with the fact that after a dozen or two of Stuart's spicy, high-acid, texturally complex dishes, you want something sweet—come on, you know you do—but may not have room for an ice cream sandwich. It's also one of the ideas that our by-the-seats-of-our-pants restaurant gave us. It wasn't carefully planned or even well thought out but it stuck because it's awesome, and trying to be awesome is essentially our only guiding principle. In another setting, dessert by the two-ounce pour might just seem weird, but at State Bird, it's weird and comforting, exhilarating and irresistible, the sweet spot in a shot.

peanut muscovado milk

Makes a generous 1 quart

make the syrup

½ cup dark muscovado sugar

½ cup water

3 Tbsp brown rice syrup

Combine the muscovado sugar, water, and rice syrup in a small saucepan and bring to a gentle simmer over medium heat, frequently stirring and scraping the pan, just until the sugar dissolves. Remove from the heat and let cool. Transfer to an airtight container and store in the fridge for up to 1 month.

make the peanut milk

1⅓ cups skin-on Spanish peanuts

4 cups whole milk

2 cups heavy cream

2 cups water

⅓ cup granulated sugar

1 vanilla bean, split lengthwise

Preheat the oven to 350°F. Spread the peanuts on a baking sheet and roast, shaking the pan often, until light golden brown beneath the skins and very aromatic, about 15 minutes.

Combine the peanuts, milk, cream, water, and granulated sugar in a large saucepan. Use a knife to scrape the seeds of the vanilla bean into the pan and then add the pod. Bring to a gentle simmer over medium heat and cook, stirring every 15 minutes or so and lowering the heat if necessary to maintain the gentle simmer, until the liquid looks a little creamier, about 1½ hours. (Even better, though, is to taste after 1 hour, then keep cooking until the liquid tastes even more peanutty, about 30 minutes more.)

Discard the vanilla bean pod. Use an immersion blender (or a regular blender, working in two batches) to pulse the mixture just enough to break the peanuts into small pieces. Don't overblend! Let the mixture cool, transfer to a container, cover, and refrigerate for at least 8 hours or up to 24 hours. The longer the better.

Strain the mixture through a medium-mesh sieve into a large airtight container and skim off the thick foam. Discard the solids. Store in the fridge for up to 4 days.

Spoon ½ to 1 tsp of the syrup into eight glasses. Stir the peanut milk well and pour ½ cup into each glass. Serve right away.

the
DESSERT
larder

FRUITY
CONDIMENTS

Fun fruit preserves tend to be an afterthought on dessert menus. I know I used to dream up a turnover or cake, then later wonder, "Hmm, now what to swirl on the plate?" But at State Bird, the opposite is often true. Because our food is so seasonally driven, we'll get a few cases of kumquats or huckleberries and get all excited to make marmalade or compote. Then we're like, "Hmm, what cake should we use to garnish the fruit?"

You'll notice that practically all of the recipes in this section follow the same formula: fruit, sugar, acid, heat. The goal is the same, too. To add just enough sugar to obtain the texture I'm after without overwhelming the flavor of the fruit, just enough acid to balance the sugar, and just enough heat to keep the best qualities of the fruit in its fresh form. The fun part to me is varying the forms of sugar and acid, finding just the right kinds for the fruit in question. Explaining why blueberries benefit from muscovado sugar while huckleberries are awesome with maple syrup can make me sound fussy. But it all makes sense once you take a bite.

slow-roasted strawberries, below

huckleberry compote, page 276

dried pear–verjus compote, page 277

slow-roasted strawberries

Makes about 1½ cups

My friend Michelle Polzine, who runs San Francisco's awesome 20th Century Café, and I used to trade recipes like baseball cards. I got the deal of a lifetime from one of these swaps when I scored her roasted strawberries. Roasting fruit is nothing new, but Michelle's genius was doing it longer and slower than I ever had. By the time she pulled her strawberries from the oven, they had gone way past the stage where roasted fruit can be watery and mushy and become something amazing— dense and intense like dried fruit but with the flavor of a fresh berry and even some of its juicy texture. Okay, Michelle, what can I trade for your bagel recipe?

3 pounds ripe strawberries, hulled, halved if large

1 cup granulated sugar

Preheat the oven to 300°F.

Arrange the strawberries in a single layer in a shallow glass or ceramic baking dish, sprinkle with the sugar, and mix briefly. Roast, stirring every hour, until the strawberries shrink significantly and the juices they release reduce to a syrup, about 3 hours. Let cool to room temperature.

Transfer the strawberries and their juices to an airtight container and store in the fridge for up to 4 days.

dried cherry compote,
page 277

kumquat marmalade, page 278

raspberry jam

Makes about 1½ cups

Paddling fresh raspberries in a stand mixer helps extract the pectin from the fruit's seeds. This way, the jam takes on a thick texture without added pectin or a flavor-eclipsing amount of sugar.

12 ounces raspberries
1 cup granulated sugar
1 Tbsp lemon juice
⅛ tsp kosher salt

Put the raspberries in a stand mixer fitted with the paddle attachment and mix on medium-low speed for 12 minutes.

Transfer the liquidy raspberries to a medium saucepan wide enough to hold the mixture in a depth of about ½ inch and stir in the sugar. Bring to a strong simmer over medium heat and cook, stirring often, until the mixture is thick enough that it drops, not drips, off of a spoon, about 8 minutes. Remove from the heat and stir in the lemon juice and salt. Pour the mixture into a wide bowl and let cool.

Transfer to an airtight container and store in the fridge for up to 1 week.

apricot-aprium jam

Makes about 2½ cups

This jam is classic in most ways, with the exception of the butter (the idea borrowed from a friend who every stone-fruit season borrows my copper jam pot). Like all good stone-fruit jams, this one takes patience, though not much effort. You break the pits and steep them in the mixture, which adds both natural pectin (to give the jam body) and a mild almondlike quality (thank you, pits!). You work in a few stages to dissolve the sugar and achieve the right texture while minimizing the time your fruit is subjected to heat, which can mush out its texture and rob its fresh flavor. If you can get only apricots (preferably a jam apricot, like Blenheim), that's totally fine, though apriums (a plum-apricot hybrid) have more acid and make for an even more livelier product.

8 ounces jam apricots
(such as Blenheim),
halved with pits reserved

8 ounces apriums
(or more apricots), halved
with pits reserved

1¼ cups granulated sugar

1 Tbsp unsalted butter

2 to 4 tsp lemon juice
(depending on the
sweetness of the fruit)

¼ tsp kosher salt

Whack the apricot and aprium pits with the bottom of a heavy pan to break them into two or three pieces. Put the pits in a piece of cheesecloth and tie it into a bundle.

Put the apricots and apriums in a large nonreactive container. Sprinkle with the sugar and use your hands to toss well to moisten the sugar. Add the bundle of pits, burying it in the fruit as best as you can. Cover with a kitchen towel and let sit at room temperature for at least 8 hours or up to 12 hours.

Transfer the apricot mixture to a medium nonreactive heavy pot, preferably a copper jam pot. Carefully squeeze the bundle to release any juices the cheesecloth absorbed, then discard. Set the pot over medium heat and cook, stirring occasionally, just until the mixture comes to a simmer. Immediately pour into a nonreactive wide bowl and let cool. Cover again with the kitchen towel and let sit at room temperature for at least 8 hours or up to 12 hours.

Return the apricot mixture to the heavy pot and bring to a simmer over medium heat. As the jam simmers, using a metal spoon, skim off any foam that rises to the surface. Continue to simmer, stirring often, until the jam reaches 220°F on an instant-read thermometer. Remove from the heat. Stir in the butter, lemon juice, and salt. Pour the mixture into a wide bowl to cool.

Transfer to an airtight container and store in the fridge for up to 3 weeks.

blueberry compote

Makes about 2½ cups

This compote is all about showing off the blueberry. Molasses-like muscovado sugar works so well with the fruit's dusky sweetness, and lime juice (or even better, fresh yuzu, if you can get it) brightens the compote and plays up the floral flavor of the berries in a way that lemon would not. For an extra boost, we pour the hot mixture over more blueberries, welcoming them into the compote while preserving their fresh flavor.

1 pound 6 ounces blueberries

2 Tbsp water

2 to 3 Tbsp dark muscovado sugar (depending on the sweetness of the fruit)

1 to 1½ Tbsp lime juice (depending on the tartness of the fruit)

1 pinch kosher salt

Put half of the blueberries in a large heatproof bowl. Set aside.

Combine the water, muscovado sugar, lime juice, and salt in a medium sauté pan or low-sided pot over medium-low heat and cook, stirring occasionally, to dissolve the sugar. Increase the heat to medium, add the remaining blueberries, and cook, stirring often, until the mixture starts to thicken and the fruit starts to burst, 3 to 5 minutes. Remove from the heat, immediately pour the mixture over the raw blueberries, and stir gently to coat the fruit. Let cool to room temperature.

Transfer to an airtight container and store in the fridge for up to 3 days. Let it come to room temperature before serving.

apple-umeboshi compote

Makes about 1½ cups

One 8-ounce sweet-tart
apple (such as Fuji or
Pink Lady), cored and
cut into ½-inch dice

⅓ cup granulated sugar

3 Tbsp lemon juice

¾ cup mirin
(sweet rice wine)

2 Tbsp umeboshi (Japanese
pickled plum) paste

1 Tbsp light muscovado sugar

2 tsp orange blossom or
wildflower honey

Combine the apple, granulated sugar, and lemon juice in a large skillet (the apple should be in more or less a single layer) over medium-low heat and cook, stirring occasionally, until the apple pieces are soft but still hold their shape, about 3 minutes. Remove from the heat and set aside.

Combine the mirin, umeboshi paste, muscovado sugar, and honey in a small saucepan, stir well, and bring to a gentle simmer over medium-low heat. Cook, stirring occasionally, until the mixture is slightly syrupy and the liquid has reduced to about ½ cup, about 8 minutes. Remove from the heat and gently stir in the apple mixture. Let the mixture cool to warm before using. It's best eaten within a few hours.

huckleberry compote

Makes about 1 cup

When tiny, delicate huckleberries come to us from Washington or Oregon, we make this quick compote with barely more than the fruit itself. The berries provide all the mouth-puckering tartness you need, while maple syrup contributes just the right kind of sweetness, highlighting the similar untamed, woodsy quality of a fruit that grows wild on forest floors.

7 ounces fresh or frozen blue
or purple huckleberries,
stemmed

2 Tbsp plus 1 tsp pure
maple syrup

⅛ tsp kosher salt

Combine the huckleberries, maple syrup, and salt in a small saucepan, stir well, and bring to a gentle simmer over medium-low heat. Cook, stirring gently and often, lowering the heat if necessary to maintain the gentle simmer, until the liquid is slightly syrupy but the berries are still intact, 6 to 8 minutes. Pour the mixture into a wide bowl to cool.

Transfer to an airtight container and store in the fridge for up to 3 days.

dried pear–verjus compote

Makes about 1 cup

Even California has a couple days out of the year when fruit isn't at its best. That's when I look to high-quality dried fruit—like pears from Bella Viva, in the Central Valley—plumping them in rum and verjus, the tart juice of unripened grapes.

4 ounces dried pear halves, cut into ¼-inch dice

¾ cup white verjus

2 Tbsp dark or light aged rum

3 Tbsp granulated sugar

Preheat the oven to 375°F.

Combine the pears, verjus, rum, and sugar in a shallow glass or ceramic baking dish in which the pears fit snugly in a single layer. Toss well and cover with aluminum foil. Bake until the pears are plump and all the liquid has been absorbed, 45 minutes to 1 hour. Let cool to room temperature.

Transfer to an airtight container and store in the fridge for up to 1 week.

dried cherry compote

Makes about 1½ cups

When it's winter and fresh fruit is scarce at farmers' markets, we look to dried cherries—a combination of the sweet and tart varieties—to make a boozy compote. Plumping them in a mixture of Moscato d'Asti and honey reinvigorates the cherries without robbing them of their satisfying chewy, fruit-leather texture.

3½ ounces dried sweet cherries

3½ ounces dried tart cherries

1 cup sweet, sparkling white wine (such as Moscato d'Asti)

2 Tbsp plus 1 tsp orange blossom or wildflower honey

2 Tbsp granulated sugar

⅛ tsp kosher salt

Combine the sweet and tart cherries, wine, honey, sugar, and salt in a small saucepan and bring to a simmer over medium heat. Continue to simmer until the cherries have started to plump, about 10 minutes. Remove from the heat and let cool to room temperature.

Transfer to an airtight container and store in the fridge for up to 1 week.

kumquat marmalade

Makes about 2 cups

This one's all Mikiko's (see page 265). She has loved preserved kumquats ever since she was a girl in Japan, where her mom candied them in a solution of vinegar and sugar. Mikiko showed me her mother's painstaking and stealthy way to extract the seeds from the whole fruits by using a toothpick and without leaving a trace on the skin. A marmalade allows Mikiko to take full advantage of the kumquat's distinctive charms—the thick, particularly sweet skin and thrillingly sour flesh. Her method is merciful to me and the other State Birdies who make it; there's no toothpick required.

9 ounces kumquats, halved crosswise

2 cups water

2¼ cups granulated sugar

½ tsp kosher salt

Use a small sharp knife to flick the seeds from the halved kumquats into a bowl, then put the seeds in a piece of cheesecloth and tie it into a bundle.

Combine the kumquats, bundle of seeds, and water in a medium saucepan and bring to a strong simmer over medium-high heat. Continue to simmer for 15 minutes, using a metal spoon to skim off any foam that rises to the surface. Remove from the heat, cover the pan with a kitchen towel, and let sit at room temperature for at least 8 hours or up to 12 hours.

Stir the sugar into the pan and bring to a boil over medium-high heat. Let boil for 1 minute, skimming, then transfer to a medium bowl. Cover again with the kitchen towel and let sit at room temperature for at least 8 hours or up to 12 hours.

Return the mixture to a medium saucepan, set over low heat, and slowly bring to a simmer. Turn the heat to medium and simmer until the mixture reaches 220°F on an instant-read thermometer, 30 to 40 minutes. Immediately remove from the heat. Skim any foam from the surface and stir in the salt. Carefully squeeze the bundle of seeds to release any liquid the cheesecloth absorbed, then discard the bundle. Pour the mixture into a wide bowl and let cool.

Transfer to an airtight container and store in the fridge for up to 3 weeks.

poached quince

Makes about 2 cups

1 pound quince

1½ cups water

1½ cups dry white wine

1 cup granulated sugar

1-inch knob ginger,
peeled and thinly sliced

Peel from 1 orange,
cut into wide strips,
white pith removed

½ vanilla bean, split
lengthwise

Peel, quarter, and core the quince. Set aside.

Combine the water, wine, sugar, ginger, and orange peel in a medium pot. Use a knife to scrape the seeds of the vanilla bean into the pot and then add the pod. Bring to a simmer over medium heat, stirring occasionally, to help the sugar dissolve.

Cut a piece of parchment paper large enough to rest inside the pot with a little room to spare. Add the quince to the pot, place the parchment on the surface, and top it with a small plate to keep the quince submerged. Lower the heat to maintain a gentle simmer and cook, without stirring, until the quince is fully tender but not falling apart, about 45 minutes.

Remove the pot from the heat and let the quince cool in the poaching liquid. Cut the quince into ½-inch pieces and transfer to a container. Strain the poaching liquid through a medium-mesh sieve into the container.

Store, covered, in the fridge for up to 3 days. Bring to room temperature before serving.

DOLLOPS,
SAUCES
&
CUSTARDS

candied ginger
whipped cream,
opposite

burnt cinnamon
whipped cream,
page 284

pecan–sherry
caramel,
page 286

fudgy chocolate sauce

Makes about 1⅔ cups

At State Bird, this ethereal sauce joins my walnut-sesame frangipane to create the filling what we call "choco-pane" for flaky lard turnovers (see page 361). But it's too good and too versatile to bury in another recipe. It's incredible that it manages to be *dense* and *light* and that it's so silky but contains neither cream or butter. My secret? I borrowed (and barely tweaked) a Nancy Silverton recipe, where the fudge was just one component of her stunning chocolate cake.

4¾ ounces coarsely chopped high-quality milk chocolate (preferably Valrhona)

2½ ounces coarsely chopped high-quality dark chocolate (about 72%; preferably Valrhona)

¾ cup alkalized (Dutch process) cocoa powder

⅓ cup plus 1 Tbsp water

¼ cup orange blossom or wildflower honey

¼ cup brown rice syrup

Pour about 2 inches of water into a medium saucepan and bring to a simmer over medium heat. Combine both chocolates in a medium heatproof bowl large enough to sit on top of the saucepan without touching the water. Set the bowl over the pan and melt the chocolate, stirring occasionally until completely smooth, about 4 minutes. Remove the bowl from the pan and set aside.

Combine the cocoa powder, water, honey, and rice syrup in a medium saucepan. Cook over medium-low heat, whisking frequently, until the mixture is smooth, 2 to 3 minutes.

A half at a time, pour the honey mixture over the chocolate and whisk until very smooth. Let cool.

Transfer to an airtight container and store in the fridge for up to 1 week. Warm in a medium saucepan over low heat before serving.

cocoa
custard,
page 290

cream cheese
custard,
page 291

candied ginger whipped cream

Makes about 2½ cups

You don't have to do like we do and candy your own ginger to add this whipped cream to your repertoire. Buy some candied ginger, chop it finely, and put your arm (or mixer) to work. Pastries made with ginger-friendly fruit, like lemon and cherry, and all manner of chocolaty things get better with a dollop of this stuff, each bite electrified by the bracing chewy chunks.

1½ cups heavy cream
3 Tbsp thinly sliced candied ginger

Refrigerate the bowl and whisk attachment of a stand mixer until cold, about 10 minutes.

Add the cream and ginger to the cold bowl and whisk on medium-low speed until the cream holds medium peaks, about 8 minutes.

If not using immediately, cover and refrigerate for up to 2 hours, gently rewhipping by hand before serving if necessary.

burnt cinnamon whipped cream

Makes about 4 cups

We burn so many things at State Bird, mostly on purpose. In this case, we torch cinnamon sticks, which sends little sparks into the air and transforms the spice's familiar, straightforward Red Hots flavor into something much more complex, floral, and smoky. We steep it in dairy to make whipped cream that showcases this new sultry side of cinnamon. It revitalizes the spice's standard partners—apple pies, pear crisps, chocolate cake—and makes new friends, like peach, blueberries, and coconut.

2 cups heavy cream
4 cinnamon sticks
½ cup sour cream
2 Tbsp light muscovado sugar

Warm the cream in a small saucepan over medium heat until just steaming. Remove from the heat and cover to keep warm.

Position an oven rack about 4 inches from the heat source and preheat the broiler.

Using a mortar and pestle, break the cinnamon sticks into large shards and spread them on a baking sheet. Broil, shaking the sheet once, until the cinnamon is blackened at the edges, about 2 minutes. Add the sticks to the warm cream. Re-cover the pan and let steep for 45 minutes. Transfer the mixture to an airtight container and refrigerate for at least 8 hours or up to 12 hours.

Refrigerate the bowl and whisk attachment of a stand mixer until cold, about 10 minutes.

Strain the chilled cream through a fine-mesh sieve into the cold bowl. Add the sour cream and sugar and whisk on medium-low speed until the mixture holds medium peaks, about 4 minutes.

If not using immediately, cover and refrigerate for up to 2 hours, gently rewhipping by hand before serving if necessary.

burnt meringue

Makes about 4 cups

This meringue could be a classic, right up until whatever dessert it graces leaves the kitchen. Then we hit it with enough heat to take its color to the brink of black. While burning meringue might make traditionalists weep, I love how the slight bitterness tames the sweetness, just like the char on a marshmallow. It's something you can do only with Italian meringue. Such intense heat would destroy its more fragile siblings, Swiss and French. While you can successfully carbonize the meringue under the broiler, we use a butane torch, which you might even have hanging out in your garage if it's not in your pantry.

3 large egg whites
(with no trace of yolks),
at room temperature

¾ cup granulated sugar

⅓ cup water

½ tsp cream of tartar

Put the egg whites in a stand mixer fitted with the whisk attachment.

Combine the sugar and water in a small saucepan and stir gently until all the sugar is moistened, trying your best to keep the sides of the pan clean.

Start whisking the egg whites on medium speed. Meanwhile, set the pan with the sugar over medium heat.

Once the whites are frothy, about 1 minute, add the cream of tartar and continue to whisk while the sugar mixture is heating up.

Once the sugar mixture registers 248°F on an instant-read thermometer, pour it into the egg whites in a thin, steady stream with the mixer running. When you've added it all, increase the speed to medium-high and continue to whisk until the mixture has cooled fully and formed stiff, shiny peaks, about 6 minutes. Transfer to an airtight container and store in the fridge for up to 3 hours.

Spoon the meringue in large dollops onto serving plates, flatten them slightly with a spoon, and use a butane torch to scorch the tops so that some parts are black and other parts are light brown. Serve right away.

pecan-sherry caramel

Makes about 3½ cups

10 Tbsp unsalted butter

¾ cup granulated sugar

⅓ cup plus 1 Tbsp
orange blossom or
wildflower honey

1¼ cups heavy cream

1 Tbsp plus 1 tsp
sherry vinegar

¼ tsp kosher salt

1 cup pecan halves, toasted
(see page 96) and cooled

Melt the butter in a medium saucepan over medium-low heat.
Turn the heat to low, add the sugar and honey, and cook, stirring,
until the sugar dissolves. Turn the heat to high, bring to a boil,
and cook, stirring occasionally, until the mixture turns a deep
amber color, about 5 minutes. Tip the pan to check the color;
otherwise the mixture will look darker than it really is.

Remove the pan from the heat. Whisk constantly as you add the
cream in a thin, steady stream, followed by the vinegar and salt.
If necessary, use a flexible heatproof spatula to stir until any
clumps have dissolved. Pour the mixture into a wide heatproof
container and let cool to room temperature (the wide container
helps it cool quickly).

Transfer to an airtight container and store in the fridge for up to
2 weeks. Warm in a medium saucepan over low heat and stir in
the nuts before serving.

lemon curd

Makes about 2 cups

Zest of 2 lemons, finely grated on a Microplane, plus ¾ cup lemon juice

½ cup plus 1 Tbsp granulated sugar

3 large eggs plus 4 large egg yolks

7 Tbsp unsalted butter, cut into pieces, at room temperature

¼ tsp kosher salt

Pour about 2 inches of water into a medium saucepan and bring to a bare simmer. Combine the lemon zest, lemon juice, sugar, eggs, and egg yolks in a heatproof mixing bowl that is large enough to sit on top of the pan without touching the water. Whisk until fairly smooth.

Set the bowl over the pan and cook, stirring occasionally at first and then stirring and scraping the sides frequently, until the mixture thickens and registers 165° to 170°F on an instant-read thermometer, about 8 minutes. Turn off the heat and continue stirring and scraping the sides until the mixture has the texture of a loose pudding, 3 to 4 minutes more. Take the bowl off the saucepan and let the mixture cool, stirring occasionally, until it registers 125°F.

Pour the mixture into a countertop blender (or, if you're using an immersion blender, leave in the bowl). Blend in the butter a third at a time, fully incorporating each portion before adding the next. Add the salt and blend well.

Strain through a fine-mesh sieve into a wide bowl, stirring and pressing with a flexible heatproof spatula. Press plastic wrap to the surface to prevent a skin from forming and then refrigerate until chilled, about 1 hour.

Transfer to an airtight container, press plastic wrap to the surface again, cover, and store in the fridge for up to 4 days.

crème fraîche tapioca

Make about 1½ cups

2 cups whole milk

1½ tsp granulated sugar

¼ cup small tapioca pearls
(not quick-cooking)

⅓ cup crème fraîche

In a small saucepan, whisk together the milk and sugar. Set over medium heat and bring to a gentle simmer, whisking occasionally to prevent scalding. Once the mixture is simmering, gradually and steadily pour in the tapioca pearls, whisking all the while. Lower the heat to maintain a gentle simmer and cook, stirring frequently, until the tapioca is tender and almost completely translucent with only the center still opaque, 12 to 16 minutes. Turn off the heat, let the mixture sit in the pan for 1 minute, and then transfer to a medium mixing bowl.

Meanwhile, prepare an ice bath in a large mixing bowl.

Set the bowl with the tapioca mixture in the ice bath, stirring occasionally until cold. When cooled fully, stir in the crème fraîche with a rubber spatula until well combined.

If not using immediately, transfer to an airtight container and store in the fridge for up to 3 days.

vanilla-bean tapioca

Make about 1½ cups

2¼ cups whole milk

1½ tsp granulated sugar

1-inch piece vanilla bean, split lengthwise

¼ cup small tapioca pearls (not quick-cooking)

In a small saucepan, whisk together the milk and sugar. Use a knife to scrape the seeds of the vanilla bean into the pan, discarding the pod. Set over medium heat and bring to a gentle simmer, whisking occasionally to prevent scalding. Once the mixture is simmering, gradually and steadily pour in the tapioca pearls, whisking all the while. Lower the heat to maintain a gentle simmer and cook, stirring frequently, until the tapioca is tender and almost completely translucent with only the center still opaque, 12 to 16 minutes. Turn off the heat, let the mixture sit in the pan for 1 minute, and then transfer to a medium mixing bowl.

Meanwhile, prepare an ice bath in a large mixing bowl.

Set the bowl with the tapioca mixture in the ice bath, stirring occasionally until cold.

If not using immediately, transfer to an airtight container and store in the fridge for up to 3 days.

cocoa custard

Makes about 3 cups

Alkalized (rather than natural) cocoa powder contributes a nostalgic flavor to this custard that brings me happily back to the pudding and hot cocoa most of us had as kids. It comes through when you make chocolate ice cream (see page 327) or when you eat the result as chocolate pudding—perhaps with strawberries, a drizzle of olive oil, and a sprinkle of flaky salt. Don't skip the bake-then-blend step, which makes the final texture particularly velvety and rich.

2 cups plus 2 Tbsp
heavy cream

½ cup granulated sugar

6 Tbsp unsalted butter,
cut into 1-inch pieces

¾ cup alkalized (Dutch
process) cocoa powder

2 Tbsp dark
muscovado sugar

1 large egg

Preheat the oven to 300°F.

Combine the cream, granulated sugar, butter, cocoa powder, and muscovado sugar in a small saucepan and set over medium-low heat. Cook, stirring and scraping the pan frequently, until the mixture gives off steam and just begins to bubble at the edges (don't let it fully simmer), 10 to 15 minutes.

Lightly beat the egg in a medium mixing bowl. Gradually pour in the chocolate mixture, about 2 Tbsp at a time, whisking constantly and vigorously for about 30 seconds after each addition. Once you've added about one-fourth of the chocolate mixture, whisk in the remaining mixture about ½ cup at a time. Pour the mixture into an 8-inch square heavy baking pan.

Bake, rotating the pan every 8 minutes, until just set at the edges but still jiggly in the center, 15 to 20 minutes.

Prepare an ice bath in a large mixing bowl.

Scrape the mixture into a medium mixing bowl and blend thoroughly with an immersion blender. Strain through a fine-mesh sieve into a bowl, stirring and pressing with a flexible heatproof spatula. Set the bowl in the ice bath, stirring occasionally until the custard is cold.

If not serving immediately, transfer to an airtight container, press plastic wrap to the surface to prevent a skin from forming, cover, and store in the fridge for up to 4 days.

cream cheese custard

Makes about 2 cups

Meant for cream cheese ice cream (see page 331) but a treat on its own, the sweet custard is balanced by the tang of cream cheese, while orange zest gives each bite a loveable Creamsicle quality.

1 cup plus 2 Tbsp cream cheese, cut into ½-inch pieces, at room temperature

2 vanilla beans, split lengthwise

1 cup crème fraîche

½ cup granulated sugar

¼ tsp kosher salt

2 large eggs, at room temperature

Zest of ½ orange, finely grated on a Microplane

1 sheet gelatin (preferably Silver Strength; 160 Bloom)

Preheat the oven to 275°F.

Put the cream cheese in the bowl of a stand mixer fitted with the paddle attachment and mix on medium speed until completely smooth and fluffy, about 2 minutes. Use a knife to scrape the vanilla bean seeds into the bowl, discarding the pods, and mix until the seeds are well incorporated, about 30 seconds.

Add the crème fraîche, ¼ cup at a time, mixing on low speed until fully incorporated after each addition. Add the sugar and salt and mix briefly. Add the eggs, one at a time, mixing on low speed until fully incorporated and scraping down the sides of the bowl after each addition. Strain the mixture through a fine-mesh sieve into a mixing bowl and then whisk in the orange zest. Pour the mixture into an 8-inch square heavy baking pan.

Bake until just set at the edges but still jiggly in the center, about 30 minutes.

Prepare an ice bath in a large mixing bowl.

Fill a small bowl with cold water and a few ice cubes. Add the gelatin sheet and let soak until it's pliable, about 3 minutes. Remove the gelatin from the water, gently squeeze to remove excess water, and add it to the hot custard. Whisk to dissolve the gelatin and then strain again into a large mixing bowl. Use an immersion blender to blend until very smooth. Set the bowl in the ice bath, stirring occasionally until the custard is cold.

If not serving immediately, transfer to an airtight container, press plastic wrap to the surface to prevent a skin from forming, cover, and store in the fridge for up to 4 days.

CRUNCHES

three chocolate crunches 296

DARK OR MILK CHOCOLATE CRUNCH 296
DOUBLE CHOCOLATE–SESAME CRUNCH 297
WHITE CHOCOLATE CRUNCH 298

toffee 299

flaky cream cheese pie crunch 300

dark chocolate crunch,
page 296

white chocolate crunch,
page 298

milk chocolate crunch,
page 296

CRUNCH AND DIPS

Stuart has his chip and dips. I have my crunch and dips. They rely on the same principle of deliciousness—crunchy plus creamy equals awesome. Comprising three or so ingredients from the larder, they team up to make full-on dishes, combinations compelling enough to be featured as one of the four desserts on our nightly menu. I have fun with the combinations, playing with the various flavors in our sweet larder, and you should too.

THE FORMULA
Put 1½ cups of creaminess in a serving bowl,
garnish with ¾ cup of fruitiness,
and serve with 12 shards of crunch.

Here are four of my favorites:

Cream Cheese
Custard
(page 291)

Huckleberry
Compote
(page 276)

Dark
Chocolate
Crunch
(page 296)

Burnt Cinnamon
Whipped Cream
(page 284)

Dried
Pear–Verjus
Compote
(page 277)

Milk
Chocolate
Crunch
(page 296)

Cocoa
Custard
(page 290)

Kumquat
Marmalade
(page 278)

Double
Chocolate–
Sesame Crunch
(page 297)

Candied Ginger
Whipped Cream
(page 283)

Dried Cherry
Compote
(page 277)

White
Chocolate
Crunch
(page 298)

three chocolate crunches

What I call "chocolate crunches" are basically chocolate bark made with *feuilletine*, magical crisp, buttery flakes of pastry that make each bite a delight. We've done many variations on the theme, but *feuilletine*'s buddy, chocolate, always joins the fun, whether it's dark, milk, a combo, or white. The process is pretty simple. We serve the crunches as a component of our desserts, typically treating them like chips to dip into something creamy. But they're great all by themselves.

Anyone looking for *feuilletine* will thank goodness for the Internet. No more hunting for the flakes at specialty stores! They keep in a cool, dry place for up to 3 months.

DARK OR MILK CHOCOLATE CRUNCH

Makes about twenty-five
3-inch shards

15 ounces coarsely chopped high-quality dark chocolate (61% to 72%) or milk chocolate (preferably Valrhona)

1¾ cups feuilletine

1 tsp flaky sea salt

Clear space in your freezer. Line two 9 by 13-inch baking sheets with parchment paper.

Pour about 1 inch of water into a medium pot and bring to a simmer. Immediately remove the pot from the heat. Put the chocolate in a heatproof bowl that is large enough to sit on top of the pot without touching the water. Set the bowl over the pot and let the chocolate melt, stirring until completely smooth. Add the feuilletine and stir gently to coat it in the melted chocolate.

Immediately transfer half of the mixture to each baking sheet and gently spread with an offset spatula to form an even layer that fills the bottom of the sheet. Sprinkle with the sea salt.

Put the baking sheets, uncovered, in the freezer until the mixture is fully frozen, about 1 hour. Run a knife around the edge of the baking sheets to release the crunch and break into approximately 3-inch shards.

If not serving immediately, transfer to airtight containers and store in the freezer for up to 1 month.

DOUBLE CHOCOLATE—SESAME CRUNCH

Makes about twenty-five
3-inch shards

1½ cups sesame seeds,
toasted (see page 96)

7½ ounces coarsely chopped
high-quality milk chocolate
(preferably Valrhona)

6 ounces coarsely chopped
high-quality dark chocolate
(about 72%; preferably
Valrhona)

2½ cups feuilletine

1 tsp flaky sea salt

Clear space in your freezer. Line two 9 by 13-inch baking sheets
with parchment paper.

Put 1¼ cups of the sesame seeds in a food processor and
alternate between running the processor for 30 seconds or so
and scraping down the sides until you have a thick, crumbly
paste, 3 to 5 minutes.

Pour about 1 inch of water into a medium pot and bring to a
simmer. Immediately remove the pot from the heat. Put all the
chocolate in a heatproof bowl that is large enough to sit on top
of the pot without touching the water. Set the bowl over the pot
and let the chocolate melt, stirring until completely smooth. Add
the sesame paste and stir to combine well. Add the feuilletine
and remaining ¼ cup sesame seeds and stir gently to coat them
in the melted chocolate.

Immediately transfer half of the mixture to each baking sheet and
gently spread with an offset spatula to form an even layer that fills
the bottom of the sheet. Sprinkle with the sea salt.

Put the baking sheets, uncovered, in the freezer until the mixture
is fully frozen, about 1 hour. Run a knife around the edge of the
baking sheets to release the crunch and break into approximately
3-inch shards.

If not serving immediately, transfer to airtight containers and
store in the freezer for up to 1 month.

WHITE CHOCOLATE CRUNCH

Makes about twenty-five
3-inch shards

1 tsp caraway seeds, toasted
(see page 96) and cooled

15 ounces coarsely chopped
high-quality white chocolate
(preferably Valrhona)

1¾ cups feuilletine

2 Tbsp bee pollen

1 tsp flaky sea salt

Clear space in your freezer. Line two 9 by 13-inch baking sheets
with parchment paper.

Briefly pound the caraway seeds in a mortar to break them slightly.

Pour about 1 inch of water into a medium pot and bring to a simmer.
Immediately remove the pot from the heat. Put the chocolate in a
heatproof bowl that is large enough to sit on top of the pot without
touching the water. Set the bowl over the pot and let the chocolate
melt, stirring until completely smooth. Add the feuilletine, bee
pollen, and caraway seeds and stir gently to coat them in the
melted chocolate.

Immediately transfer half of the mixture to each baking sheet and
gently spread with an offset spatula to form an even layer that fills
the bottom of the sheet. Sprinkle with the sea salt.

Put the baking sheets, uncovered, in the freezer until the mixture
is fully frozen, about 1 hour. Run a knife around the edge of the
baking sheets to release the crunch and break into approximately
3-inch shards.

If not serving immediately, transfer to airtight containers and
store in the freezer for up to 1 month.

toffee

Makes about 4 cups
chopped toffee

1 cup plus 2 Tbsp
unsalted butter

1¾ cups granulated sugar

1 Tbsp plus 2 tsp kosher salt

1 Tbsp orange blossom or
wildflower honey

Line a 13 by 18-inch baking sheet with a silicone baking mat.

Melt the butter in a medium saucepan over medium-low heat, but don't let it bubble. Add the sugar, salt, and honey, then use a flexible heatproof spatula to stir constantly and vigorously, scraping the sides and bottom frequently, until the mixture turns light golden brown and its temperature registers 320°F on an instant-read thermometer, 12 to 15 minutes. Don't be tempted to stop stirring or step away from the stove or the toffee could burn.

Pour the mixture onto the prepared baking sheet and use the spatula to help it spread so it's about an inch away from the edge of the pan on all sides. Let cool to room temperature, about 10 minutes. Pry the toffee from the silicone mat and break into large pieces.

Transfer to an airtight container and store at room temperature for up to 1 week.

flaky cream cheese pie-crunch

Makes about 12 large shards

SPECIAL EQUIPMENT
Digital kitchen scale

Oh my god, she's here. Rose Levy Beranbaum had just arrived at State Bird to dine with me, and I was freaking out. For a baking nerd like me, hosting her was kind of like Stuart cooking for Michel Bras. During dinner, I could barely eat. I was too worried about what she'd think of my desserts. When they finally arrived, I watched her bite into a sort of free-form pie, crisp layers of flaky dough stacked with blueberry compote and topped with burnt meringue. It was an ode to the blueberry meringue pie my mom used to get from American-food chain Marie Callender's.

I swear, just as Rose took her first bite, I remembered where I'd gotten the recipe for those incredible flaky layers: *The Pie and Pastry Bible* written by none other than Rose Levy Beranbaum. It was the pastry, she'd written, that took *years* to perfect. Because I loved it so, I'd been using it for years, baking it without filling and with a good dusting of cinnamon-sugar, then serving it with a variety of creamy, delicious things. I'd been making it for so long that I'd forgotten who created it. And now here she was, smiling and complimenting *me!* The moment I decided to come clean, I saw her eyes widen. "This is my crust!" she said. My heart sank until her eyes welled up. She wasn't angry. She was touched.

I've tweaked the recipe slightly over the years. I've even added a touch of sour cream, which, for my purposes, makes it easier to break the baked pastry into big shards without crumbling. At least I think it does. I've never tasted them side by side. I bet you only Rose could tell the difference.

make the dough

85 grams/6 Tbsp
unsalted butter

105 grams/¾ cup
all-purpose flour

30 grams/⅓ cup cake flour

3 Tbsp fine semolina flour

⅛ tsp kosher salt

⅛ tsp baking powder

50 grams/¼ cup cream
cheese, chilled, cut into
about 4 chunks

1 Tbsp sour cream

1 Tbsp ice-cold water

1½ tsp apple cider vinegar

Cut the butter into ½-inch chunks, cover, and freeze for 30 minutes.

Combine the all-purpose flour, cake flour, semolina flour, salt, and baking powder in a mixing bowl and stir well. Transfer to a resealable bag and freeze for 30 minutes.

Transfer the flour mixture to a food processor. Add the cream cheese and pulse several times. Add the butter and pulse until the mixture has no clumps larger than large peas. Add the sour cream, ice-cold water, and vinegar and pulse until the butter clumps are no larger than the size of small peas.

Transfer the mixture to a lightly floured work surface and knead until it becomes a rough ball of dough. Cut the dough into half, pat each piece to form a rough rectangle. Wrap in plastic wrap and refrigerate for at least 2 hours or up to 12 hours.

finish the dish

2 Tbsp dark
muscovado sugar

2 Tbsp turbinado sugar

¼ tsp ground cinnamon

⅛ tsp kosher salt

1 egg, lightly beaten

1 Tbsp water

Preheat the oven to 350°F. Line two 9 by 13-inch baking sheets with parchment paper.

In a small bowl, stir together the muscovado sugar, turbinado sugar, cinnamon, and salt.

In another small bowl, combine the egg and water and beat lightly to combine.

On a lightly floured work surface, roll each piece of dough into an approximately 7 by 10½-inch rectangle about ⅛ inch thick. Transfer to the prepared baking sheets.

Poke both dough rectangles with a fork, every inch or so, then brush them with the egg mixture and evenly sprinkle with the cinnamon-sugar.

Bake until when you carefully lift an edge to check the bottom of the crust, it's golden brown at the edges, about 20 minutes, switching the positions of the baking sheets and rotating them halfway through. Remove from the oven and let cool to room temperature. Break each crust into six large shards.

Transfer to an airtight container and store at room temperature for up to 2 days.

DRINKS

It would be a bummer if customers who don't or can't drink alcohol were stuck with seltzer. So we always have a few sodas on the menu, simple concoctions based on whatever's in season—from yuzu citrus to roses to fig leaves. Sometimes we even ferment fruit, like plums and strawberries, which is a fun project and gives the soda a slight boozy quality. It would also be a bummer if readers, unlike diehards who wait in line on chilly evenings, didn't get a sweet reward; so we've included the recipe for our Saturday "thank you" cocoa.

rose petal–meyer lemonade

Serves 6

1½ cups firmly packed organic rose petals

¾ cup granulated sugar

¾ cup freshly squeezed Meyer lemon juice

⅛ tsp kosher salt

Ice cubes

4 cups seltzer, cold

Combine the rose petals and sugar in a food processor and process to a wet paste that has taken on the tint of the roses. Transfer the sugar mixture to a bowl and stir in the lemon juice and salt. Strain through a fine-mesh sieve into a separate container, pressing to extract as much liquid as possible and then discarding the solids.

Fill each tall glass with ice, pour in ¼ cup rose-lemon syrup, top with ⅔ cup seltzer, and stir well. Serve right away, with a straw.

fermented plum-strawberry soda

Serves 20

1 Tbsp vodka or another high-proof alcohol

1¾ pounds pitted, quartered very ripe plums

1 pound hulled, halved very ripe strawberries

1 Tbsp apple cider vinegar

2¼ pounds Japanese rock sugar

Ice cubes

13 cups seltzer, cold

Wash and dry a 2-quart glass jar with an airtight lid. Pour in the vodka, swirl it around so it makes contact with the walls and bottom of the jar, then discard.

In a medium mixing bowl, combine the plums, strawberries, and vinegar and toss well. Put about half the sugar in the jar, followed by about half the fruit mixture, then the remaining sugar and remaining fruit mixture, pressing on the fruit if necessary to fit it in the jar. Cover with the lid.

Put the jar on a plate (in case it leaks a little), then keep in a place that's approximately 65°F and away from direct sunlight and let ferment for 3 weeks. Most of the sugar will have dissolved (there might be a few pieces at the bottom) and the surface will be slightly foamy. The flavor will be sweet and tart with a mild booziness.

Strain the mixture through a fine-mesh sieve into a separate container, pressing to extract as much liquid as possible and then discarding the solids. If not immediately using, cover and refrigerate for up to 1 month.

Fill each tall glass with ice, pour in ¼ cup fermented plum-strawberry syrup, top with ⅔ cup seltzer, and stir well. Serve right away, with a straw.

fig leaf–lime soda

Serves 6

6 large fresh fig leaves

2 cups granulated sugar

1 cup water

3 Tbsp freshly squeezed lime juice, plus 6 strips lime peel (each about 3 by 1 inch), white pith removed

Ice cubes

4 cups seltzer, cold

One at a time, hold each fig leaf with tongs about 6 inches above an open flame, such as a gas burner on the stove top, and toast for about 15 seconds per side. This brings out the aroma of the leaves.

In a small saucepan, combine the sugar and water, set over medium heat, and cook until the sugar dissolves and the mixture reaches a simmer. Stir in the fig leaves, turn off the heat, and cover the pan. Let steep for 20 minutes, then strain through a medium-mesh sieve. Transfer to an airtight container and store in the fridge for up to 1 week.

In a container with a spout, stir together the lime juice and ½ cup plus 1 Tbsp fig leaf syrup.

Fill each tall glass with ice, pour in 2 Tbsp fig-lime syrup, top with ⅔ cup seltzer, and stir well. Twist a strip of lime peel over the glass to release the oils and add the peel to the drink. Serve right away, with a straw.

yuzu-shiso soda

Serves 6

1 cup granulated sugar

½ cup water

1½ cups bottled yuzu juice

Ice cubes

12 purple or green shiso leaves

4 cups seltzer, cold

In a small saucepan, combine the sugar and water, set over medium heat, and cook, stirring, just until the sugar dissolves. Let the mixture cool fully, then stir in the yuzu juice. Transfer to an airtight container and store in the fridge for up to 1 week.

Combine a few ice cubes and 2 shiso leaves in each tall glass and muddle to slightly bruise the leaves. Fill the glasses with ice, pour in 2 Tbsp yuzu syrup, top with ⅔ cup seltzer, and stir well. Serve right away, with a straw.

saturday cocoa

Serves 6

Hours after the news came out that *Bon Appétit* had named us the country's best new restaurant, and just nine months after we opened, State Bird was overrun. Every table was booked and every evening there was a line stretching down Fillmore Street, full of hungry people hoping to score one of the fifty spots per night we reserved for walk-ins. We were thrilled and overcome with gratitude, particularly for those who braved a long wait in the city's famously temperamental weather to eat at our strange little experiment. Saturdays were particularly brutal. At the time, they were our only weekend night, and the line formed hours before we opened. We decided to show these supporters some State Bird love, so we brought everyone hot cocoa as a thank-you. We even served it iced on those rare warm San Francisco afternoons.

The recipe changed often as we played around with ingredients. Heavy cream, coconut milk, almond milk, and even leftover flavored sabayon for the base; dark, milk, and white chocolate for flavor; and maple syrup, honey, and muscovado sugar for the sweetener. So feel free to use the following directions as a jumping-off place. Once cooled, you can transfer the mixture to an airtight container and store in the fridge for up to 4 days. Reheat gently, uncovered and whisking occasionally, over medium-low heat until hot.

Whatever you do, serve it to friends who deserve a treat.

2 cups heavy cream

2 cups whole milk

1 cup water

¼ cup granulated sugar

¼ tsp kosher salt

¼ cup alkalized (Dutch process) cocoa powder

6 ounces high-quality dark chocolate (66 to 72%; preferably Valrhona), broken into several pieces, or to taste

Combine the cream, milk, and water in a medium pot and bring to a gentle simmer over medium heat. Whisk in the sugar and salt, then whisk in the cocoa powder. Let the liquid return to a simmer, whisking constantly, then continue to cook, whisking occasionally, for 3 minutes.

Turn the heat to very low and add the chocolate, whisking until it has completely melted, about 5 minutes. Gradually add more chocolate to taste, which will make the cocoa sweeter, thicker, and more intense. Strain through a medium-mesh sieve into mugs. Serve right away.

the
SWEET
recipes

STATE BIRD
ICE CREAM
SANDWICHES

While we call State Bird's signature dessert "ice cream" sandwiches and they eat like ice cream sandwiches, they're technically frozen sabayon sandwiches. Because when we first opened, we had neither the extra money nor the space for a giant commercial ice-cream maker. So I did something tricky and tweaked classic sabayon—a sort of light, ethereal version of custard and the French version of Italian zabaglione—so it would turn out like ice cream when frozen. It was so good that I went wild, infusing it with all sorts of flavors from oolong tea to Sichuan peppercorn and mixing in lemon curd and cocoa custard.

At the same, my partner in pastry, Mikiko, and I almost ruined our lives making macarons in an overcrowded kitchen. As if the cookie weren't already hard enough, we tried to produce them in a space that we shared with Stuart's savory team, who would be mincing and butchering on the same counters where we were carefully piping, and would be braising and roasting in the same temperamental oven we used to bake off our macarons. We got fed up. And then we got smart.

In what will strike only the kitchen-efficiency nerds among you as a stroke of great inspiration, we decided to fuse two troublesome desserts. For the macarons, we nixed the laborious piping and filling. Instead, we just spread the batter in one thin layer on sheet pans, then baked and froze them. We used these big sheets of macaron as the "bread" in our ice cream sandwich, a different dessert that we had been making with delicious chocolate cookies. Frozen cookies can be awesome, but not in this context—when you cut into or bite down on the hard cookie, the ice cream escapes out the sides. It's messy. It sucks. Also, this new component of State Bird's signature dessert is that rarest of cookbook miracles—when the restaurant version of a dish is easier, not harder, for the home cook.

And even though I now have an ice-cream maker in the dedicated pastry kitchen that services both State Bird and our second restaurant, The Progress, I still make a sabayon ice cream for the ice cream sandwiches. Since it's not as dense as regular ice cream, it lets us cut through the frozen dessert to make neat edges (I dare you to try slicing a traditional ice cream sandwich). But more important, it's incredibly good, so why change it? At home, you might decide to make the frozen sabayon—ice cream that doesn't require an ice-cream maker!—and not the sandwich. That's great! Simply pour into airtight containers and freeze for at least 8 hours before eating or store for up to 5 days. You can even include the individual sandwich garnishes, but not the macarons, to turn a simple scoop into a proper dish.

saffron ice cream sandwiches
with raspberry, peaches, and hazelnuts,
page 324

cacao nib–lemon verbena
ice cream sandwiches
with blueberry compote,
page 320

cacao nib–lemon verbena ice cream sandwiches with blueberry compote

make the cacao nib macaron

285 grams/2⅓ cups sifted confectioners' sugar

175 grams/1¾ cups sifted almond flour

50 grams/⅓ cup coarsely chopped cacao nibs

5 large egg whites (with no trace of yolks), at room temperature

½ tsp cream of tartar

50 grams/¼ cup granulated sugar

½ tsp flaky sea salt

Preheat the oven to 300°F. Coat the baking sheets (including the sides) with nonstick cooking spray. Lay the parchment paper in the sheets so it covers the edges of the long sides, pressing so it adheres. Lay the baking mats on top of the parchment.

In a large mixing bowl, whisk together confectioners' sugar, almond flour, and cacao nibs. Set aside.

Wipe the bowl of the stand mixer clean (lingering oil prevents the egg whites from whipping properly) and add the egg whites. Fit the mixer with the whisk attachment. Blend on medium-low speed to break up the egg whites, 30 to 45 seconds, then increase the speed to medium and beat until the surface is frothy, about 1 minute.

With the machine running, add the cream of tartar, then add the granulated sugar, about 1 Tbsp at a time. Continue beating on medium speed until soft peaks form, about 5 minutes.

Remove the bowl from the mixer and add the almond flour mixture. Use a rubber spatula to fold and stir well (no need to be delicate), just until there's very little loose flour visible, about 30 seconds. Use the dough scraper to scoop, flip, and smoosh the mixture against the walls of the bowl until there are no pockets of egg white remaining, about 45 seconds.

Divide the mixture evenly into the prepared baking sheets and use the offset spatula to spread into even layers that completely cover each surface. Sprinkle the sea salt evenly over each layer.

Bake, rotating the sheets every 6 minutes, just until the surface of the macarons is a shade darker in spots, the edges are firm and just begin to pull away from the sides, and the center is set but still gives slightly to pressure, 30 to 35 minutes. Let cool, uncovered, to room temperature.

Once the macarons are cool, use the offset spatula to loosen the edges. One at a time, put a cutting board on top of each baking sheet, lift and secure the sheet and cutting board, and invert the two so that the macaron releases onto the cutting board. Carefully peel off the parchment paper and baking mat. Line the baking sheets with the parchment paper again and slide the macarons

onto the parchment paper. (The side of the macaron to which the baking mat used to be attached should now be facing up.)

If not using immediately, wrap the whole baking sheets completely in plastic wrap and store at room temperature for up to 2 days.

make the lemon verbena ice cream

610 grams/2½ cups heavy cream, plus more as needed

8 grams/½ cup fresh lemon verbena leaves

7 large egg yolks

2 Tbsp granulated sugar, plus 100 grams/½ cup

3 Tbsp water

⅛ tsp kosher salt

——

2 cups Blueberry Compote (page 275)

Warm the cream in a small saucepan over medium-low heat until it steams but doesn't simmer (145°F), 4 to 5 minutes. Remove from the heat, add the lemon verbena, and stir. Cover and let steep for 15 minutes. Strain through a fine-mesh sieve into a container and let cool. You should have about 2¼ cups; if not, add more cold cream to get that amount. Cover and refrigerate for at least 4 hours or up to 12 hours.

Put a large stainless-steel mixing bowl and the balloon whisk in the fridge or freezer to chill, about 30 minutes. When they're cold, wipe the bowl dry, add the lemon verbena cream, and whip to soft peaks, 4 to 6 minutes. Refrigerate, uncovered, while you beat the egg yolks.

In the stand mixer fitted with the whisk attachment, combine the egg yolks and 2 Tbsp granulated sugar. Whip on medium-high speed and let the machine run.

Meanwhile, combine the water and remaining 100 grams/½ cup sugar in a small saucepan and stir until all the sugar is moistened. Set over medium-high heat, let the mixture liquefy and bubble, and cook, swirling occasionally, until it registers 245°F on the instant-read thermometer, 4 to 6 minutes. Tilt the pan and let the mixture pool on one side to take the temperature reading.

As soon as the sugar syrup is ready, with the mixer running, pour it into the egg yolks in a steady stream and continue to whip until the mixture is fully cooled and thicker than whipped cream (when you lift the whisk, it should fall in what look like ribbons), 8 to 10 minutes.

Remove the whipped cream from the fridge, add the kosher salt, and briefly whisk to beat in a little more air. Add half of the whipped cream to the egg mixture and gently fold just until the mixture is a single color. Fold in the remaining cream.

Assemble, freeze, and cut the ice cream sandwiches as directed on page 316. Arrange on plates and top with the compote. Serve right away.

poppy seed–lemon ice cream sandwiches with cherries and fennel

make the poppy seed macaron

285 grams/2⅓ cups sifted confectioners' sugar

175 grams/1¾ cups sifted almond flour

60 grams/6 Tbsp poppy seeds

5 large egg whites (with no trace of yolks), at room temperature

½ tsp cream of tartar

50 grams/¼ cup granulated sugar

½ tsp flaky sea salt

Preheat the oven to 300°F. Coat the baking sheets (including the sides) with nonstick cooking spray. Lay the parchment paper in the sheets so it covers the edges of the long sides, pressing so it adheres. Lay the baking mats on top of the parchment.

In a large mixing bowl, whisk together the confectioners' sugar, almond flour, and poppy seeds. Set aside.

Wipe the bowl of the stand mixer clean (lingering oil prevents the egg whites from whipping properly) and add the egg whites. Fit the mixer with the whisk attachment. Blend on medium-low speed to break up the egg whites, 30 to 45 seconds, then increase the speed to medium and beat until the surface is frothy, about 1 minute.

With the machine running, add the cream of tartar, then add the granulated sugar, about 1 Tbsp at a time. Continue beating on medium speed until soft peaks form, about 5 minutes.

Remove the bowl from the mixer and add the almond flour mixture. Use a rubber spatula to fold and stir well (no need to be delicate), just until there's very little loose flour visible, about 30 seconds. Use the dough scraper to scoop, flip, and smoosh the mixture against the walls of the bowl until there are no pockets of egg white remaining, about 45 seconds.

Divide the mixture evenly into the prepared baking sheets and use the offset spatula to spread into even layers that completely cover each surface. Sprinkle the sea salt evenly over each layer.

Bake, rotating the baking sheets every 6 minutes, just until the surface of the macarons is a shade darker in spots, the edges are firm and just begin to pull away from the sides, and the center is set but still gives slightly to pressure, 30 to 35 minutes. Let cool, uncovered, to room temperature.

Once the macarons are cool, use the offset spatula to loosen the edges. One at a time, put a cutting board on top of each baking sheet, lift and secure the sheet and cutting board, and invert the two so that the macaron releases onto the cutting board. Carefully peel off the parchment paper and baking mat. Line the baking

sheets with the parchment paper again and slide the macarons onto the parchment paper. (The side of the macaron to which the baking mat used to be attached should now be facing up.)

If not using immediately, wrap the whole baking sheets completely in plastic wrap and store at room temperature for up to 2 days.

make the lemon curd ice cream

240 grams/1 cup heavy cream, cold

6 large egg yolks

2 Tbsp granulated sugar, plus 65 grams/⅓ cup

3 Tbsp water

230 grams/1 cup Lemon Curd (page 287), cold

¼ tsp kosher salt

———

1 medium fennel bulb, trimmed, outer layer removed, and shaved thin on a mandoline, tossed with 1 Tbsp fruity olive oil (such as Arbequina)

1½ cups Dried Cherry Compote (page 277)

1 Meyer lemon

Put a large stainless-steel mixing bowl and the balloon whisk in the fridge or freezer to chill, about 30 minutes. When they're cold, wipe the bowl dry, add the cream, and whip to soft peaks, 4 to 6 minutes. Refrigerate, uncovered, while you beat the egg yolks.

In the stand mixer fitted with the whisk attachment, combine the egg yolks and 2 Tbsp granulated sugar. Whip on medium-high speed and let the machine run.

Meanwhile, combine the water and remaining 65 grams/⅓ cup sugar in a small saucepan and stir until all the sugar is moistened. Set over medium-high heat, let the mixture liquefy and bubble, and cook, swirling occasionally, until it registers 245°F on the instant-read thermometer, 4 to 5 minutes. Tilt the pan and let the mixture pool on one side to take the temperature reading.

As soon as the sugar syrup is ready, with the mixer running, pour it into the egg yolks in a steady stream and continue to whip until the mixture is fully cooled and thicker than whipped cream (when you lift the whisk, it should fall in what look like ribbons), 8 to 10 minutes.

Put the lemon curd in another large mixing bowl. Add a third of the egg mixture at a time and fold gently but well, just until combined, before the next addition.

Remove the whipped cream from the fridge, add the kosher salt, and briefly whisk to beat in a little more air. Add half of the whipped cream to the egg mixture and gently fold just until the mixture is a single color. Fold in the remaining cream.

Assemble, freeze, and cut the ice cream sandwiches as directed on page 316. Arrange on plates, drape with the fennel, top with the compote, and grate a little Meyer lemon zest over each. Serve right away.

saffron ice cream sandwiches with raspberry, peaches, and hazelnuts

make the saffron macaron

1 pinch saffron threads

50 grams/¼ cup granulated sugar

285 grams/2⅓ cups sifted confectioners' sugar

175 grams/1¾ cups sifted almond flour

5 large egg whites (with no trace of yolks), at room temperature

½ tsp cream of tartar

½ tsp flaky sea salt

Preheat the oven to 300°F. Coat the baking sheets (including the sides) with nonstick cooking spray. Lay the parchment paper in the sheets so it covers the edges of the long sides, pressing so it adheres. Lay the baking mats on top of the parchment.

In a mortar, combine the saffron and 2 Tbsp of the granulated sugar. Pound to a fine powder, then stir into the remaining granulated sugar and set aside.

In a large mixing bowl, whisk together the saffron sugar, confectioners' sugar, and almond flour. Set aside.

Wipe the bowl of the stand mixer clean (lingering oil prevents the egg whites from whipping properly) and add the egg whites. Fit the mixer with the whisk attachment. Blend on medium-low speed to break up the egg whites, 30 to 45 seconds, then increase the speed to medium and beat until the surface is frothy, about 1 minute.

With the machine running, add the cream of tartar, then add the saffron-sugar, about 1 Tbsp at a time. Continue beating on medium speed until soft peaks form, about 5 minutes.

Remove the bowl from the mixer and add the almond flour mixture. Use a rubber spatula to fold and stir well (no need to be delicate), just until there's very little loose flour visible, about 30 seconds. Use the dough scraper to scoop, flip, and smoosh the mixture against the walls of the bowl until there are no pockets of egg white remaining, about 45 seconds.

Divide the mixture evenly into the prepared baking sheets and use the offset spatula to spread into even layers that completely cover each surface. Sprinkle the sea salt evenly over each layer.

Bake, rotating the baking sheets every 6 minutes, just until the surface of the macarons is a shade darker in spots, the edges are firm and just begin to pull away from the sides, and the center is set but still gives slightly to pressure, 30 to 35 minutes. Let cool, uncovered, to room temperature.

Once the macarons are cool, use the offset spatula to loosen the edges. One at a time, put a cutting board on top of each baking sheet, lift and secure the sheet and cutting board, and invert the two so that the macaron releases onto the cutting board. Carefully peel off the parchment paper and baking mat. Line the baking sheets with the parchment paper again and slide the macarons onto the parchment paper. (The side of the macaron to which the baking mat used to be attached should now be facing up.)

If not using immediately, wrap the whole baking sheets completely in plastic wrap and store at room temperature for up to 2 days.

make the ice cream

540 grams/2¼ cups heavy cream, cold

7 large egg yolks

2 Tbsp granulated sugar, plus 100 grams/½ cup

3 Tbsp water

⅛ tsp kosher salt

———

1½ cups Raspberry Jam (page 273)

1 large ripe peach, pitted and cut into bite-size pieces

1 cup raw hazelnuts, toasted (see page 96), cooled, and coarsely chopped

1 cup raspberries

Put a large stainless-steel mixing bowl and the balloon whisk in the fridge or freezer to chill, about 30 minutes. When they're cold, wipe the bowl dry, add the cream, and whip to soft peaks, 4 to 6 minutes. Refrigerate, uncovered, while you beat the egg yolks.

In the stand mixer fitted with the whisk attachment, combine the egg yolks and 2 Tbsp granulated sugar. Whip on medium-high speed and let the machine run.

Meanwhile, combine the water and remaining 100 grams/½ cup sugar in a small saucepan and stir until all the sugar is moistened. Set over medium-high heat, let the mixture liquefy and bubble, and cook, swirling occasionally, until it registers 245°F on the instant-read thermometer, 4 to 5 minutes. Tilt the pan and let the mixture pool on one side to take the temperature reading.

As soon as the sugar syrup is ready, with the mixer running, pour it into the egg yolks in a steady stream and continue to whip until the mixture is fully cooled and thicker than whipped cream (when you lift the whisk, it should fall in what look like ribbons), 8 to 10 minutes.

Remove the whipped cream from the fridge, add the kosher salt, and briefly whisk to beat in a little more air. Add half of the whipped cream to the egg mixture and gently fold just until the mixture is a single color. Fold in the remaining cream.

Assemble, freeze, and cut the ice cream sandwiches as directed on page 316. Arrange on plates and top with the jam, peach, hazelnuts, and raspberries. Serve right away.

double-chocolate ice cream sandwiches with apricot-aprium jam and cacao nibs

make the chocolate macaron

285 grams/2⅓ cups sifted confectioners' sugar

175 grams/1¾ cups sifted almond flour

20 grams/¼ cup sifted alkalized (Dutch process) cocoa powder

6 large egg whites (with no trace of yolks), at room temperature

½ tsp cream of tartar

50 grams/¼ cup granulated sugar

½ tsp flaky sea salt

Preheat the oven to 300°F. Coat the baking sheets (including the sides) with nonstick cooking spray. Lay the parchment paper in the sheets so it covers the edges of the long sides, pressing so it adheres. Lay the baking mats on top of the parchment.

In a large mixing bowl, whisk together the confectioners' sugar, almond flour, and cocoa powder. Set aside.

Wipe the bowl of the stand mixer clean (lingering oil prevents the egg whites from whipping properly) and add the egg whites. Fit the mixer with the whisk attachment. Blend on medium-low speed to break up the egg whites, 30 to 45 seconds, then increase the speed to medium and beat until the surface is frothy, about 1 minute.

With the machine running, add the cream of tartar, then add the granulated sugar, about 1 Tbsp at a time. Continue beating on medium speed until soft peaks form, about 5 minutes.

Remove the bowl from the mixer and add the almond flour mixture. Use a rubber spatula to fold and stir well (no need to be delicate), just until there's very little loose flour visible, about 30 seconds. Use the dough scraper to scoop, flip, and smoosh the mixture against the walls of the bowl until there are no pockets of egg white remaining, about 45 seconds.

Divide the mixture evenly into the prepared baking sheets and use the offset spatula to spread into even layers that completely cover each surface. Sprinkle the sea salt evenly over each layer.

Bake, rotating the baking sheets every 6 minutes, just until the surface of the macarons is a shade darker in spots, the edges are firm and just begin to pull away from the sides, and the center is set but still gives slightly to pressure, 30 to 35 minutes. Let cool, uncovered, to room temperature.

Once the macarons are cool, use the offset spatula to loosen the edges. One at a time, put a cutting board on top of each baking sheet, lift and secure the sheet and cutting board, and invert the two so that the macaron releases onto the cutting board. Carefully peel off the parchment paper and baking mat. Line the baking

sheets with the parchment paper again and slide the macarons onto the parchment paper. (The side of the macaron to which the baking mat used to be attached should now be facing up.)

If not using immediately, wrap the whole baking sheets completely in plastic wrap and store at room temperature for up to 2 days.

make the chocolate ice cream

240 grams/1 cup heavy cream, cold

6 large egg yolks

2 Tbsp granulated sugar, plus 65 grams/⅓ cup

3 Tbsp water

230 grams/1 cup Cocoa Custard (page 290), cold

¼ tsp kosher salt

——

½ cup Apricot-Aprium Jam (page 274)

½ cup cacao nibs tossed with 1 Tbsp olive oil

1 tsp flaky sea salt

Put a large stainless-steel mixing bowl and the balloon whisk in the fridge or freezer to chill, about 30 minutes. When they're cold, wipe the bowl dry, add the cream, and whip to soft peaks, 4 to 6 minutes. Refrigerate, uncovered, while you beat the yolks.

In the stand mixer fitted with the whisk attachment, combine the egg yolks and 2 Tbsp granulated sugar. Whip on medium-high speed and let the machine run.

Meanwhile, combine the water and remaining 65 grams/⅓ cup sugar in a small saucepan and stir until all the sugar is moistened. Set over medium-high heat, let the mixture liquefy and bubble, and cook, swirling occasionally, until it registers 245°F on the instant-read thermometer, 4 to 5 minutes. Tilt the pan and let the mixture pool on one side to take the temperature reading.

As soon as the sugar syrup is ready, with the mixer running, pour it into the egg yolks in a steady stream and continue to whip until the mixture is fully cooled and thicker than whipped cream (when you lift the whisk, it should fall in what look like ribbons), 8 to 10 minutes.

Put the custard in another large mixing bowl. Add a third of the egg mixture at a time and fold gently but well, just until combined, before the next addition.

Remove the whipped cream from the fridge, add the kosher salt, and briefly whisk to beat in a little more air. Add half of the whipped cream to the egg mixture and gently fold just until the mixture is a single color. Fold in the remaining cream.

Assemble, freeze, and cut the ice cream sandwiches as directed on page 316. Arrange on plates and add a spoonful of jam to each. Top with the cacao nibs and sprinkle with the sea salt. Serve right away.

black pepper–olive oil ice cream sandwiches with blackberries, oregano, and pecorino

make the black pepper macaron

285 grams/2⅓ cups sifted confectioners' sugar

175 grams/1¾ cups sifted almond flour

1 tsp coarsely ground black pepper

5 large egg whites (with no trace of yolks), at room temperature

½ tsp cream of tartar

50 grams/¼ cup granulated sugar

½ tsp flaky sea salt

Preheat the oven to 300°F. Coat the baking sheets (including the sides) with nonstick cooking spray. Lay the parchment paper in the sheets so it covers the edges of the long sides, pressing so it adheres. Lay the baking mats on top of the parchment.

In a large mixing bowl, whisk together the confectioners' sugar, almond four, and pepper. Set aside.

Wipe the bowl of the stand mixer clean (lingering oil prevents the egg whites from whipping properly) and add the egg whites. Fit the mixer with the whisk attachment. Blend on medium-low speed to break up the egg whites, 30 to 45 seconds, then increase the speed to medium and beat until the surface is frothy, about 1 minute.

With the machine running, add the cream of tartar, then add the granulated sugar, about 1 Tbsp at a time. Continue beating on medium speed until soft peaks form, about 5 minutes.

Remove the bowl from the mixer and add the almond flour mixture. Use a rubber spatula to fold and stir well (no need to be delicate), just until there's very little loose flour visible, about 30 seconds. Use the dough scraper to scoop, flip, and smoosh the mixture against the walls of the bowl until there are no pockets of egg white remaining, about 45 seconds.

Divide the mixture evenly into the prepared baking sheets and use the offset spatula to spread into even layers that completely cover each surface. Sprinkle the sea salt evenly over each layer.

Bake, rotating the baking sheets every 6 minutes, just until the surface of the macarons is a shade darker in spots, the edges are firm and just begin to pull away from the sides, and the center is set but still gives slightly to pressure, 30 to 35 minutes. Let cool, uncovered, to room temperature.

Once the macarons are cool, use the offset spatula to loosen the edges. One at a time, put a cutting board on top of each baking sheet, lift and secure the sheet and cutting board, and invert the two so that the macaron releases onto the cutting board. Carefully peel off the parchment paper and baking mat. Line the baking sheets with the parchment paper again and slide the macarons onto the parchment paper. (The side of the macaron to which the baking mat used to be attached should now be facing up.)

If not using immediately, wrap the whole baking sheets completely in plastic wrap and store at room temperature for up to 2 days.

make the olive oil ice cream

360 grams/1½ cups heavy cream, cold

7 large egg yolks

1 Tbsp granulated sugar, plus 65 grams/⅓ cup

3 Tbsp water

95 grams/⅓ cup plus 1 Tbsp fruity olive oil (such as Arbequina)

¼ tsp kosher salt

———

2 cups blackberries, halved

4 ounces shaved aged pecorino (preferably Fiore Sardo)

1 Tbsp fresh oregano leaves

Fruity olive oil (such as Arbequina) for finishing

Put a large stainless-steel mixing bowl and the balloon whisk in the fridge or freezer to chill, about 30 minutes. When they're cold, wipe the bowl dry, add the cream, and whip to soft peaks, 4 to 6 minutes. Refrigerate, uncovered, while you beat the egg yolks.

In the stand mixer fitted with the whisk attachment, combine the egg yolks and 1 Tbsp granulated sugar. Whip on medium-high speed and let the machine run.

Meanwhile, combine the water and remaining 65 grams/⅓ cup sugar in a small saucepan and stir until all the sugar is moistened. Set over medium-high heat, let the mixture liquefy and bubble, and cook, swirling occasionally, until it registers 245°F on the instant-read thermometer, 4 to 5 minutes. Tilt the pan and let the mixture pool on one side to take the temperature reading.

As soon as the sugar syrup is ready, with the mixer still running, pour it into the egg yolks in a steady stream. Next, very, very gradually, add the olive oil—a drop at a time for the first minute or so, then in a very thin stream. Once you've added all the oil, continue to whip until the mixture is fully cooled and thicker than whipped cream (when you lift the whisk, it should fall in what look like ribbons), 8 to 10 minutes.

Remove the whipped cream from the fridge, add the kosher salt, and briefly whisk to beat in a little more air. Add half of the whipped cream to the egg mixture and gently fold just until the mixture is a single color. Fold in the remaining cream.

Assemble, freeze, and cut the ice cream sandwiches as directed on page 316. Arrange on plates; top with the blackberries, pecorino, and oregano; and finish with olive oil. Serve right away.

white sesame–cream cheese ice cream sandwiches with roasted strawberries

make the white sesame macaron

---

285 grams/2⅓ cups sifted confectioners' sugar

175 grams/1¾ cups sifted almond flour

50 grams/6 Tbsp sesame seeds, toasted (see page 96)

5 large egg whites (with no trace of yolks), at room temperature

½ tsp cream of tartar

50 grams/¼ cup granulated sugar

½ tsp flaky sea salt

Preheat the oven to 300°F. Coat the baking sheets (including the sides) with nonstick cooking spray. Lay the parchment paper in the sheets so it covers the edges of the long sides, pressing so it adheres. Lay the baking mats on top of the parchment.

In a large mixing bowl, whisk together the confectioners' sugar, almond flour, and sesame seeds. Set aside.

Wipe the bowl of the stand mixer clean (lingering oil prevents the egg whites from whipping properly) and add the egg whites. Fit the mixer with the whisk attachment. Blend on medium-low speed to break up the egg whites, 30 to 45 seconds, then increase the speed to medium and beat until the surface is frothy, about 1 minute.

With the machine running, add the cream of tartar, then add the granulated sugar, about 1 Tbsp at a time. Continue beating on medium speed until soft peaks form, about 5 minutes.

Remove the bowl from the mixer and add the almond flour mixture. Use a rubber spatula to fold and stir well (no need to be delicate), just until there's very little loose flour visible, about 30 seconds. Use the dough scraper to scoop, flip, and smoosh the mixture against the walls of the bowl until there are no pockets of egg white remaining, about 45 seconds.

Divide the mixture evenly into the prepared baking sheets and use the offset spatula to spread into even layers that completely cover each surface. Sprinkle the sea salt evenly over each layer.

Bake, rotating the baking sheets every 6 minutes, just until the surface of the macarons is a shade darker in spots, the edges are firm and just begin to pull away from the sides, and the center is set but still gives slightly to pressure, 30 to 35 minutes. Let cool, uncovered, to room temperature.

Once the macarons are cool, use the offset spatula to loosen the edges. One at a time, put a cutting board on top of each baking sheet, lift and secure the sheet and cutting board, and invert the two so that the macaron releases onto the cutting board. Carefully peel off the parchment paper and baking mat. Line the baking sheets with the parchment paper again and slide the macarons onto the parchment paper. (The side of the macaron to which the baking mat used to be attached should now be facing up.)

If not using immediately, wrap the whole baking sheets completely in plastic wrap and store at room temperature for up to 2 days.

make the cream cheese ice cream

240 grams/1 cup heavy cream, cold

6 large egg yolks

2 Tbsp granulated sugar, plus 65 grams/⅓ cup

3 Tbsp water

230 grams/1 cup Cream Cheese Custard (page 291)

⅛ tsp kosher salt

——

1½ cups Slow-Roasted Strawberries (page 272)

2 cups strawberries, hulled and quartered

Put a large stainless-steel mixing bowl and the balloon whisk in the fridge or freezer to chill, at least 30 minutes. When they're cold, wipe the bowl dry, add the cream, and whip to soft peaks, 4 to 6 minutes. Refrigerate, uncovered, while you beat the egg yolks.

In the stand mixer fitted with the whisk attachment, combine the egg yolks and 2 Tbsp granulated sugar. Whip on medium-high speed and let the machine run.

Meanwhile, combine the water and remaining 65 grams/⅓ cup sugar in a small saucepan and stir until all the sugar is moistened. Set over medium-high heat, let the mixture liquefy and bubble, and cook, swirling occasionally, until it registers 245°F on the instant-read thermometer, 4 to 5 minutes. Tilt the pan and let the mixture pool on one side to take the temperature reading.

As soon as the sugar syrup is ready, with the mixer running, pour it into the egg yolks in a steady stream and continue to whip until the mixture is fully cooled and thicker than whipped cream (when you lift the whisk, it should fall in what look like ribbons), 8 to 10 minutes.

Put the custard in another large mixing bowl. Add a third of the egg mixture at a time and fold gently but well, just until combined, before the next addition.

Remove the whipped cream from the fridge, add the kosher salt, and briefly whisk to beat in a little more air. Add half of the whipped cream to the egg mixture and gently fold just until the mixture is a single color. Fold in the remaining cream.

Assemble, freeze, and cut the ice cream sandwiches as directed on page 316. Arrange on plates and top with the roasted and fresh strawberries. Serve right away.

candy cap–walnut ice cream sandwiches with quince and manchego

make the candy cap macaron

285 grams/2⅓ cups sifted confectioners' sugar

175 grams/1¾ cups sifted almond flour

1 tsp sifted candy cap mushroom powder

5 large egg whites (with no trace of yolks), at room temperature

½ tsp cream of tartar

50 grams/¼ cup granulated sugar

½ tsp flaky sea salt

Preheat the oven to 300°F. Coat the baking sheets (including the sides) with nonstick cooking spray. Lay the parchment paper in the sheets so it covers the edges of the long sides, pressing so it adheres. Lay the baking mats on top of the parchment.

In a large mixing bowl, whisk together the confectioners' sugar, almond flour, and mushroom powder. Set aside.

Wipe the bowl of the stand mixer clean (lingering oil prevents the egg whites from whipping properly) and add the egg whites. Fit the mixer with the whisk attachment. Blend on medium-low speed to break up the egg whites, 30 to 45 seconds, then increase the speed to medium and beat until the surface is frothy, about 1 minute.

With the machine running, add the cream of tartar, then add the granulated sugar, about 1 Tbsp at a time. Continue beating on medium speed until soft peaks form, about 5 minutes.

Remove the bowl from the mixer and add the almond flour mixture. Use a rubber spatula to fold and stir well (no need to be delicate), just until there's very little loose flour visible, about 30 seconds. Use the dough scraper to scoop, flip, and smoosh the mixture against the walls of the bowl until there are no pockets of egg white remaining, about 45 seconds.

Divide the mixture evenly into the prepared baking sheets and use the offset spatula to spread into even layers that completely cover each surface. Sprinkle the sea salt evenly over each layer.

Bake, rotating the baking sheets every 6 minutes, just until the surface of the macarons is a shade darker in spots, the edges are firm and just begin to pull away from the sides, and the center is set but still gives slightly to pressure, 30 to 35 minutes. Let cool, uncovered, to room temperature.

Once the macrons are cool, use the offset spatula to loosen the edges. One at a time, put a cutting board on top of each baking sheet, lift and secure the sheet and cutting board, and invert the two so that the macaron releases onto the cutting board. Carefully peel off the parchment paper and baking mat. Line the baking sheets with the parchment paper again and slide the macarons

onto the parchment paper. (The side of the macaron to which the baking mat used to be attached should now be facing up.)

If not using immediately, wrap the whole baking sheets completely in plastic wrap and store at room temperature for up to 2 days.

make the walnut ice cream

780 grams/3¼ cups heavy cream, cold, plus more as needed

130 grams/1½ cups walnuts, toasted (see page 96)

7 large egg yolks

2 Tbsp granulated sugar, plus 100 grams/½ cup

3 Tbsp water

¼ tsp kosher salt

―――

2 cups drained Poached Quince (page 279)

4 ounces shaved aged manchego

½ cup walnuts, toasted (see page 96)

Warm the cream in a small saucepan over medium-low heat until it steams but doesn't simmer (145°F), 4 to 5 minutes. Remove from the heat, add the walnuts, and stir. Cover and let steep for 15 minutes. Strain through a fine-mesh sieve into a container and let cool. You should have about 2¼ cups; if not, add more cold cream to get that amount. Cover and refrigerate for at least 4 hours or up to 12 hours.

Put a large stainless-steel mixing bowl and the balloon whisk in the fridge or freezer to chill, about 30 minutes. When they're cold, wipe the bowl dry, add the walnut cream, and whip to soft peaks, 4 to 6 minutes. Refrigerate, uncovered, while you beat the egg yolks.

In the stand mixer fitted with the whisk attachment, combine the egg yolks and 2 Tbsp granulated sugar. Whip on medium-high speed and let the machine run.

Meanwhile, combine the water and remaining 100 grams/½ cup sugar in a small saucepan and stir until all the sugar is moistened. Set over medium-high heat, let the mixture liquefy and bubble, and cook, swirling occasionally, until it registers 245°F on the instant-read thermometer, 4 to 5 minutes. Tilt the pan and let the mixture pool on one side to take the temperature reading.

As soon as the sugar syrup is ready, with the mixer running, pour it into the egg yolks in a steady stream and continue to whip until the mixture is fully cooled and thicker than whipped cream (when you lift the whisk, it should fall in what look like ribbons), 8 to 10 minutes.

Remove the whipped cream from the fridge, add the kosher salt, and briefly whisk to beat in a little more air. Add half of the whipped cream to the egg mixture and gently fold, just until the mixture is a single color. Fold in the remaining cream.

Assemble, freeze, and cut the ice cream sandwiches as directed on page 316. Arrange on plates and top with the quince and manchego. Using a Microplane, finely grate the walnuts over the sandwiches. Serve right away.

coconut-shiso ice cream sandwiches with figs, melon, and olive oil

make the coconut macaron

285 grams/2⅓ cups sifted confectioners' sugar

175 grams/1¾ cups sifted almond flour

50 grams/7 Tbsp unsweetened desiccated coconut

5 large egg whites (with no trace of yolks), at room temperature

½ tsp cream of tartar

50 grams/¼ cup granulated sugar

½ tsp flaky sea salt

Preheat the oven to 300°F. Coat the baking sheets (including the sides) with nonstick cooking spray. Lay the parchment paper in the sheets so it covers the edges of the long sides, pressing so it adheres. Lay the baking mats on top of the parchment.

In a large mixing bowl, whisk together the confectioners' sugar, almond flour, and coconut. Set aside.

Wipe the bowl of the stand mixer clean (lingering oil prevents the egg whites from whipping properly) and add the egg whites. Fit the mixer with the whisk attachment. Blend on medium-low speed to break up the egg whites, 30 to 45 seconds, then increase the speed to medium and beat until the surface is frothy, about 1 minute.

With the machine running, add the cream of tartar, then add the granulated sugar, about 1 Tbsp at a time. Continue beating on medium speed until soft peaks form, about 5 minutes.

Remove the bowl from the mixer and add the almond flour mixture. Use a rubber spatula to fold and stir well (no need to be delicate), just until there's very little loose flour visible, about 30 seconds. Use the dough scraper to scoop, flip, and smoosh the mixture against the walls of the bowl until there are no pockets of egg white remaining, about 45 seconds.

Divide the mixture evenly into the prepared baking sheets and use the offset spatula to spread into even layers that completely cover each surface. Sprinkle the sea salt evenly over each layer.

Bake, rotating the baking sheets every 6 minutes, just until the surface of the macarons is a shade darker in spots, the edges are firm and just begin to pull away from the sides, and the center is set but still gives slightly to pressure, 30 to 35 minutes. Let cool, uncovered, to room temperature.

Once the macarons are cool, use the offset spatula to loosen the edges. One at a time, put a cutting board on top of each baking sheet, lift and secure the sheet and cutting board, and invert the two so that the macaron releases onto the cutting board. Carefully peel off the parchment paper and baking mat. Line the baking sheets with the parchment paper again and slide the macarons

onto the parchment paper. (The side of the macaron to which the baking mat used to be attached should now be facing up.)

If not using immediately, wrap the whole baking sheets completely in plastic wrap and store at room temperature for up to 2 days.

make the shiso ice cream

610 grams/2½ cups heavy cream, plus more as needed

20 grams/½ cup torn fresh green shiso leaves

7 large egg yolks

2 Tbsp granulated sugar, plus 100 grams/½ cup

3 Tbsp water

⅛ tsp kosher salt

———

4 ripe fresh Black Mission or Kadota figs, quartered

1 cup cubed Charentais or other orange-fleshed melon (½-inch cubes)

Fruity olive oil (such as Arbequina) for drizzling

½ cup micro shiso leaves

Warm the cream in a small saucepan over medium-low heat until it steams but doesn't simmer (145°F), 4 to 5 minutes. Remove from the heat, add the shiso leaves, and stir. Cover and let steep for 30 minutes. Strain through a fine-mesh sieve into a container and let cool. You should have about 2¼ cups; if not, add more cold cream to get that amount. Cover and refrigerate for at least 4 hours or up to 12 hours.

Put a large stainless-steel mixing bowl and the balloon whisk in the fridge or freezer to chill, about 30 minutes. When they're cold, wipe the bowl dry, add the shiso cream, and whip to soft peaks, 4 to 6 minutes. Refrigerate, uncovered, while you beat the egg yolks.

In the stand mixer fitted with the whisk attachment, combine the egg yolks and 2 Tbsp granulated sugar. Whip on medium-high speed and let the machine run.

Meanwhile, combine the water and remaining 100 grams/½ cup sugar in a small saucepan and stir until all the sugar is moistened. Set over medium-high heat, let the mixture liquefy and bubble, and cook, swirling occasionally, until it registers 245°F on the instant-read thermometer, 4 to 5 minutes. Tilt the pan and let the mixture pool on one side to take the temperature reading.

As soon as the sugar syrup is ready, with the mixer running, pour it into the egg yolks in a steady stream and continue to whip until the mixture is fully cooled and thicker than whipped cream (when you lift the whisk, it should fall in what look like ribbons), 8 to 10 minutes.

Remove the whipped cream from the fridge, add the kosher salt, and briefly whisk to beat in a little more air. Add half of the whipped cream to the egg mixture and gently fold just until the mixture is a single color. Fold in the remaining cream.

Assemble, freeze, and cut the ice cream sandwiches as directed on page 316. Arrange on plates, scatter on the figs and melon, drizzle with the olive oil, and sprinkle with the shiso. Serve right away.

pepita-oolong ice cream sandwiches
with apple-umeboshi compote

make the pepita macaron

285 grams/2⅓ cups sifted confectioners' sugar

175 grams/1¾ cups sifted almond flour

50 grams/⅓ cup pepitas (pumpkin seeds), toasted (see page 96), cooled, and fairly finely chopped

5 large egg whites (with no trace of yolks), at room temperature

½ tsp cream of tartar

50 grams/¼ cup granulated sugar

½ tsp flaky sea salt

Preheat the oven to 300°F. Coat the baking sheets (including the sides) with nonstick cooking spray. Lay the parchment paper in the sheets so it covers the edges of the long sides, pressing so it adheres. Lay the baking mats on top of the parchment.

In a large mixing bowl, whisk together the confectioners' sugar, almond flour, and pepitas. Set aside.

Wipe the bowl of the stand mixer clean (lingering oil prevents the egg whites from whipping properly) and add the egg whites. Fit the mixer with the whisk attachment. Blend on medium-low speed to break up the egg whites, 30 to 45 seconds, then increase the speed to medium and beat until the surface is frothy, about 1 minute.

With the machine running, add the cream of tartar, then add the granulated sugar, about 1 Tbsp at a time. Continue beating on medium speed until soft peaks form, about 5 minutes.

Remove the bowl from the mixer and add the almond flour mixture. Use a rubber spatula to fold and stir well (no need to be delicate), just until there's very little loose flour visible, about 30 seconds. Use the dough scraper to scoop, flip, and smoosh the mixture against the walls of the bowl until there are no pockets of egg white remaining, about 45 seconds.

Divide the mixture evenly into the prepared baking sheets and use the offset spatula to spread into even layers that completely cover each surface. Sprinkle the sea salt evenly over each layer.

Bake, rotating the baking sheets every 6 minutes, just until the surface of the macarons is a shade darker in spots, the edges are firm and just begin to pull away from the sides, and the center is set but still gives slightly to pressure, 30 to 35 minutes. Let cool, uncovered, to room temperature.

Once the macrons are cool, use the offset spatula to loosen the edges. One at a time, put a cutting board on top of each baking sheet, lift and secure the sheet and cutting board, and invert the two so that the macaron releases onto the cutting board. Carefully peel off the parchment paper and baking mat. Line the baking sheets with the parchment paper again and slide the macarons

onto the parchment paper. (The side of the macaron to which the baking mat used to be attached should now be facing up.)

If not using immediately, wrap the whole baking sheets completely in plastic wrap and store at room temperature for up to 2 days.

make the oolong ice cream

610 grams/2½ cups heavy cream, plus more as needed

3 Tbsp oolong tea leaves

7 large egg yolks

2 Tbsp granulated sugar, plus 100 grams/½ cup

3 Tbsp water

⅛ tsp kosher salt

——

1½ cups Apple-Umeboshi Compote (page 276)

Warm the cream in a small saucepan over medium-low heat until it steams but doesn't simmer (145°F), 4 to 5 minutes. Remove from the heat, add the oolong leaves, and stir. Cover and let steep for 35 minutes. Strain through a fine-mesh sieve into a container and let cool. You should have about 2¼ cups; if not, add more cold cream to get that amount. Cover and refrigerate for at least 4 hours or up to 12 hours.

Put a large stainless-steel mixing bowl and the balloon whisk in the fridge or freezer to chill, about 30 minutes. When they're cold, wipe the bowl dry, add the oolong cream, and whip to soft peaks, 4 to 6 minutes. Refrigerate, uncovered, while you beat the egg yolks.

In the stand mixer fitted with the whisk attachment, combine the egg yolks and 2 Tbsp granulated sugar. Whip on medium-high speed and let the machine run.

Meanwhile, combine the water and remaining 100 grams/½ cup sugar in a small saucepan and stir until all the sugar is moistened. Set over medium-high heat, let the mixture liquefy and bubble, and cook, swirling occasionally, until it registers 245°F on the instant-read thermometer, 4 to 5 minutes. Tilt the pan and let the mixture pool on one side to take the temperature reading.

As soon as the sugar syrup is ready, with the mixer running, pour it into the egg yolks in a steady stream and continue to whip until the mixture is fully cooled and thicker than whipped cream (when you lift the whisk, it should fall in what look like ribbons), 8 to 10 minutes.

Remove the whipped cream from the fridge, add the kosher salt, and briefly whisk to beat in a little more air. Add half of the whipped cream to the egg mixture and gently fold just until the mixture is a single color. Fold in the remaining cream.

Assemble, freeze, and cut the ice cream sandwiches as directed on page 316. Arrange on plates and top with the compote. Serve right away.

chicory-coffee ice cream sandwiches with toffee

make the chicory macaron

285 grams/2⅓ cups sifted confectioners' sugar

175 grams/1¾ cups sifted almond flour

20 grams/¼ cup sifted alkalized (Dutch process) cocoa powder

2 Tbsp dried chicory root, ground in a mortar to coffee-grounds texture

5 large egg whites (with no trace of yolks), at room temperature

½ tsp cream of tartar

50 grams/¼ cup granulated sugar

½ tsp flaky sea salt

Preheat the oven to 300°F. Coat the baking sheets (including the sides) with nonstick cooking spray. Lay the parchment paper in the sheets so it covers the edges of the long sides, pressing so it adheres. Lay the baking mats on top of the parchment.

In a large mixing bowl, whisk together the confectioners' sugar, almond flour, cocoa powder, and chicory root. Set aside.

Wipe the bowl of the stand mixer clean (lingering oil prevents the egg whites from whipping properly) and add the egg whites. Fit the mixer with the whisk attachment. Blend on medium-low speed to break up the egg whites, 30 to 45 seconds, then increase the speed to medium and beat until the surface is frothy, about 1 minute.

With the machine running, add the cream of tartar, then add the granulated sugar, about 1 Tbsp at a time. Continue beating on medium speed until soft peaks form, about 5 minutes.

Remove the bowl from the mixer and add the almond flour mixture. Use a rubber spatula to fold and stir well (no need to be delicate), just until there's very little loose flour visible, about 30 seconds. Use the dough scraper to scoop, flip, and smoosh the mixture against the walls of the bowl until there are no pockets of egg white remaining, about 45 seconds.

Divide the mixture evenly into the prepared baking sheets and use the offset spatula to spread into even layers that completely cover each surface. Sprinkle the sea salt evenly over each layer.

Bake, rotating the baking sheets every 6 minutes, just until the surface of the macarons is a shade darker in spots, the edges are firm and just begin to pull away from the sides, and the center is set but still gives slightly to pressure, 30 to 35 minutes. Let cool, uncovered, to room temperature.

Once the macarons are cool, use the offset spatula to loosen the edges. One at a time, put a cutting board on top of each baking sheet, lift and secure the sheet and cutting board, and invert the two so that the macaron releases onto the cutting board. Carefully peel off the parchment paper and baking mat. Line the baking

sheets with the parchment paper again and slide the macarons onto the parchment paper. (The side of the macaron to which the baking mat used to be attached should now be facing up.)

If not using immediately, wrap the whole baking sheets completely in plastic wrap and store at room temperature for up to 2 days.

make the coffee ice cream

610 grams/2½ cups heavy cream

65 grams/½ cup plus 2 Tbsp whole roasted coffee beans (preferably decaffeinated)

7 large egg yolks

2 Tbsp granulated sugar, plus 100 grams/½ cup

3 Tbsp water

⅛ tsp kosher salt

———

1 cup coarsely chopped toffee (see page 299)

Combine the cream and coffee beans in a bowl, stir together, cover, and refrigerate for at least 12 hours or up to 24 hours. Strain through a fine-mesh sieve.

Put a large stainless-steel mixing bowl and the balloon whisk in the fridge or freezer to chill, about 30 minutes. When they're cold, wipe the bowl dry, add the coffee cream, and whip to soft peaks, 4 to 6 minutes. Refrigerate, uncovered, while you beat the egg yolks.

In the stand mixer fitted with the whisk attachment, combine the egg yolks and 2 Tbsp granulated sugar. Whip on medium-high speed and let the machine run.

Meanwhile, combine the water and remaining 100 grams/½ cup sugar in a small saucepan and stir until all the sugar is moistened. Set over medium-high heat, let the mixture liquefy and bubble, and cook, swirling occasionally, until it registers 245°F on the instant-read thermometer, 4 to 5 minutes. Tilt the pan and let the mixture pool on one side to take the temperature reading.

As soon as the sugar syrup is ready, with the mixer running, pour it into the egg yolks in a steady stream and continue to whip until the mixture is fully cooled and thicker than whipped cream (when you lift the whisk, it should fall in what look like ribbons), 8 to 10 minutes.

Remove the whipped cream from the fridge, add the kosher salt, and briefly whisk to beat in a little more air. Add half of the whipped cream to the egg mixture and gently fold just until the mixture is a single color. Fold in the remaining cream.

Assemble, freeze, and cut the ice cream sandwiches as directed on page 316. Arrange on plates and sprinkle with the toffee. Serve right away.

cacao nib–sichuan peppercorn ice cream sandwiches with pecan caramel

make the sichuan peppercorn ice cream

610 grams/2½ cups heavy cream, plus more as needed

20 grams/¼ cup Sichuan peppercorns

7 large egg yolks

2 Tbsp granulated sugar, plus 100 grams/½ cup

3 Tbsp water

⅛ tsp kosher salt

———

1 recipe Cacao Nib Macaron (page 320)

2 cups Pecan-Sherry Caramel (page 286)

1 cup diced peeled, cored Bosc pears

Warm the cream in a small saucepan over medium-low heat until it steams but doesn't simmer (145°F), 4 to 5 minutes. Remove from the heat, add the peppercorns, and stir. Cover and let steep for 10 minutes. Strain through a fine-mesh sieve into a container and let cool. You should have about 2¼ cups; if not, add more cold cream to get that amount. Cover and refrigerate for at least 4 hours or up to 12 hours.

Put a large stainless-steel mixing bowl and the balloon whisk in the fridge or freezer to chill, about 30 minutes. When they're cold, wipe the bowl dry, add the pepper cream, and whip to soft peaks, 4 to 6 minutes. Refrigerate, uncovered, while you beat the egg yolks.

In the stand mixer fitted with the whisk attachment, combine the egg yolks and 2 Tbsp granulated sugar. Whip on medium-high speed and let the machine run.

Meanwhile, combine the water and remaining 100 grams/½ cup sugar in a small saucepan and stir until all the sugar is moistened. Set over medium-high heat, let the mixture liquefy and bubble, and cook, swirling occasionally, until it registers 245°F on the instant-read thermometer, 4 to 5 minutes. Tilt the pan and let the mixture pool on one side to take the temperature reading.

As soon as the sugar syrup is ready, with the mixer running, pour it into the egg yolks in a steady stream and continue to whip until the mixture is fully cooled and thicker than whipped cream (when you lift the whisk, it should fall in what look like ribbons), 8 to 10 minutes.

Remove the whipped cream from the fridge, add the kosher salt, and briefly whisk to beat in a little more air. Add half of the whipped cream to the egg mixture and gently fold just until the mixture is a single color. Fold in the remaining cream.

Assemble, freeze, and cut the ice cream sandwiches as directed on page 316. Arrange on plates, drizzle with the caramel, and top with the pears. Serve right away.

MACARONS

The macaron is an argument against recipes, if there ever was one. Because to get the traditional macaron right—and thank goodness, ours is *not* traditional—you have to be a veteran of the process, to have the sort of instincts that can't be put into words. And even then, you might mess up.

When I worked at Rubicon, I had a pastry assistant named Sara Cox. Sara was my main squeeze and a true Francophile. A few years before the American Macaron Craze of 2014, when every bakery suddenly seemed to be exhibiting colorful rows of the Parisian cookie, she became obsessed with making macarons for the petit-four plate we put out after dessert. Poor girl. Because of all things to get obsessed with, she was hooked by one of the most difficult.

Macarons are simple in the same way sushi is. At their most basic, they require only a few ingredients, essentially just egg whites, sugar, and almond flour—but turning these ingredients into something worthy of the title takes practice and a bit of culinary witchcraft. Even expert macaron makers have days when the universe conspires to ruin their batch. Sara was too young to be a master pâtissier, but she was pretty damn good. And though she had probably made macarons every day for five years, she failed as often as she succeeded.

While most sweets made with egg whites—meringues, marshmallows, angel food cake—require whipping the whites to a fluffy consistency and then tenderly folding them into the remaining ingredients, macarons require the opposite. You use a plastic bench scraper to smash and smear the mixture of egg whites, sugar, and almond flour against the side of the bowl. As you batter that batter, you occasionally lift the scraper, let the mixture drop into the bowl, and then assess the mound it forms. Sara would keep at it until the mound spread at just the right rate—leisurely but not sluggishly, a distinction only a veteran can recognize.

One week, she'd seem to have cracked the code, and for six days straight she'd pull from the oven a tray of perfectly smooth, glossy domes, each with a slim craggy ring at the base—what the macaron community calls a "foot." She'd meticulously pipe pastry cream or jam onto the flat side of one feather-light cookie and sandwich the filling with another. I'd take a bite, through the most delicate crispy crust and into the light but somehow also dense and chewy cookie, and I'd just smile. I couldn't help it. Then day seven would come and whatever had worked so well for Sara would suddenly produce grotesquely giant feet or bumpy, lopsided, or cracked domes. This sort of mystifying macaron mutiny is so common that cookbooks dedicated to the cookie are like printer manuals—with pages and pages of troubleshooting tips. I'd say the only thing more frustrating than using a printer is making macarons.

GRANITAS

apple granita with crème fraîche tapioca
and blackberries **345**

cherry granita with vanilla-bean tapioca,
rooibos gelée, apricots, and shiso **346**

strawberry granita with vanilla-bean tapioca,
caramelized honey, and dates **348**

chocolate mint granita
with honeyed crème fraîche
and pears **350**

There's always granita on the dessert menu, a reality inspired by my love of icy fruit and, as was the case with frozen sabayons, the fact that we didn't have an ice-cream machine when we opened. That's one reason granita won out over sorbet, which is fine with me—the glorious slush doesn't require as much sugar, so you can achieve a purer fruit flavor. Though the components change with the season and our whims, the composition remains the same—icy thing plus cold creamy thing plus fresh fruit. This gives you a bunch of different textures. And because granitas inevitably melt before you can finish them, it also means that the icy fruit doesn't just end up as syrup at the bottom of the bowl, but instead mingles with the creamy element to deliver Creamsicle-like pleasure.

apple granita
with crème
fraîche tapioca
and blackberries,
opposite

cherry granita
with vanilla-bean
tapioca, rooibos
gelée, apricots,
and shiso,
page 346

strawberry
granita with
vanilla-bean
tapioca,
caramelized
honey, and dates,
page 348

chocolate
mint granita
with honeyed
crème fraîche
and pears,
page 350

apple granita with crème fraîche tapioca and blackberries

Serves 4

Mikiko, my much-missed Number Two, introduced me to this ingenious method—you freeze apples whole, defrost them, then squeeze out the soft flesh. The resulting liquid has an intense, concentrated flavor, the sweetness and tartness heightened. Plus the liquid doesn't oxidize like it would if you had just juiced it. Instead it takes on a pretty pink hue.

make the granita

2½ pounds crisp, sweet-tart apples (preferably Gravenstein or Red Gala)

2 tsp lemon juice

½ cup sparkling water

¼ cup maple syrup

¼ tsp kosher salt

About 1 day before you plan to serve the granita, clear space in your freezer. Arrange the apples on a large baking sheet in a single layer, and freeze uncovered for about 8 hours.

Defrost the apples at room temperature until they're completely thawed (the flesh will be very soft), about 3 hours.

Pour the lemon juice into a medium mixing bowl. Set a fine-mesh sieve over the bowl. Using your hands, squeeze each apple into the sieve, discarding the peels, stems, and seeds and stirring and pressing on the solids to help extract as much juice as possible. Discard the solids. Whisk in the sparkling water, maple syrup, and salt until well combined.

Pour the mixture into a 9 by 13-inch baking pan and freeze, uncovered, until the mixture has an icy border, about 1 hour. Take out of the freezer and scrape and stir with a fork to loosen the frozen portions and evenly distribute them throughout the mixture.

Return the pan to the freezer, scraping with a fork every 30 minutes or so to turn any frozen portions into flaky ice crystals, until the mixture is all flaky, fluffy ice, 2 to 3 hours more. Cover and keep in the freezer up to 4 days.

finish the dish

1 recipe Crème Fraîche Tapioca (page 288)

20 blackberries

½ cup chervil (thin stems and leaves)

Divide the tapioca among serving bowls. Top with a scoop or two of granita, the blackberries, and chervil. Serve right away.

cherry granita with vanilla-bean tapioca, rooibos gelée, apricots, and shiso

Serves 4

While, in many ways, freezing makes fruit extra fun, it does tend to dull flavor. To counteract this, and to balance the other sweet elements in our granita desserts, we pay especially close attention to acid. That's why in the spring, we look to sour cherries to make sweet cherries taste even more like themselves. Smoky rooibos tea and shiso supply welcome, if unexpected, accents.

make the granita

1 pound 5 ounces sweet cherries, stemmed but not pitted

7 ounces sour cherries, stemmed but not pitted

1½ cups water

4½ Tbsp granulated sugar

Scant ½ tsp kosher salt

2 tsp lime juice

Clear space in your freezer.

Combine the sweet cherries, sour cherries, and water in a small pot, set over medium heat, and let come to a simmer. Lower the heat slightly to cook at a gentle simmer, stirring occasionally, until the cherries are plumped and softened but not mushy, 4 to 5 minutes. Blend the cherries, pits and all, with an immersion blender (or in a regular blender) until the flesh is a pulpy puree and the seeds are broken.

Prepare an ice bath in a large mixing bowl.

Strain the cherry mixture through a fine-mesh sieve into a medium mixing bowl, stirring and pressing to extract as much liquid as possible, discarding the solids. Add the sugar and salt and stir until they dissolve. Set the bowl in the ice bath, stirring occasionally, until the mixture has cooled fully. Stir in the lime juice.

Pour the mixture into a 9 by 13-inch baking pan and freeze, uncovered, until the mixture has an icy border, about 1 hour. Take out of the freezer and scrape and stir with a fork to loosen the frozen portions and evenly distribute them throughout the mixture.

Return the pan to the freezer, scraping with a fork every 30 minutes or so to turn any frozen portions into flaky ice crystals, until the mixture is all flaky, fluffy ice, 2 to 3 hours more. Cover and keep in the freezer for up to 4 days.

make the tea gelée

3 sheets gelatin (preferably Silver Strength; 160 Bloom)

2 cups water

2 Tbsp rooibos tea leaves

Fill a small shallow container with cold water and a few ice cubes. Add the gelatin sheets in a single layer and let them soak until they're pliable, about 10 minutes.

Meanwhile, bring the 2 cups water to a boil in a small pot. Add the tea leaves, turn off the heat, and let steep for 3 minutes. Strain through a fine-mesh sieve into a small mixing bowl, discarding the leaves.

Remove the gelatin sheets from the water, gently squeeze them to remove excess water, and add them to the warm tea. Whisk to dissolve the gelatin. Let the mixture cool, then cover and refrigerate until set, about 2 hours. (Store in the fridge for up to 2 days.)

make the shiso syrup

¼ cup water

¼ cup granulated sugar

3 green shiso leaves

Combine the water and sugar in a very small saucepan. Tear the shiso into small pieces, add them to the pan, and stir well. Bring to a boil over high heat, stirring occasionally, then turn off the heat and let steep for 20 minutes. Strain through a fine-mesh sieve into a container. Cover and refrigerate until cool, about 10 minutes. (Store in the fridge for up to 1 week.)

finish the dish

1 recipe Vanilla-Bean Tapioca (page 289)

4 large apricots, pitted and quartered

Divide the tapioca among serving bowls. Spoon four or five quarter-size pieces of gelée onto each, drizzle with the shiso syrup, and top with a scoop or two of granita and the apricots. Serve right away.

strawberry granita with vanilla-bean tapioca, caramelized honey, and dates

Serves 4

make the granita

2 pounds 4 ounces ripe strawberries, hulled and halved lengthwise

¾ cup granulated sugar

1 tsp kosher salt

1 cup water

½ cup sweet, sparkling white wine (such as Moscato d'Asti)

¼ cup plus 3 Tbsp Meyer lemon juice

Clear space in your freezer.

Put the strawberries in a medium pot, set over low heat, and cook, stirring occasionally, until the berries release enough liquid to almost cover them and are fully softened, 25 to 30 minutes. Stir in the sugar and salt until they dissolve.

Prepare an ice bath in a large mixing bowl.

Scrape the strawberry mixture into a medium mixing bowl. Set in the ice bath, stirring occasionally, until the mixture has cooled fully. Stir in the water, wine, and lemon juice. Blend with an immersion blender (or in a regular blender) until smooth.

Pour the mixture into a 9 by 13-inch baking pan and freeze, uncovered, until the mixture has an icy border, about 1 hour. Take out of the freezer and scrape and stir with a fork to loosen the frozen portions and evenly distribute them throughout the mixture.

Return the pan to the freezer, scraping with a fork every 30 minutes or so to turn any frozen portions into flaky ice crystals, until the mixture is all flaky, fluffy ice, 2 to 3 hours more. Cover and keep in the freezer for up to 4 days.

finish the dish

¼ cup orange blossom or wildflower honey

2 Tbsp water

1 Tbsp clarified butter (see page 38)

4 dried dates (preferably Deglet Noor), halved and pitted

1 recipe Vanilla-Bean Tapioca (page 289)

Pour the honey into a small sauté pan and set over high heat. Cook, constantly swirling the pan to prevent burning, until the honey bubbles and turns one shade darker, 2 to 3 minutes. Stir briefly with a flexible heatproof spatula, add the water, and stir until well combined. Scrape into a small bowl and let cool.

Melt the butter in a small sauté pan over medium-high heat, let it get hot, and then add the dates. Cook, flipping them once, until they soften and darken slightly, about 10 seconds. Remove the pan from the heat, let the dates cool, chop them into bite-size pieces, and stir them into the honey.

Divide the tapioca among serving bowls. Spoon on the honey mixture and top with a scoop or two of granita. Serve right away.

chocolate mint granita with honeyed crème fraîche and pears

Serves 4

make the granita

½ cup cacao nibs
⅔ cup granulated sugar
3⅔ cups water
2 cups mint leaves, torn
1 Tbsp Madeira
¼ tsp kosher salt

Clear space in your freezer.

Put the cacao nibs in a small sauté pan, set over medium heat, and toast, shake the pan often, until they turn a shade darker, about 1 minute.

Combine the sugar and ⅔ cup of the water in a small saucepan. Bring to a boil over high heat, stirring occasionally, about 3 minutes. Turn off the heat, add the cacao nibs, and let steep for 30 minutes. Strain through a fine-mesh sieve into a medium mixing bowl and set aside.

Meanwhile, in a medium pot, bring the remaining 3 cups water to a boil over high heat. Remove from the heat, add the mint, and let steep for 15 minutes. Strain through a fine-mesh sieve into the cacao nib syrup. Stir in the Madeira and salt.

Pour the mixture into a 9 by 13-inch baking pan and freeze, uncovered, until the mixture has an icy border, about 1 hour. Take out of the freezer and scrape and stir with a fork to loosen the frozen portions and evenly distribute them throughout the mixture.

Return the pan to the freezer, scraping with a fork every 30 minutes or so to turn any frozen portions into flaky ice crystals, until the mixture is all flaky, fluffy ice, 2 to 3 hours more. Cover and keep in the freezer for up to 4 days.

make the honeyed crème fraîche

¼ cup orange blossom or
wildflower honey

2 tsp water

⅓ cup heavy cream

1½ cups crème fraîche

½ tsp kosher salt

Put the honey into a small sauté pan and set over high heat. Cook, constantly swirling the pan to prevent burning, until the honey bubbles and turns one shade darker, 2 to 3 minutes. Stir briefly with a flexible heatproof spatula, add the water, and stir until well combined. Scrape into a medium mixing bowl and let cool.

Prepare an ice bath in another medium mixing bowl.

Once the honey is cool, add about 2 Tbsp of the cream and whisk to combine. Add another 2 Tbsp cream and whisk to combine well. Add the remaining cream, the crème fraîche, and salt. Set the bowl in the ice bath and use a balloon whisk or handheld mixer to whip the mixture to soft peaks, 3 to 4 minutes.

finish the dish

2 Bosc pears, halved, cored,
and cut into wedges

½ cup cacao nibs tossed
with 1 Tbsp olive oil

Divide the crème fraîche mixture among serving bowls. Top with the pears, a scoop or two of granita, and the cacao nibs. Serve right away.

WILD CARDS

dutch crunch "bao"
with carrot halwa 355

peach leaf rice pudding with
cream cheese pie-crunch, nectarines,
and hazelnuts 359

flaky lard turnovers with choco-pane,
figs, and whipped crème fraîche 361

sweet corn tres leches cake
with cloud cream and
blueberry compote 365

To focus our overactive imaginations, we created three dessert categories—crunch and
dips, ice cream sandwiches, and granitas—that would always be on the menu. Then
we added a fourth category I think of as Wild Cards, because it has no fixed theme or
blueprint. This is where my rogue ideas sneak out of the boxes I built to contain them.

dutch crunch "bao" with carrot halwa

Serves 12

SPECIAL EQUIPMENT
Digital kitchen scale

One day, years ago, an Indian pastry chef reminded me how much I don't know about sweets. She was making a dessert called *halwa*, and I thought that meant *halvah*, the Middle Eastern candy that's like a fudgy mixture of tahini and sugar syrup. What she made was entirely different. She cooked grated carrots in butter, added scalded milk, and simmered until the dairy disappeared. Somehow, the carrots kept their shape and, instead of turning to mush, they took on a wonderful custardy texture. I couldn't get enough. I've been making a version of that sweet ever since.

In the early days of State Bird, we served it with *bao*—a wink at our dim sum–style service, though they were really just big profiteroles—which you tore into and used to scoop up the halwa. To make the bao extra-cool, we topped the pâte à choux with a layer of cookie dough so that when they baked, their tops looked cracked like Dutch crunch bread, a Californian oddity I grew up on.

The sauce couldn't be easier, an unlikely but awesome combo of sweet condensed milk, lemon zest, and curry powder.

make the dutch crunch

100 grams/7 Tbsp unsalted butter, at room temperature

75 grams/¼ cup plus 2 Tbsp granulated sugar

50 grams/3½ Tbsp turbinado sugar

105 grams/¾ cup all-purpose flour

2 Tbsp buckwheat flour

Clear space in your freezer.

Combine the butter, granulated sugar, and turbinado sugar in the bowl of a stand mixer fitted with the paddle attachment. Beat on low speed until the butter is smooth (though you'll still be able to see the grains of turbinado sugar), 3 to 4 minutes.

Add the all-purpose flour and buckwheat flour to the bowl and mix on low speed until all the flour is incorporated, about 1 minute. Take the bowl off the mixer and use your hands to briefly scrunch, mix, and press the crumbly mixture into a fairly smooth dough.

Divide the dough in half and place one half on each of two pieces of parchment paper. Flatten each half with your hands into a rough rectangle that's about 5 by 8 inches. One rectangle at a time, cover with another sheet of parchment paper, then roll into an approximately 9 by 12-inch rectangle of even thickness (just a little thicker than paper). Because the parchment paper tends to bunch as you roll, occasionally flip over, remove the top sheet, lay it flat, and continue rolling.

Stack the two dough rectangles, still between the parchment paper, on a baking sheet and freeze until firm, about 15 minutes.

Remove the dough and parchment from the freezer and place on a work surface. Use a 3-inch ring cutter to cut each rectangle of dough into eight rounds. Use an offset spatula to transfer the rounds to the reserved sheets of parchment paper. Gather the scraps, use your hands to press them into a rough rectangle of dough, then roll it out and use the ring cutter to cut another eight rounds. Stack the sheets of parchment, and return to the freezer. Freeze for 15 minutes, then transfer to an airtight container, still separated by parchment paper, and store in the freezer for up to 3 months.

make the sauce

¾ cup sweetened
condensed milk

1½ tsp finely grated
(on a Microplane)
Meyer lemon zest

¾ tsp Madras curry powder

¼ tsp kosher salt

Combine the condensed milk, lemon zest, curry powder, and salt in an airtight container and stir well. (Store in the fridge for up to 1 week. Let it come to room temperature before serving.)

make the halwa

9 Tbsp unsalted butter

8 cups peeled grated
(on the large holes of
a box grater) carrots

3¾ cups whole milk

¼ cup granulated sugar

¾ tsp kosher salt

Melt the butter in a 12-inch sauté pan over medium heat. Add the carrots, stir well, and cover the pan. Cook, stirring occasionally at first but more frequently as you cook, until the carrots are tender but not mushy, about 10 minutes.

Meanwhile, in a small pot, warm the milk over medium-high heat, stirring occasionally, until it steams, about 5 minutes.

When the carrots are ready, pour in the milk and stir well. Bring to a simmer, then lower the heat to maintain a gentle simmer and cook, uncovered, stirring frequently, until the milk has been completely absorbed but the mixture still looks moist, 40 to 50 minutes.

Stir in the sugar and salt, then continue to cook until any liquid has evaporated, about 5 minutes more. Transfer to a bowl and let cool. (Store at room temperature for up to 2 hours.)

make the bao

180 grams/¾ cup water

3 Tbsp whole milk

1 tsp kosher salt

85 grams/6 Tbsp
unsalted butter

160 grams/1 cup plus
2 Tbsp all-purpose flour

4 large eggs

12 rounds Dutch crunch
(see page 355)

———

Confectioners' sugar
for dusting

Preheat the oven to 400°F. Line two 13 by 18-inch baking sheets with silicone baking mats.

Combine the water, milk, and salt in a sauté pan and set aside.

Melt the butter in a small light-colored skillet over medium-low heat. Let it froth and bubble, occasionally stirring and pushing the froth aside to check on the color, until the butter turns a caramel hue, 6 to 8 minutes.

Pour the brown butter into the milk mixture, scraping in any browned bits. Stir well and bring the mixture to a simmer over medium heat. Add the flour and cook, stirring and scraping constantly with a wooden spoon, until a smooth dough forms, about 30 seconds. Continue to cook, stirring and smashing constantly to incorporate and cook the flour, until the dough feels slightly stiffer as you stir, 2 to 3 minutes. Transfer the dough to the bowl of a stand mixer fitted with the paddle attachment and let cool for a minute or two.

Beat the dough on medium-high speed for 10 seconds. Turn the speed to medium and add the eggs, one at a time, stopping to scrape down the sides and bottom after each addition and waiting until each egg is fully incorporated before adding the next. Continue beating until when you stop the mixer, the mixture slowly slumps for about 3 seconds. If it slumps for more than 3 seconds, continue beating for 20 seconds before checking again.

Immediately transfer the dough to a pastry bag fitted with a plain ½-inch tip, and twist the open part of the bag to force the mixture toward the tip. Holding the bag steady over one of the prepared baking sheets, pipe enough of the dough to form a 3½-inch circle. Repeat with the remaining dough, spacing the circles about 2 inches apart. Place the Dutch crunch rounds onto the center of each circle.

Bake until the bao are puffed, light golden brown, and slightly cracked on the tops, about 20 minutes, rotating the bao on the edges of the sheet by 180 degrees after 10 minutes.

Remove the sheets from the oven, immediately use a small knife to poke four evenly spaced holes on the sides of each bao, and let cool.

Put the halwa in serving bowls and drizzle with the sauce. Place the bao on individual plates and dust with confectioners' sugar just before serving.

peach leaf rice pudding with cream cheese pie-crunch, nectarines, and hazelnuts

Serves 6

This is a borrowed dessert. The dough for shards of flaky pie-crunch come from Rose Levy Beranbaum's brilliant *The Pie and Pastry Bible*. The technique for the rice pudding comes from Kate Zuckerman's *The Sweet Life*, where I learned that anglaise could stand in for rice starch as a thickener and give the modest pudding a luxurious texture. The flavor inspiration comes from Alice Waters' *Chez Panisse Café Cookbook*, where I found a crème brûlée infused with peach leaves and the excitement to experiment with the floral flavor and amaretto-like quality they bring. And the garnish comes straight from Mother Nature's cookbook via the folks at Oregon's Trufflebert Farm, where they grow perfect hazelnuts so delicious that they sell out every year.

On a practical note, you don't need to have a peach tree to access the leaves. Most friendly farmers would gladly bring you a few branches if you ask nicely. Feel free to swap in other leafy green herbs like lemon verbena and rose geranium.

make the peach leaf anglaise

2 cups heavy cream

1 cup whole milk

1 cup peach leaves, torn into several pieces

½ cup granulated sugar, plus 2 Tbsp

1 large egg plus 5 large egg yolks, at room temperature

Combine the cream, milk, peach leaves, and ½ cup sugar in a medium saucepan. Set over medium-high heat, stirring occasionally, until the mixture steams, about 8 minutes. Turn off the heat and let steep, tasting every 5 minutes, until the mixture has taken on a subtle floral, amaretto-like flavor from the peach leaves but before it tastes bitter, about 15 minutes. Strain through a medium-mesh sieve, discarding the leaves, and return the cream mixture to the saucepan.

Combine the egg, egg yolks, and remaining 2 Tbsp sugar in a medium mixing bowl and whisk to combine. (Wrap a damp towel around the base of the bowl to keep it steady.)

Bring the cream mixture to a gentle simmer over medium heat and then, in a thin, steady stream, pour about ½ cup into the egg, whisking constantly. Pour the egg mixture into the saucepan, set over medium heat, and cook, stirring frequently, until the anglaise thickens enough to coat the back of a spoon and registers 180°F on an instant-read thermometer, about 5 minutes.

Prepare an ice bath in a large mixing bowl.

Strain the mixture through a fine-mesh sieve into a medium mixing bowl. Set the bowl in the ice bath and stir occasionally until the anglaise has fully cooled. Transfer to an airtight container and store in the fridge for up to 3 days or in the freezer for up to 3 months.

make the rice pudding

½ cup jasmine rice

1 cup whole milk

2 Tbsp granulated sugar

½ tsp kosher salt

1 cup peach leaf anglaise (see page 359)

Preheat the oven to 350°F.

Put the rice in a small mixing bowl, cover with water, stir well, then empty the water. Repeat until the water looks clear after stirring. Drain well.

Transfer the rice to a small ovenproof saucepan and add enough water to cover by about 1 inch. Set over medium-high heat, let come to a simmer, stir once, and then immediately drain the rice.

Return the rice to the saucepan. Add ¾ cup water, the milk, sugar, and salt and stir to combine. Set over medium-high heat and let come to a boil. Immediately turn off the heat, cover tightly with aluminum foil, and transfer to the oven. Bake until the rice is tender but not mushy and there's just a little liquid remaining at the bottom, 15 to 18 minutes.

Meanwhile, prepare an ice bath in a large mixing bowl.

When the rice is done, transfer it to a medium mixing bowl. Set the bowl in the ice bath and stir continuously until the rice has cooled. Stir in the 1 cup anglaise, cover, and refrigerate for at least 1 hour or up to 3 days.

finish the dish

½ cup peach leaf anglaise (see page 359)

¼ cup Lemon Curd (page 287)

1 recipe Flaky Cream Cheese Pie-Crunch (page 300)

2 large nectarines, pitted and cut into bite-size pieces

½ cup raw hazelnuts, coarsely chopped

Combine the ½ cup anglaise and lemon curd in a small mixing bowl and stir well.

Divide the rice pudding among serving bowls. Top each with the lemon curd mixture and two shards of the pie-crunch. Scatter with the nectarines and hazelnuts. Serve right away.

flaky lard turnovers with choco-pane, figs, and whipped crème fraîche

Serves 6 to 12

SPECIAL EQUIPMENT
Digital kitchen scale

make the turnover dough

105 grams/¾ cup all-purpose flour, plus more for dusting

60 grams/⅓ cup plus 2 Tbsp pastry flour

50 grams/⅓ cup plus 2 Tbsp whole-grain (dark) rye flour

1 tsp granulated sugar

½ tsp kosher salt

115 grams/8 Tbsp unsalted butter, cold, cut into ¼-inch cubes

3 Tbsp rendered pork lard, cold

75 grams/¼ cup plus 1 Tbsp cold water

Clear space in your freezer.

Whisk together the all-purpose flour, pastry flour, rye flour, sugar, and salt in a large bowl. Add the butter and lard and use your fingertips to mix and work the fat into the flour until the mixture resembles a coarse meal with some pea-size lumps. Add the water and mix until just incorporated. Gather the dough together, divide it in half, and shape each into a rough rectangular block. Wrap each piece in plastic wrap and refrigerate until firm, at least 1 hour or up to overnight.

Remove the dough from the refrigerator and let rest for 10 minutes.

On two sheets of parchment paper, roll out the pieces of dough into 8 by 12 inch rectangles (about ⅛ inch thick) and stack on a prepared baking sheet with parchment between them. Cover the baking sheet with plastic wrap and freeze until ready to use, at least 30 minutes or up to 3 weeks.

make the walnut-sesame frangipane

6 Tbsp unsalted butter

⅓ cup plus 1 Tbsp pretoasted black sesame seeds

½ cup plus 2 Tbsp granulated sugar

1 cup walnuts, toasted (see page 96) and cooled

¾ cup almond flour

1 large egg plus 1 large egg yolk, at room temperature

¼ tsp kosher salt

Melt the butter in a small skillet over medium-low heat. Let it froth and bubble, occasionally stirring and pushing the froth aside to check on the color, until the butter turns a caramel hue, about 6 minutes. Pour into a small bowl and set aside to cool.

Meanwhile, put the sesame seeds in a food processor and pulse until they resemble coarsely ground pepper, about 30 seconds. Add the sugar and pulse until the mixture resembles gray sand, about 30 seconds. Add the walnuts and almond flour and pulse until the walnuts are fairly finely ground, about 30 seconds.

Add the egg, egg yolk, and salt and pulse until well combined, about 20 seconds.

When the butter has cooled, add it to the processor and process to a well-combined, loose paste, about 20 seconds. Set aside.

finish the dish

1½ cups Fudgy Chocolate Sauce (page 282), at room temperature

1 pound ripe fresh Black Mission figs, each cut into 6 wedges, plus 6 figs thinly sliced

4 Tbsp unsalted butter, melted and cooled

2 Tbsp granulated sugar

⅔ cup heavy cream

⅓ cup crème fraîche

¼ tsp kosher salt

2 Tbsp pretoasted black sesame seeds, coarsely pounded

Combine the frangipane and chocolate sauce in a small mixing bowl and stir to mix well. Cover and refrigerate until well chilled, at least 1 hour or up to 5 days. Form the frangipane mixture into two 11-inch logs.

Preheat the oven to 375°F and line a large baking sheet with parchment paper.

Lay out each piece of parchment with the rectangles of frozen dough so the long edge faces you and then add a frangipane log to each, positioning them about 1 inch from the bottom edge of the dough and about ¾ inch from the shorter edges. Pat each log to form a 3 by 11-inch rectangle. Line the frangipane mixture with two rows of the fig wedges, so that all the wedges are touching.

At this point the dough should be thawed just enough so that it can be folded. Use the parchment to lift and fold the top edge of the dough over the filling to meet the bottom edge. Use a fork or your fingers to crimp and seal the three open edges. Use a sharp knife to cut four equally spaced 3-inch-long slits across the top of the crust. Brush with the melted butter and sprinkle with the sugar. Transfer to the prepared baking sheet.

Bake, rotating once, until the crust is golden brown, about 20 minutes. Use a spatula to loosen the turnovers from the parchment. Let the turnovers cool until warm or fully cool, whichever you prefer.

Meanwhile, combine the cream, crème fraîche, and salt in a medium mixing bowl, set in a bowl of ice water, and use a balloon whisk to whip to soft peaks. Cover and refrigerate until ready to use, up to 1 hour.

Cut each turnover into six pieces and top with a dollop of the whipped cream and a few slices of fig. Sprinkle with the sesame seeds. Serve right away.

sweet corn tres leches cake with cloud cream and blueberry compote

Serves 12

SPECIAL EQUIPMENT
Digital kitchen scale

The tradition began at Rubicon. Whenever a longtime kitchen-staff member celebrated a birthday or moved on to another gig, we'd make two giant hotel pans' worth of tres leches cake as a thank-you. We kept the tradition alive at State Bird, then decided the dessert was so good it belonged on the menu. That's when we started to get creative.

An unremarkable cake made remarkable after a good soaking in a mixture of three forms of milk (hence the name), and because virtually anything can flavor that milk, tres leches lends itself to so many fun twists. Like sweet corn! A concentrated infusion elevates corn from its common role as quirky dessert accent to front-and-center flavor. Blueberries underline the summer fun, lime zest adds dimension, and the maple caramel in the whipped cream makes the corn taste even more like corn.

make the cakes

6 medium ears corn, shucked

970 grams/4 cups whole milk

485 grams/2 cups heavy cream

225 grams/¾ cup sweetened condensed milk

¼ tsp kosher salt

5 large eggs, at room temperature

150 grams/¾ cup granulated sugar

105 grams/¾ cup all-purpose flour

Zest of 2 limes, finely grated on a Microplane

Cut the corn kernels from the ears, then break each cob in half. Combine the kernels, cobs, whole milk, cream, condensed milk, and salt in a large saucepan and bring to a simmer over medium heat. Remove from the heat, cover, and let steep for 1 hour. Discard the cobs. Using a slotted spoon, remove 1½ cups of the kernels from the pan and set aside in a bowl.

Combine the remaining kernels and milk mixture in a blender and pulse several times just to break up the kernels. Strain through a fine-mesh sieve back into the saucepan and discard the solids. Set aside.

Preheat the oven to 325°F.

Put twelve 8-ounce ramekins on two large baking sheets. Put 2 Tbsp of the reserved corn kernels in the bottom of each ramekin.

Combine the eggs and sugar in a stand mixer fitted with the whisk attachment. Whisk on medium-high speed until very light and fluffy, 8 to 10 minutes. Remove the bowl from the mixer, add the flour and lime zest, and use a balloon whisk to gently fold until just combined. Pour into the ramekins to fill each halfway.

Bake until the cakes are golden and spring back when touched, 30 to 35 minutes. Transfer the ramekins to a wire rack and let cool to room temperature. Using a small, sharp knife, poke each cake, all the way to the ramekin, about eight times.

Bring the corn liquid to a simmer over medium heat. Spoon about 2 Tbsp of the hot liquid over each cake. Wait 1 minute, then do it again until you've used all the liquid. Use your finger to tap the surface of the cakes to help the liquid soak in.

make the cloud cream

1½ cups heavy cream

2 Tbsp pure maple syrup

½ cup granulated sugar

¼ cup water

2 Tbsp unsalted butter, at room temperature

⅛ tsp kosher salt

½ cup cream cheese, at room temperature

½ cup crème fraîche

Combine ½ cup of the cream and the maple syrup in a small saucepan and set over medium heat until steaming but not simmering. Cover and keep warm.

Combine the sugar and water in another small saucepan and stir gently until all the sugar is moistened, trying your best to keep the sides of the pan clean. Cover and bring to a simmer over medium-high heat.

Once the bubbles in the sugar mixture go from small and rapid to large and lazy, 4 to 5 minutes, remove the lid and continue to cook until it turns a tan color, about 2 minutes. Turn the heat to low and continue to cook, gently swirling the pan, until the mixture turns a medium amber color, about 30 seconds more. Remove from the heat and then whisk constantly as you add the warm cream mixture in a thin, steady stream. If necessary, use a flexible heatproof spatula to stir until any clumps have dissolved. Whisk in the butter and salt. Transfer the caramel to a bowl to fully cool.

In a stand mixer fitted with the paddle attachment, beat the cream cheese on medium speed until smooth and fluffy, about 1 minute. With the mixer running, add the maple caramel, 1 Tbsp at a time, letting the paddle incorporate each addition before adding the next, and beat just until fully incorporated.

In a medium bowl, use a balloon whisk to whip the remaining 1 cup heavy cream and the crème fraîche to very soft peaks. About a third at a time, add the whipped cream, using a flexible spatula to very gently fold it into the cream cheese mixture until just barely combined. (You'll see streaks of the maple cream.) During the last addition, gently fold until just fully combined. (If not using immediately, transfer to an airtight container and store in the fridge for up to 3 days. Fold briefly just before using.)

finish the dish

1½ cups Blueberry Compote (page 275)

Add a dollop of the cloud cream to each cake and spread to cover. Spoon on the blueberry compote. Serve right away.

acknowledgments

Thank you to Danielle Svetcov, for planting the seed, even before we were ready, and periodically watering it until what grew was too exciting to ignore. We could not have asked for a better advocate or a better voice when we needed one that was not our own.

To the entire Ten Speed team: Jenny Wapner, for your belief that the matrix would come together and for allowing us to meander down our own paths while still firmly leading the way toward somewhere wonderful. To Betsy Stromberg, for designing a beautiful book that somehow feels like our restaurant. To Aaron Wehner, for seeing a book long before we even knew we would have the bandwidth to write one. And to Serena Sigona and Doug Ogan, for helping to bring all the pieces of this book together.

To JJ Goode, you amaze us every day with your ability to distill years worth of knowledge into engaging stories and recipes. You embody our philosophy of "we take what we do very seriously but we don't take ourselves seriously."

To Ed Anderson, this book is not only full of recipes but of images of people, food, art, and landscapes. You captured so astutely what we strive to embody and convey every dinner service. And an extra thank-you for keeping your designer's eye on the whole and not just the parts.

To Kevyn Allard, for patiently and repeatedly fermenting, braising, roasting, baking, and frying in your home kitchen and sharing your thoughtful notes. And to Kat Craddock, for nerding out on sourdough starter and breads.

To our partners: Elizabeth DePalmer, for keeping all the important details organized so we never had to worry about where to find them. From the very first cookbook meeting to the planning of the release, you helped make this journey less bumpy for all of us. To Jason Alexander, for supporting The Progress team while we were deep in the cookbook.

To Rumpasri Chicharoen, after you spent nearly four years in the kitchen at State Bird, starting as our first a.m. saucier to the women commanding all stations and eventually becoming sous chef, it was obvious that when the cookbook needed an organizer you were the one for the task. The list of accomplishments is long, but to name a few: your legendary spreadsheets, the early-morning recipe testing, and your photo-filled progress reports that impressed even the publisher. All of these made you indispensable, and the book shines with your work.

To Mikiko Yui, we are so lucky you came back from Japan to open a restaurant with us, first as a pastry assistant (and occasional pancake line cook) and then as an unbelievably talented pastry chef and collaborator. We worked in hallways, spread hundreds of macarons, and scraped endless amounts of granita together, always heading toward a goal that kept evolving. We miss you.

To Gaby Maeda, who rose through the ranks to chef de cuisine and whose infectious enthusiasm and continuous creativity embody the spirit of SBP.

To Caitlin Donahue, our general manager. Every day you impress us with your leadership and your boundless sense of hospitality to our guests and staff.

To Glenn Kang, one of our first employees for the restaurant and someone who probably had a better idea than anyone, including (sometimes) us, of what this restaurant was meant to be! You became a catalyst for its success with your voice and spirit.

To Kevin Law, who brought focus and an incredible work ethic for the kitchen when it needed it most.

To all the kitchen and dining room staff, who bring fun and excitement to the restaurant every day, who so often step out of your comfort zones, who offer hospitality with true personality.

To our artists: Leah Rosenberg, for bringing color into our pegboard palace. Terri Chastain, for the moody, brilliant, always inspiring etchings Jimmy Chen, for the humor only you can tease out of a broccoli floret. Caitlin Freeman, one-time map maker and tireless supporter. Wylie Price, the designer we engaged a few months after we opened to help add a few lights and a seated bar and who has continued to push the "workshop" restaurant idea with us for five years running.

To our families, who were there to support us without question and who, when there weren't enough hours in the day to be at the restaurant and with our son, Jasper, gave us and him the gift of their time and love.

And finally, to all of our guests: Without you, we wouldn't have a restaurant, let alone a cookbook. Thank you for filling SBP every night with your spirit and eagerness to try new things, like fried quail and peanut milk.

index